AF504058

ABIDING BUDDHA

The Sculpture of Tranquillity

ABIDING BUDDHA

The Sculpture of Tranquillity

XU BIN JUEYI

FOREWORD BY
EDWARD LUCIE-SMITH

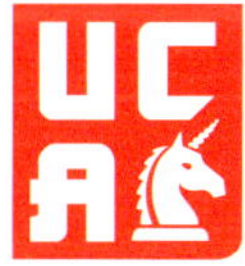

First published by Unicorn

an imprint of Unicorn Publishing Group LLP, 2018

5 Newburgh Street

London W1F 7RG

www.unicornpublishing.org

All rights reserved. No part of the contents of this book may be
reproduced, stored in or introduced into a retrieval system, or
transmitted, in any form or by any means (electronic, mechanical,
photocopying, recording or otherwise), without the prior written
permission of the copyright holder and the above publisher
of this book.

Every effort has been made to trace copyright holders and to obtain
their permission for the use of copyright material. The publisher
apologises for any errors or omissions in the above list and would be
grateful if notified of any corrections that should be incorporated
in future reprints or editions of this book.

Text / illustrations © Xu Bin Jueyi

10 9 8 7 6 5 4 3 2 1

ISBN 978-1-911604-34-1

Design by Matt Carr

Translation by Sarah Waldram

Printed in Belgium by Graphius

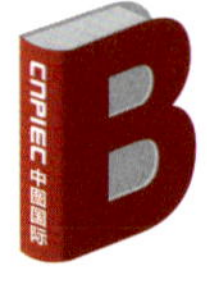
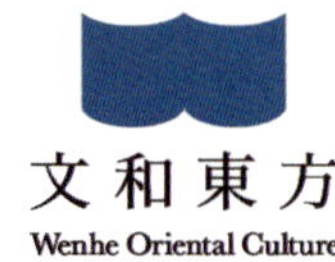

Contents

Looking from the West, eastwards
- Edward Lucie-Smith

One of the surprising, and still not fully acknowledged, characteristics of Modernist – and following that Post Modernist – art is its dependence on what one might call religious emotion. One can even make the claim that, in a certain sense, the great museums that offer the public exhibitions of contemporary art, have replaced, in terms of function, the temples and cathedrals of the past. Like these venerable institutions in their prime, they attract a large populist attendance. They transcend boundaries of race and class and are frequented by all generations.

Many of these attendees would, I think, find it difficult to define in words what it is that draws them to these institutions, but it seems clear that they are looking for experiences that take them through, and beyond, the barriers of the self. The links between traditional forms of religious experience and what is available through contemporary art have become particularly marked with the recent rise of so-called 'performance art', with its emphasis both on the power of ritual, and on the idea of the power of personal charisma to leap over barriers, without much help from actual objects. In art of this kind, personified in the most literal sense by charismatics such as Marina Abramovic, the links between certain sectors of the contemporary art world and traditional shamanism have become very evident.

They are not in fact new. They are, for example, very much present in one of the seminal texts of the Modern Movement, Kandinsky's *Concerning the Spiritual in Art*, published in 1910. Some of the things Kandinsky has to say are worth repeating here. For instance this:

[In great art] the spectator does feel a corresponding thrill in himself. Such harmony or even contrast of emotion cannot be superficial or worthless; indeed the Stimmung of a picture can deepen and purify that of the spectator. Such works of art at least preserve the soul from coarseness; they 'key it up', so to speak, to a certain height, as a tuning-key the strings of a musical instrument.

And also this:

The spiritual life, to which art belongs and of which it is one of the mightiest elements, is a complicated but definite and easily definable movement forwards and upwards. This movement is the movement of experience. It may take different forms, but it holds at bottom to the same inner thought and purpose.

Xu Bin Jueyi, the artist celebrated in this book, belongs to a different culture from the Western artists who have, for more than a century, interested themselves in matters of this kind. He also, however, belongs to a situation in which very diverse cultures have, through a revolution in communications, been set free to communicate with one another. His art is inspired by Buddhism, a non-Western creed, but is published in English, and addressed to Western readers.

While the image of the Buddha is very much featured here, it is certainly not the only subject of Xu Bin Jueyi's art, this despite his publicly announced ambition to spend the rest of his life making 3000 such sculptures. Those featured here are often very thin, deliberately elongated from the normal pattern of human proportions. In classical Buddhist sculpture emaciated figures of this sort allude directly to the Buddha's enlightenment: how he, born as a prince, became a yogi ascetic, and meditated continuously for forty-nine days, at the end of his ordeal achieving enlightenment, and freedom from all worldly desires.

In addition, some of the sculptures, where the figure is shown poised on one foot, allude not to Buddhist representations, but to Hindu ones: images of the god Shiva dancing, in a Natarajsana pose. His dance, in images of this sort, symbolizes the release of cosmic energy, expressing the relationship between humanity and nature.

In these elongated sculptures, his inspiration comes from the lengthened shadows of Tibetan pilgrims cast by the setting sun, representing a kind of extension of goodness. Where the thin figure seems to stride forward, however, one is immediately reminded of Giacometti's most characteristic works.

And these are not the only echoes of the tropes of Western Modernism. In some of the Buddha figures the modelling is faceted in a way that immediately recalls the characteristic language of Cubist sculpture. Linked to the proto-Cubist works there is one work, entitled *Flight of Beauty*, that seems to be purely abstract – a stack of V-shaped forms, one rising above the other. This might, however, also be interpreted as very abstracted image of a supernatural winged being.

Another set of associations is evoked by a piece called *The Deer King*. This evokes a story about a huntsman king, who was dissuaded from the hunt by a deer who spoke to him in human language. Greatly moved, the king ceased to hunt. The king here is the emblem of the Buddha in his past life before he achieved Enlightenment. The sculpture consists of a pair of stag's horns, planted on the summit of a cluster of three abstract forms that evoke the image of a human figure seated on a throne.

A number of works are installations. One evokes the idea of a Buddhist grotto, with a multitude of small figures, each installed in its own niche or compartment. There is also a Spider Fort, so-named, that features a patchwork of graffiti in different scripts, some in Chinese characters, some in English. There are a few drawings as well — a human face, a spindly tree, and a life-like portrayal of the spider of the title. In fact, the graffiti enables the countless visitors to the Fort unconsciously to engage in shared creation of the installation.

From these one moves, as the book progresses, to works of a more directly public kind. One of the most striking of these is a large statue of a formidable female figure, seated hands on knees. Called Lady Xian, she was born in the sixth century. A military heroine, she put down civil disturbances and helped to establish a more stable society. She became a long-lasting Chinese legend, many temples being built in her honour. The largest and most important of these is in Gaozhou. A festival is now held there every year on the 24th day of the 11th lunar month. The temple was listed in 2002 by the Guangdong Provincial Government as a key cultural protection site. Former Chinese President Jiang Zemin paid an official visit to it in the year 2000, just before this recognition. He praised Lady Xian as 'the role model that the later generations should learn forever'. Even before this, Zhou Enlai, Premier under Chairman Mao, had described her as 'the First Heroine of China'.

Also striking is a large bronze group of Tibetan *Pilgrims* in Lhasa. These are shown praying. Each is in the form of a herm — a torso, abbreviated, and perched on a pillar. It is noticeable that the handling is much rougher and freer than the smooth surfaces of the statue of Lady Xian, reminiscent to a European eye of some characteristic works by Rodin. Smooth surfaces return in the 88 figures of Buddha made for the Liurong Temple in Guangzhou.

Other major monuments are different again. The Linyi War Memorial and the Hakka Cultural Park will, I think, tend to remind the seasoned traveller, or indeed the seasoned reader of art books, of certain public monuments in Mexico, most notably the work of the three major muralists who celebrated the Mexican Revolution — Diego Rivera, José Clemente Orozco and David Siquieros. Though these were painters, not sculptors, the resemblance is, I feel, unmistakable. Xu Bin Jueyi is, just as they were, celebrating the building of a new society in these works. He is also, just as they did, looking back at very ancient cultural traditions, rooted in the soil, and finding new uses for them. These big commemorative works have a self-confidence that is usually lacking in Western equivalents of the same recent date.

According to Xu Bin Jueyi, his Buddha images are not Buddhas in a traditional sense. We can choose to call them *xinti* or 'heart-bodies'. *Xinti*, in Chinese philosophy, refers to, as well as the physical body itself, those abstract aspects of spirit, soul, wisdom, reflection, feelings, will, and so on. In creating each piece of work, Xu Bin Jueyi claims to take such a grand cosmic and world view. He wishes to use his life to make heart-likenesses of ordinary people in the mortal world. With this creative approach, he seeks to establish a spiritual connection with each person, so that every participant unconsciously becomes involved in the activity of sculpting their *xinti*. In this 'art programme', Xu Bin Jueyi says he enables people to understand better the source of their spirituality, and through the image of the *xinti*, reflect on themselves, using the mirror of virtue as a lesson. This is a mirror both for one's immediate clan and for broader society.

Peace

Converse with the soul of heaven and earth
through the art of sculpture, and retain a
magnificent existence for your own life and the
life of all beings. In years to come, when vast
tomes and the flow of words have passed away,
sculptures will remain. And, whatever changes
language and writing undergo, these sculptures
will still quietly murmur, bringing understanding
to their discoverers. The idea that humanity is
connected through the art of sculpture is not
devoid of import.

- Yu Qiuyu

Hands that speak
- Zhao Chuanrong

(On seeing Xu Bin Jueyi's sculpture exhibition)

A pair of hands that speak

Between the past and the future, explore

In the vast starry sky

A group of lonely constellations

Those military figures made of clay

Bronze war horses

Carved jade sacrifices, Buddha and distant places

Suffering, detachment

Like monks, moving from realization to awareness

A pair of hands that speak

Between metal and stone, combine

Materials, images

Notes of eminent scholars

Without words, only lines

Pattern, geometry

Transforming weapons to jade

Changing decay into magic

On this shore and the other side, walking

A pair of hands that speak

Bringing spring wind, summer rain

Autumn moon, and thick falling snow

The happy sparrow flying

Auspicious clouds curling

The riot of life, multi-coloured life

Full of the temptations of the boundless world

In hands that speak

The chains are released

The self is created

Perhaps, that is indeed the end

You, me, Tathāgata

Art is a Spiritual Practice
- Xu Bin Jueyi
('Awareness of the One')

My works seek to convey the philosophical thought and beauty of the major religions. Rather than talking about it, I choose to express myself through art. I am looking for a way of life, free and unrestrained, and my understanding of the major religions is presented through the means of art.

I grew up in China, so naturally Confucianism, Buddhism and Daoism have had the deepest influence on me. As I was learning about the world, China was too: reforming and opening up, with the Internet becoming increasingly accessible. To go anywhere in the world or to acquire any information seemed achievable instantaneously. We are not like the monk Xuanzang who travelled to what was then remotest India to bring back the sutras. The Buddha image, from the end of the Eastern Han to today, has borne the contemporary culture of each period it has seen, and in today's topsy-turvy world culture is becoming a global fusion, while the peace, compassion and love that all spiritual religions share are known to all the people of the world.

From 2014 I have had a wish: to use the rest of my life to make 3,000 Buddhas and to communicate with people I was predestined to meet to create heart-likenesses of themselves. Buddha is merely the element I use to make manifest the artistic creation; Buddha is really not the Buddha, it is the name of Buddha. The 'Myriad Buddha Programme' is an expression of the Buddha, of Jesus and of Mohammed; at the same time, it expresses neither the Buddha, nor Jesus, nor Mohammed. It is yourself, you are that Buddha statue; with you, I sculpt a mirror of your inwardness, a mirror in which to make true your heart and awareness.

For many years, I walked in mountains and along rivers, travelling the world. I loved this. My works are a reflection of my experience of life; indeed, my works are the process of my life. There is the youthful joy of entering the world, the appreciation of the beauty of life, of doubt and the worship of heaven, as in the *I Ching* ('Book of Changes') series, the sculptures *Pilgrims* and *Qinghai-Tibetan Plateau*, and so on. Some are considerations of the self, of other people and of society and explorations of the universe – for example, the *Considering the Fracture* series and the *Awareness* series. My works and myself at this period are fresh, just concerned with, 'Looking up to the vastness of the universe, looking down at the myriad creative works' (a quote from *Lantingji Xu*, 'Orchid Pavilion Collection Preface', a poem about composing poetry by a stream and the fleeting nature of life). Then, accumulating all sorts of emotions, I put them into each subsequent piece of work or fill the details with them.

The mood I most care about is, 'See the Buddha and be happy, see God and feel joy.' I have not converted to any religion; my inner heart has respect for every religion. As time slowly runs away from my life, everything is manifest in the present; things that consciousness either can or cannot penetrate are fleeting – like smoke or clouds – and are no longer important. If you do as Buddhism says – 'Go direct to the heart; the heart is the Buddha'– the remainder is the understanding of all life. It may not be a profound and unfathomable knowledge, and if it is not the Truth that the people of the world seek, then it is a discovery of gradual enlightenment. At this time, I do not shut myself away in my studio, but on the contrary open my door to connections with people of all walks of life, inviting them to participate in the 'Myriad Buddha Programme'. Every day, like a Buddhist disciple (literally 'disciple of "the empty door"') reading the scriptures and chanting, or sweeping the floor and eating a meal, I treat the process of communicating with each person as a spiritual practice in 'fording' the person and the self. Every time I attentively render a statue in clay, it is without making any demand and without any specified purpose. When I create a work, I do not need to think hard, in the moment of creation I seem to have a connection with the universe, and everything happens naturally. The Buddhas I shape are not recognised by everyone as Buddhas in the traditional sense. I hope viewers see my work as a reflection of conflicts in the world and look more deeply into themselves.

Everything I want to say concerns perceptions about life, but it does not seem to require language to express, because enlightenment itself is a thing that 'can only be intuited and not be spoken'. I am not good with words, cannot expound on the sutras as lofty monks do, and cannot rely on words to transform the Buddhist philosophy to the people of the world. Making images is the way I present these truths. I put elements from the world's culture and concepts from the major religions into my work; if people of the world get something from my works, then that is the most gratifying thing for me. If people of the world experience the sacredness of religion in contemporary images or if, in the process of, or after, the sculpting, they propagate a little more goodwill, then I obtain my heart's delight – that kind of post-enlightenment, burden-less and heartfelt delight. I want to sculpt 3,000 people in the form of the Buddha, so that they participate in the creation of heart-likenesses of themselves. The statues become a view on their inwardness. This is what I call the *'360-Degree Redemption' Beauty of Compassion* – or the Myriad Buddha Programme.

The first emperor of the Tang, Emperor Taizong, Li Shimin, once said, 'If a person uses bronze as a mirror, he can adjust his robes and hat; if you take the past as your mirror, you can understand the rise and fall of history; if human beings are your mirror, you understand gain and loss.' Today, we have the heart-likeness of self as a mirror. What will happen? No god concept requires substance: personal god followers regard idol worship as taboo and would rather 'save' their followers through virtue. Alternatively, the people of the world can see their spiritual side as a true existence. This is a kind of mindfulness, an ideal, a pursuit of perfection.

The well-known Buddhist monk Huiyuan (AD 334–416) of the Wei-Jin period was once commended by his master: 'If someone is to carry forward the Dharma on this piece of land, it will be Huiyuan and no-one else.' And he was able, because he used the widely accepted Confucianism and Daoism to explain the Dharma, in the metaphysics of the Wei-Jin period, like a clear stream. I cannot do any more than him; my spiritual practice is to use art to help people of the world plant a Bodhi seed for themselves amid the hustle and bustle, and to create

a mirror to their soul of their true heart and awareness. When statue after statue is put up in myriads of households, then the religions warn the people of the world to restrain their desires and to respect the practice of virtue, each day to improve their hearts and, even if it is trivial to repeat, this is also religious practice.

Art is life, art is spiritual practice, art is a social responsibility. If each person comes to the world with a mission, then this is my mission.

Religion
has no
boundaries,
and peace
is above
religion.

Awareness 1: The Light of Peace
Stainless steel, 54×36×220cm
2014

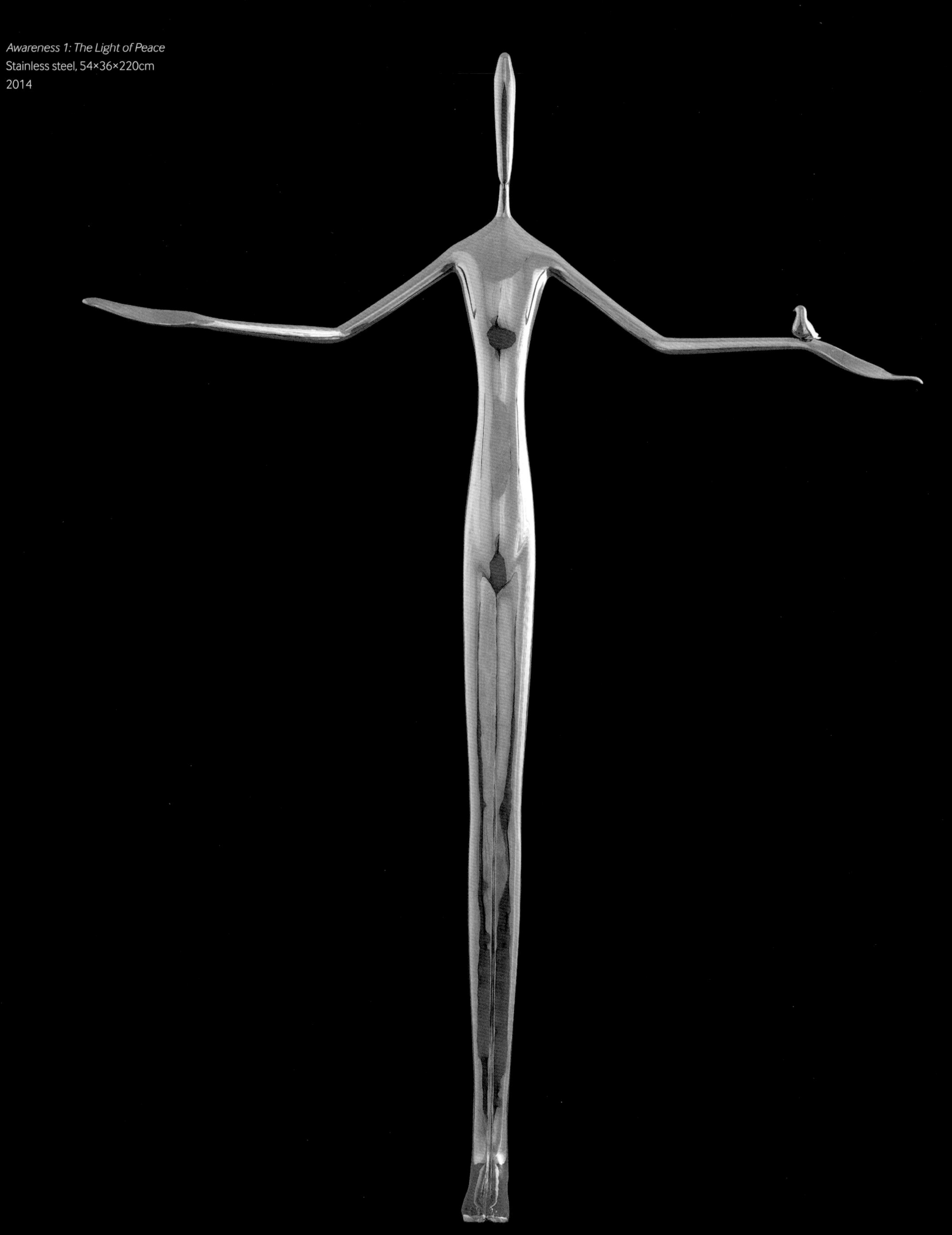

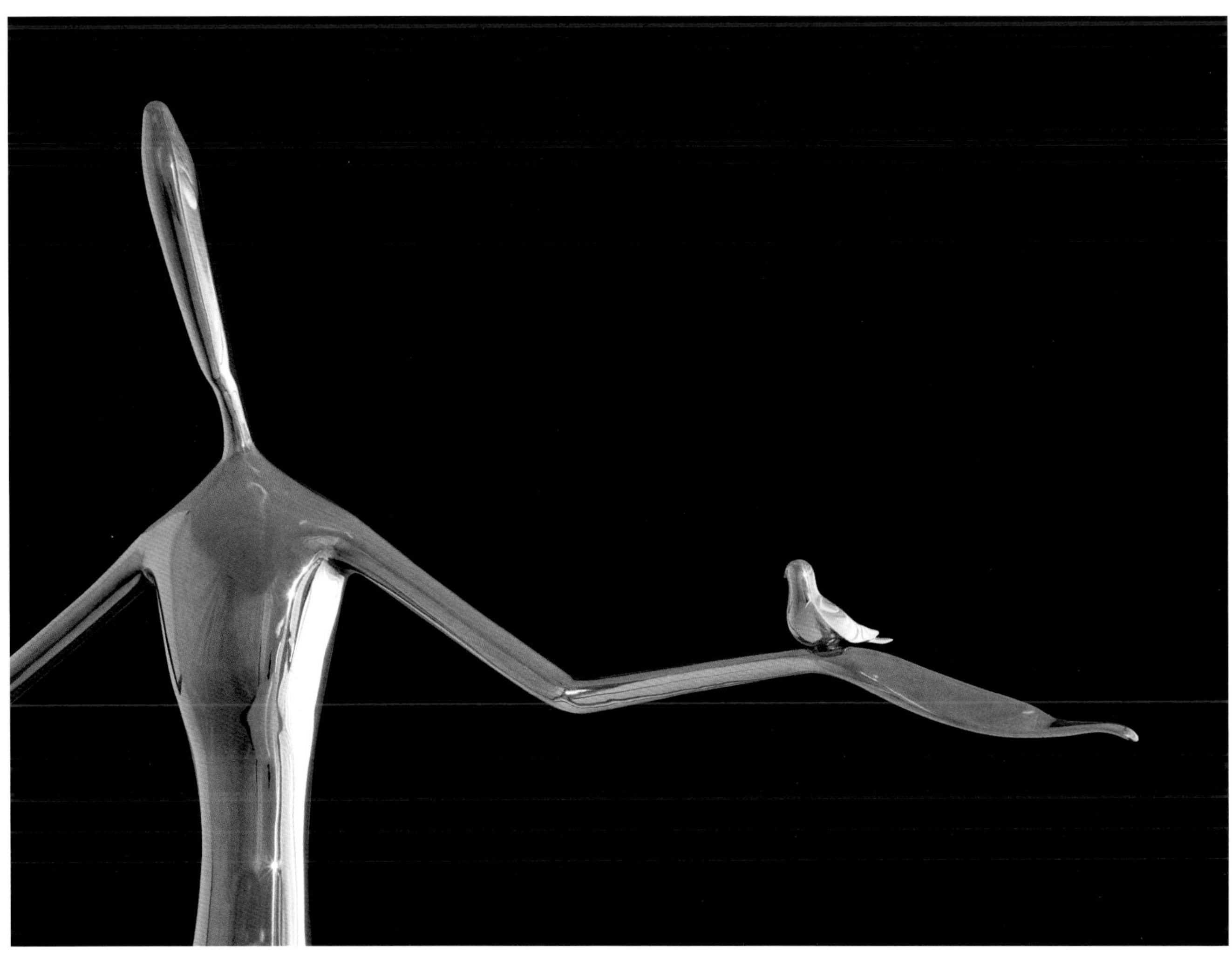

Awareness

The conscious elongation technique combines the Eastern pursuit
of the natural realm with the Western reverence for metaphysical
spirit. The lengthened Buddha and its shadow are a reference to the
journey of people passing through the barrier of material desires and
recognizing the internal, ethereal, unrestrained Buddha heart. The
Buddha and bodhisattva's facial expressions and pleated clothing
are concise and generalized. This is a breakthrough by the artist
in the traditional Buddhist sculptural language, a transformation
in consciousness. The purpose is to intensify the time spent in the
psychological experience of the spiritual world of Buddha, to replace
visual possession with psychological continuity, to exchange the
thickness of material things for the length of the soul.

Awareness 3
Stainless steel, 60×36×250cm
2014

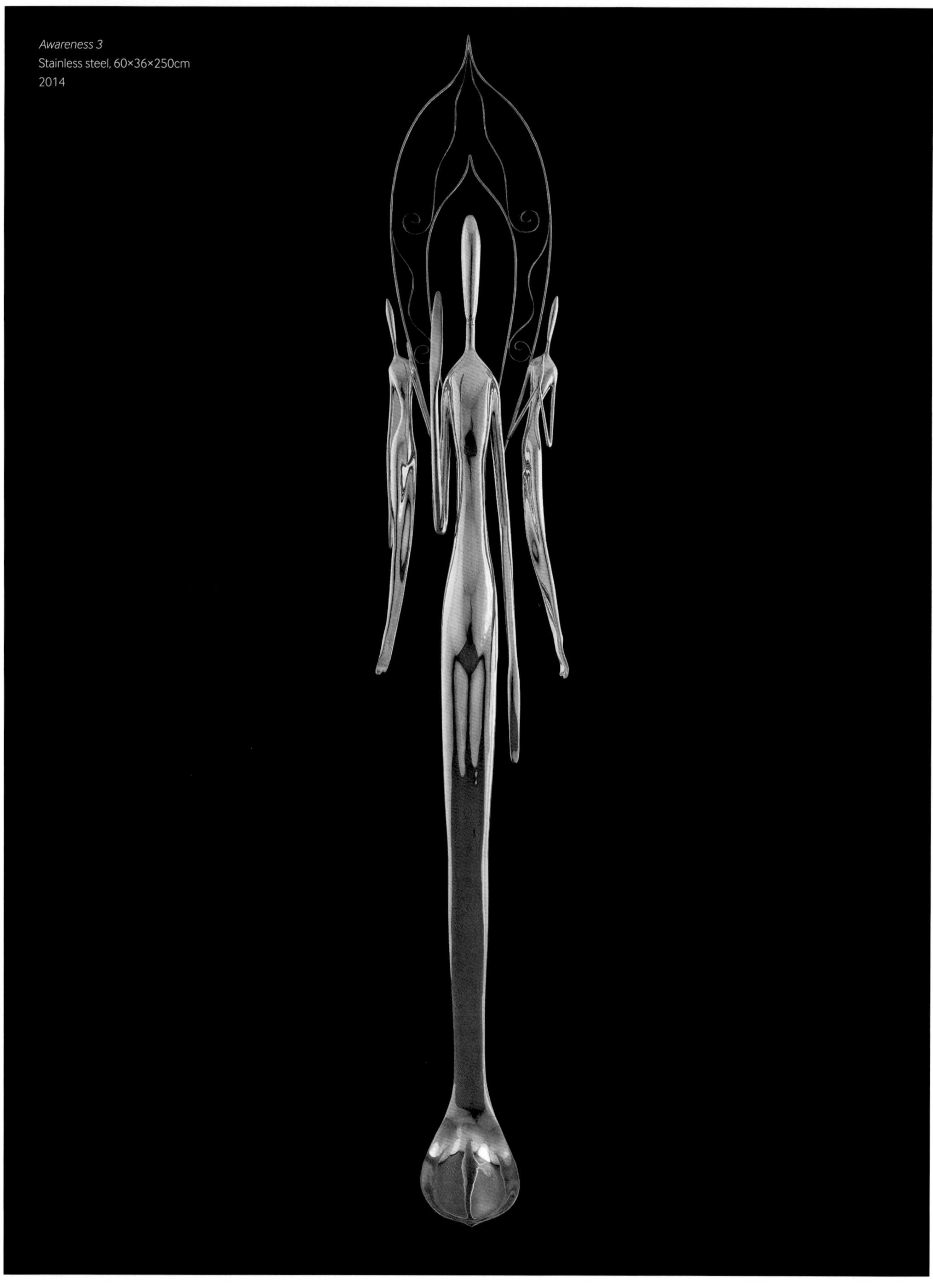

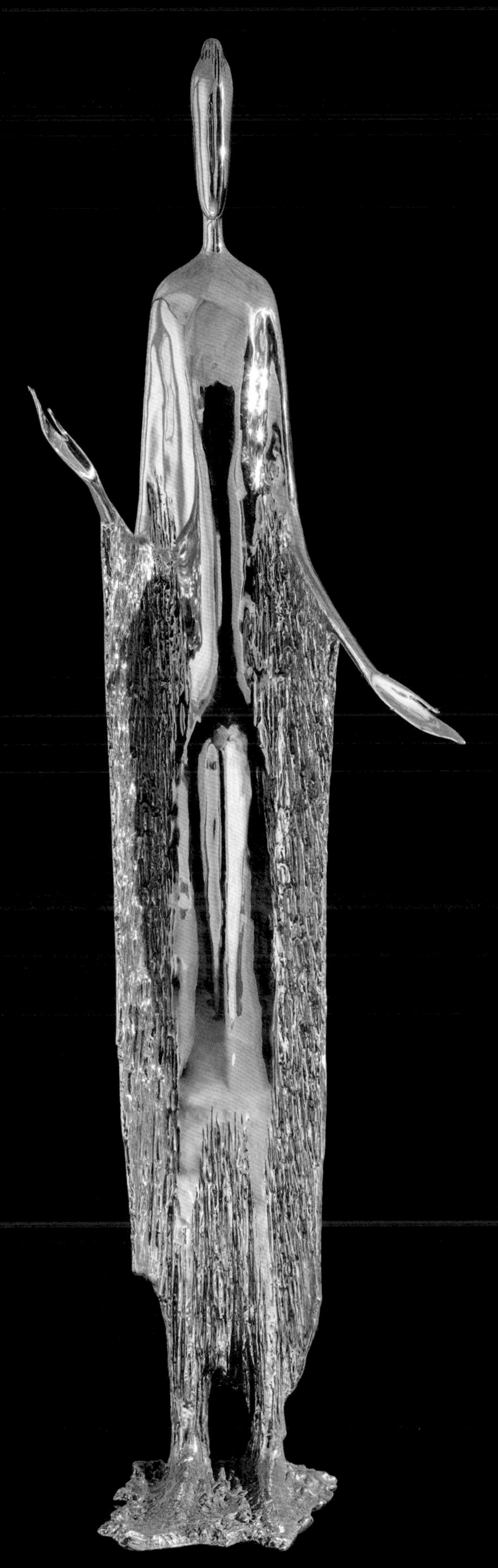

Awareness 2: State of Mind,
Becoming Aware
Stainless steel, 68×68×280cm
2013

Awareness 4
Bronze, 40×40×196cm
2014

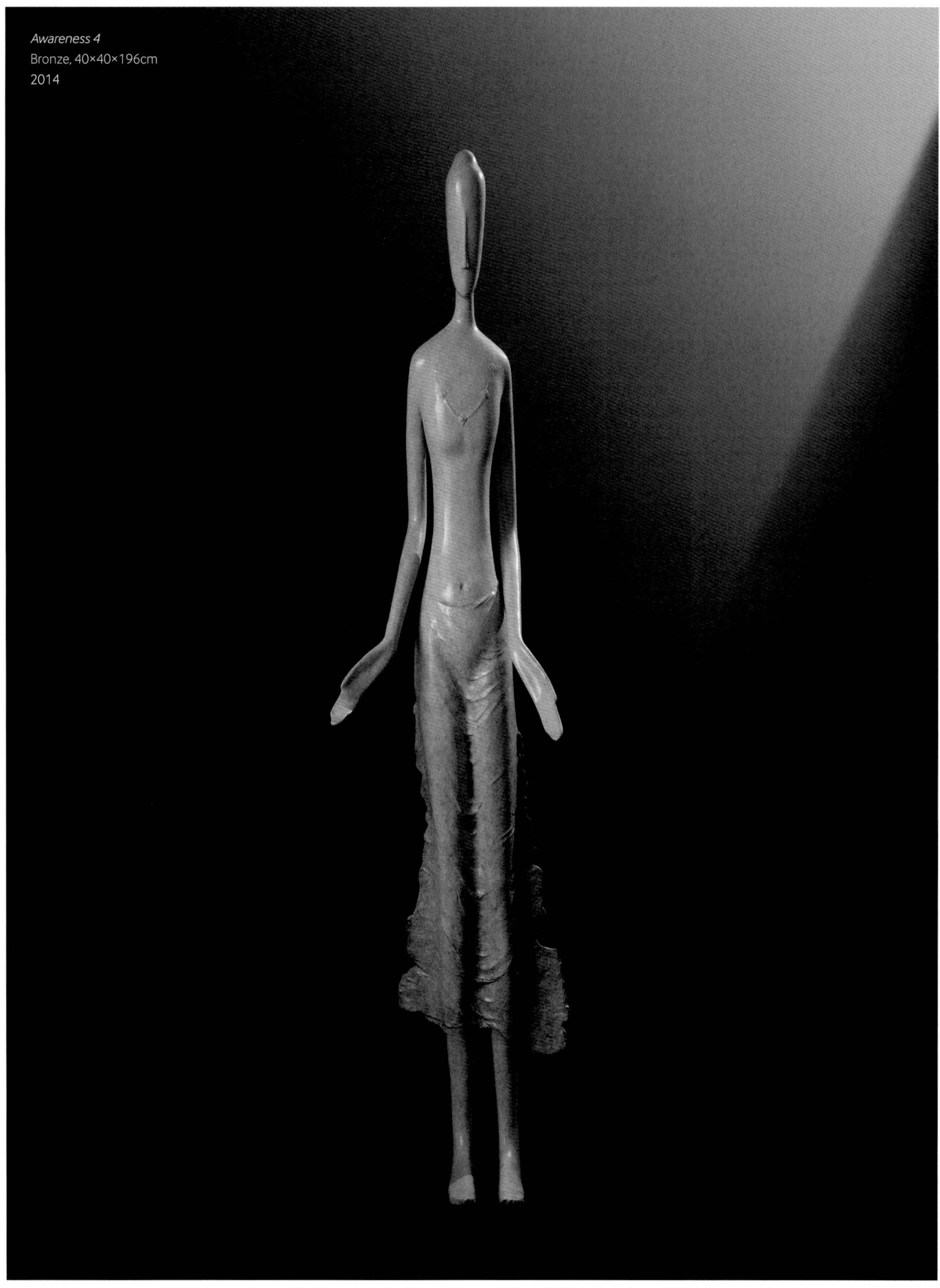

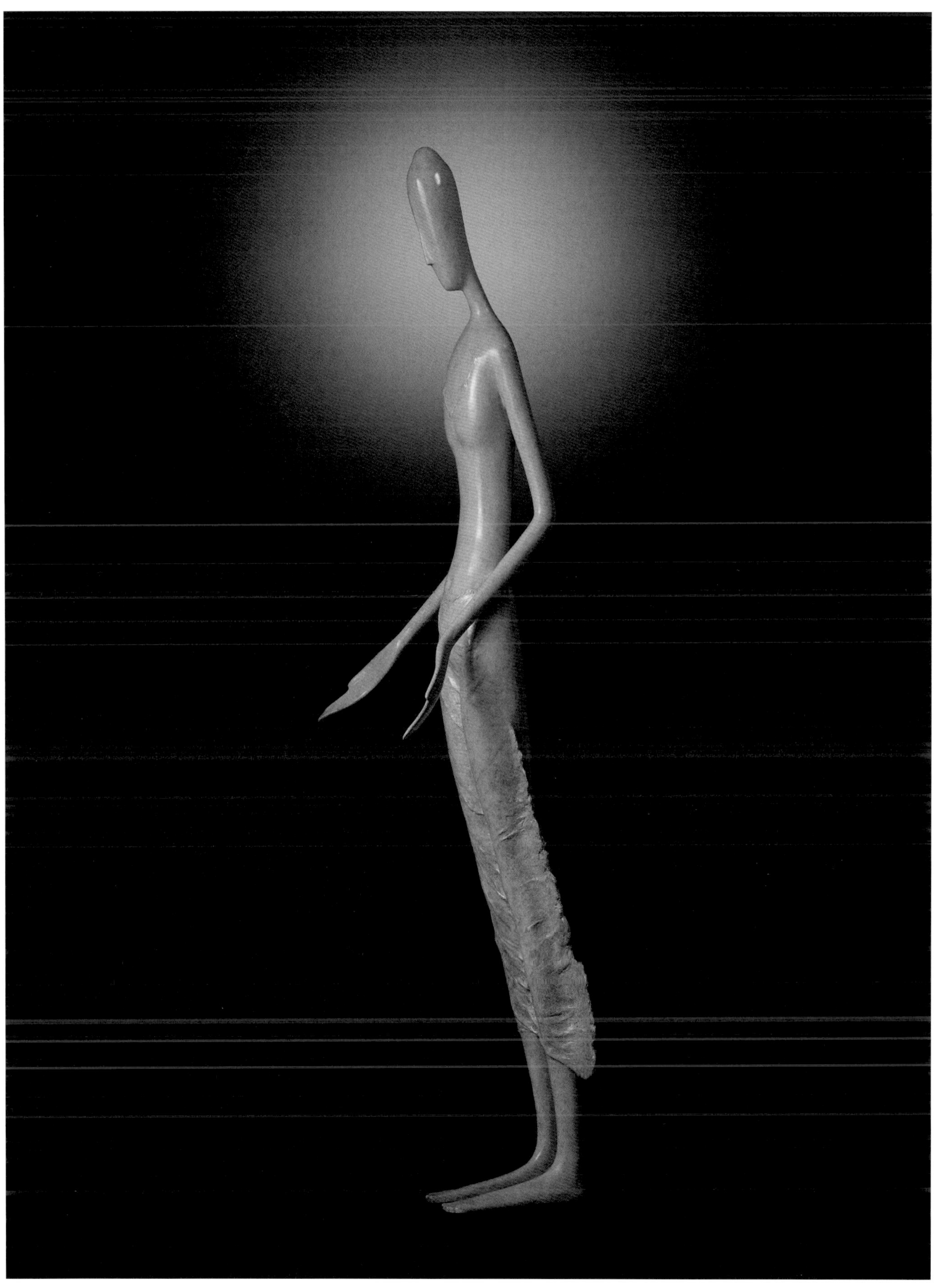

Awareness 5
Bronze, 60×40×200cm
2014

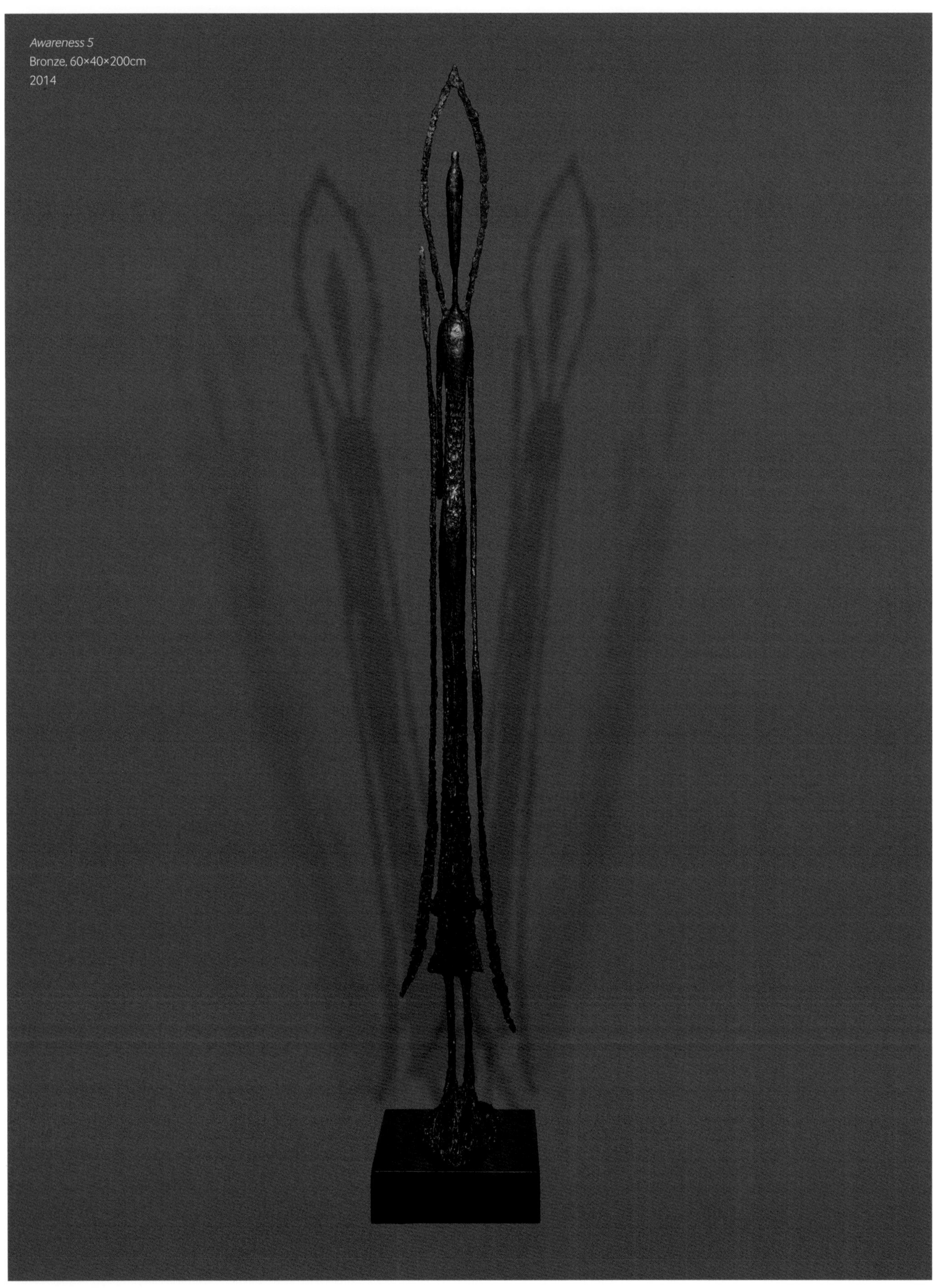

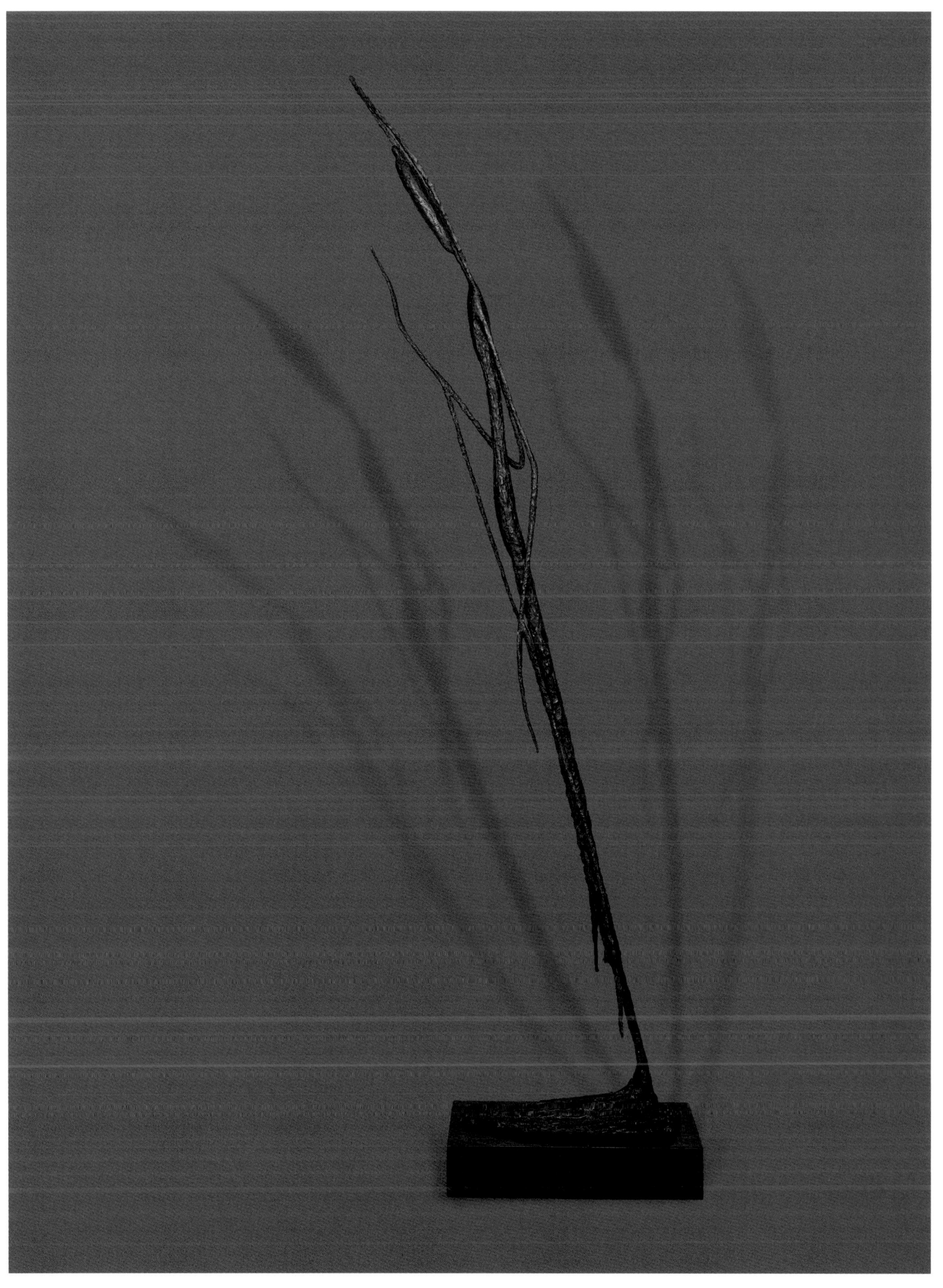

Awareness 7
Bronze, 70×70×187cm
2014

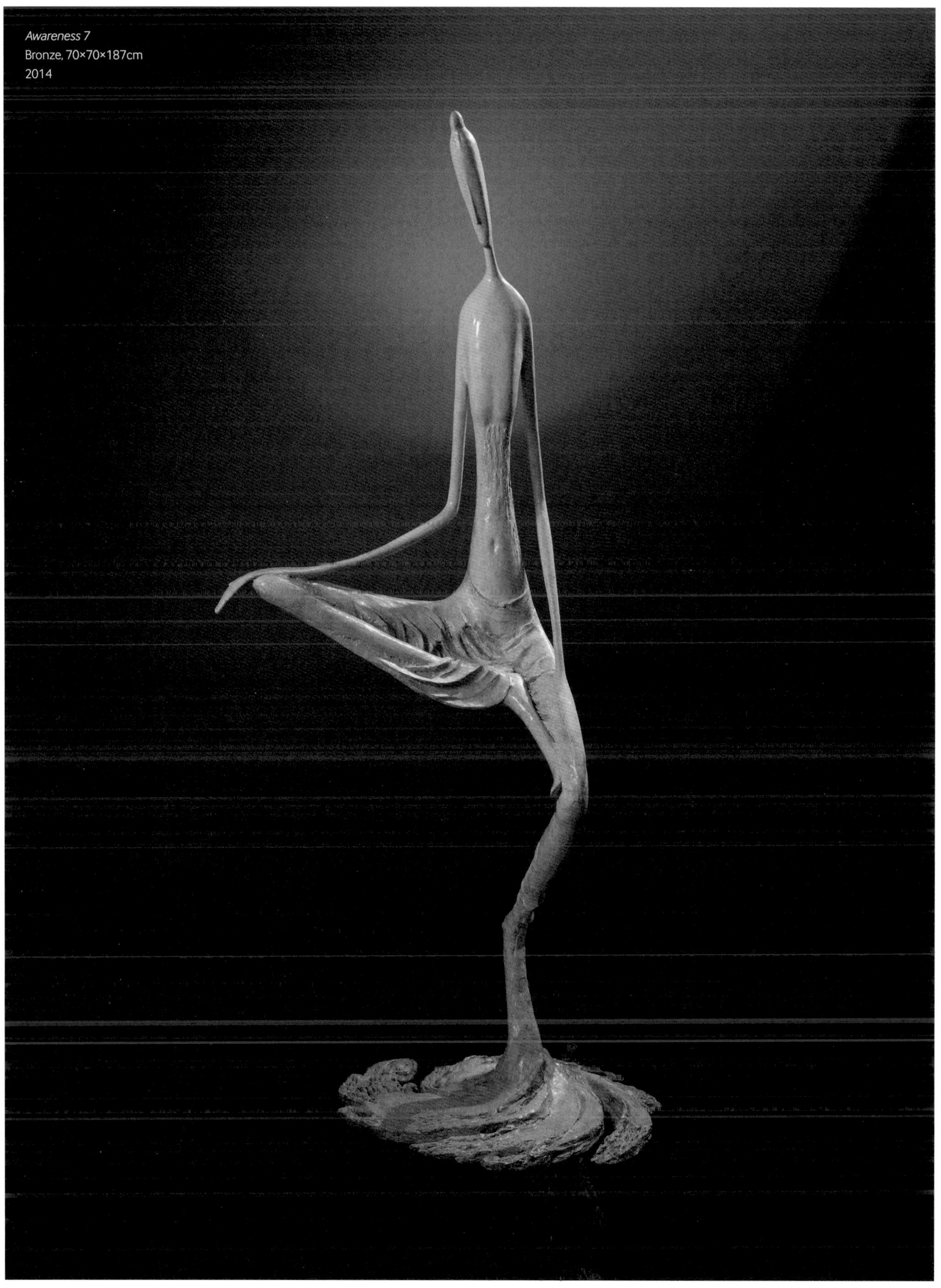

Awareness 8
Bronze, 50x50x260cm
2014

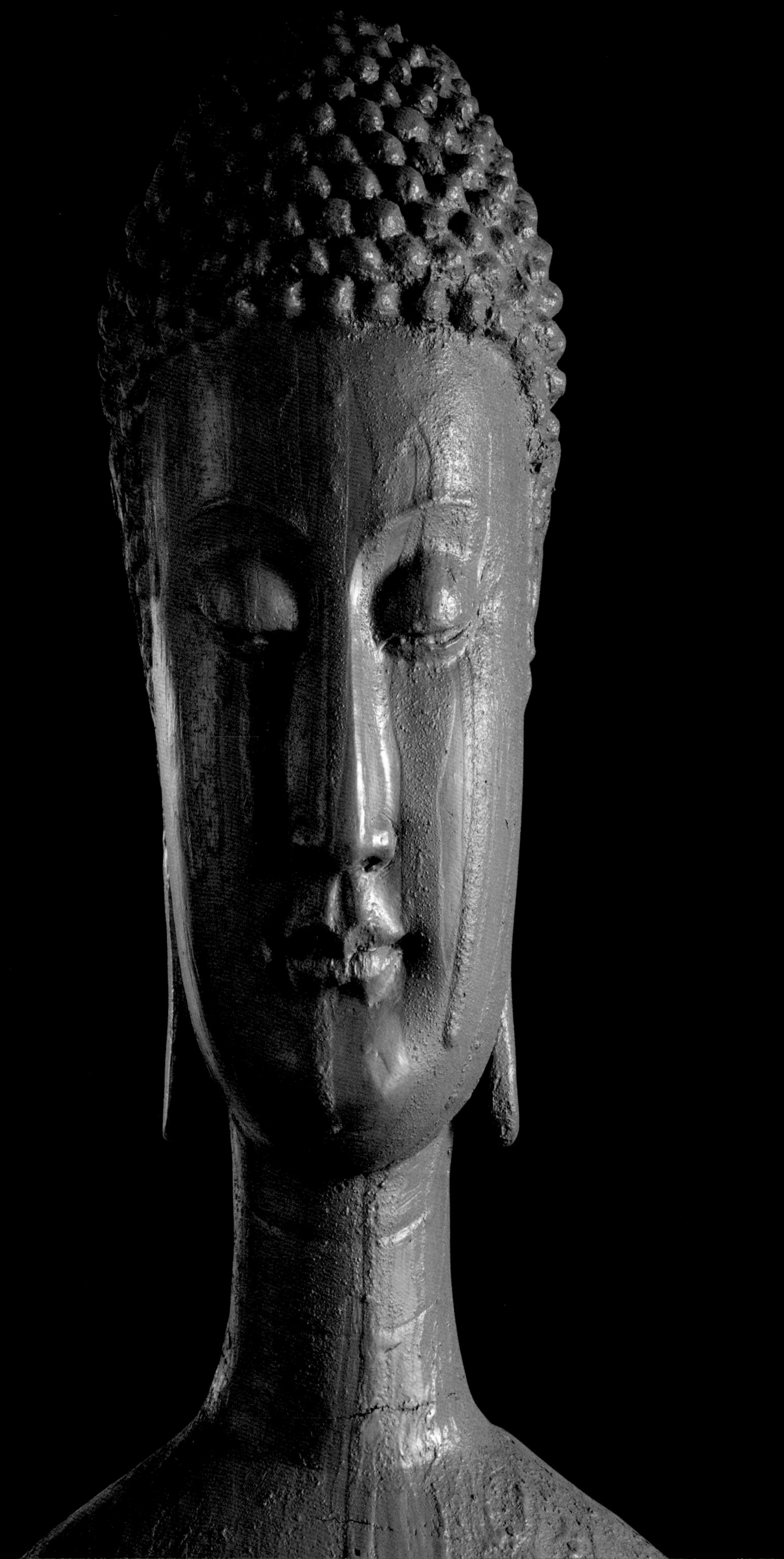

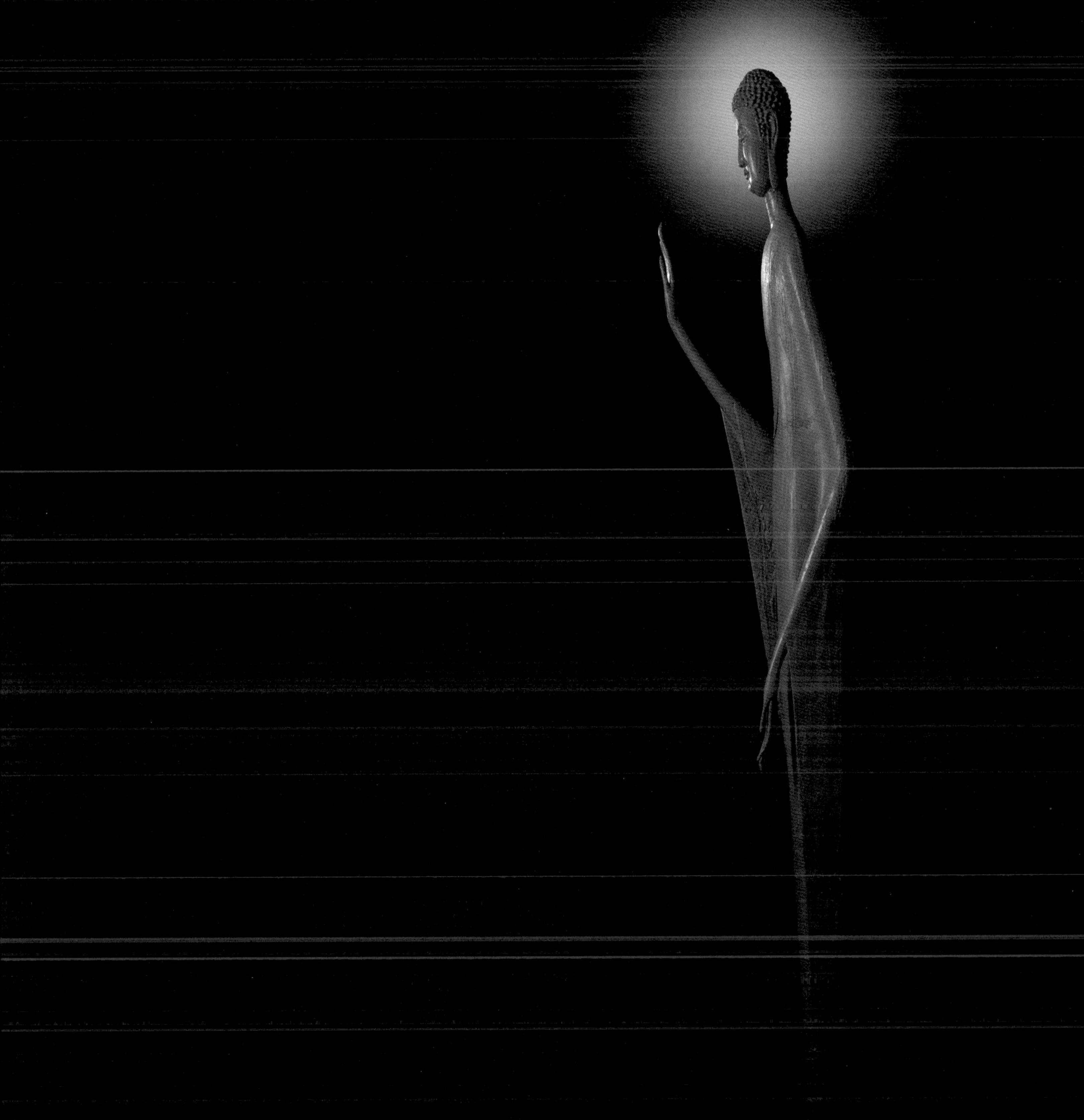

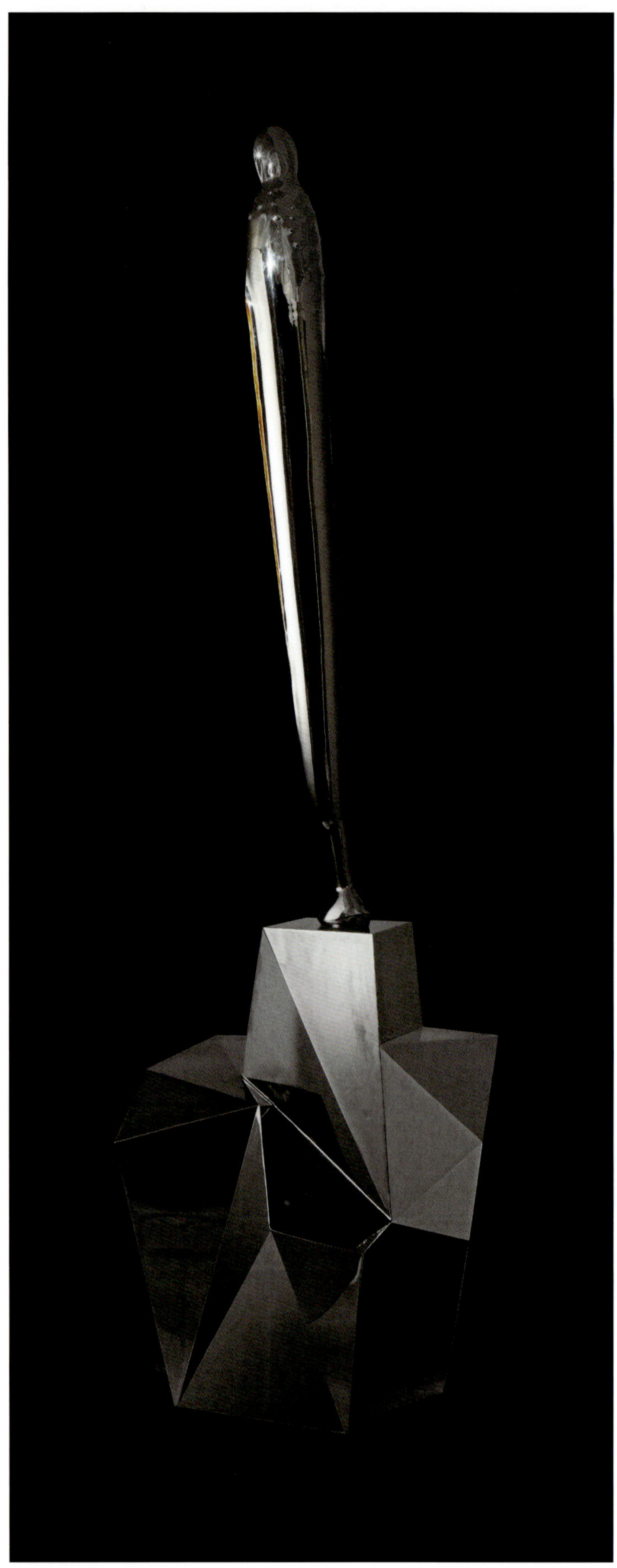

Awareness 9
Stainless steel, 40×40×196cm
2014

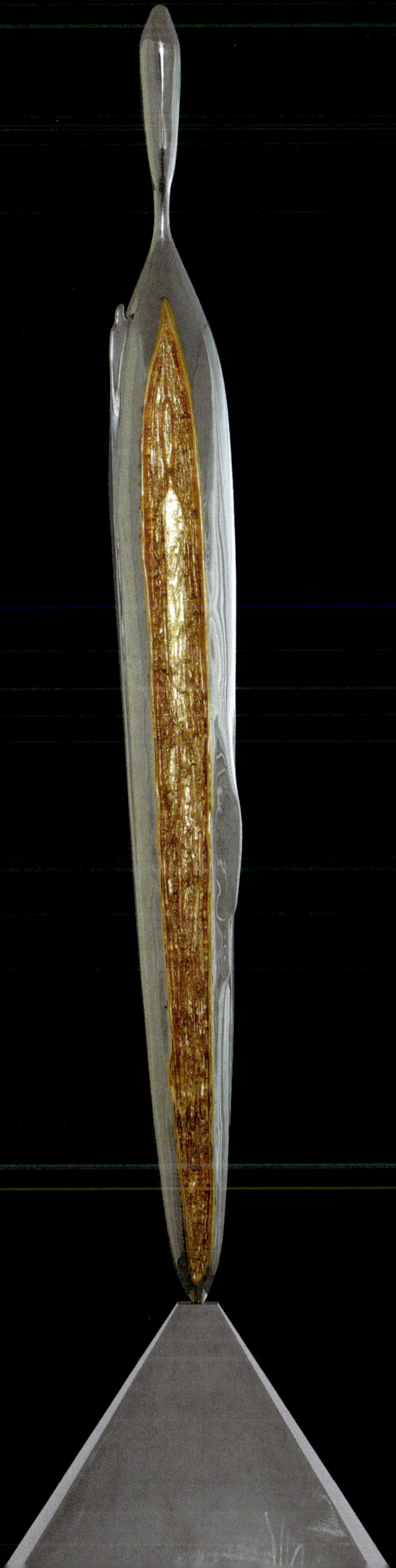

Awareness 10
Stainless steel, gold foil, 70×70×228cm
2014

Awareness 11
Stainless steel, gold foil, 40×30×190cm
2014

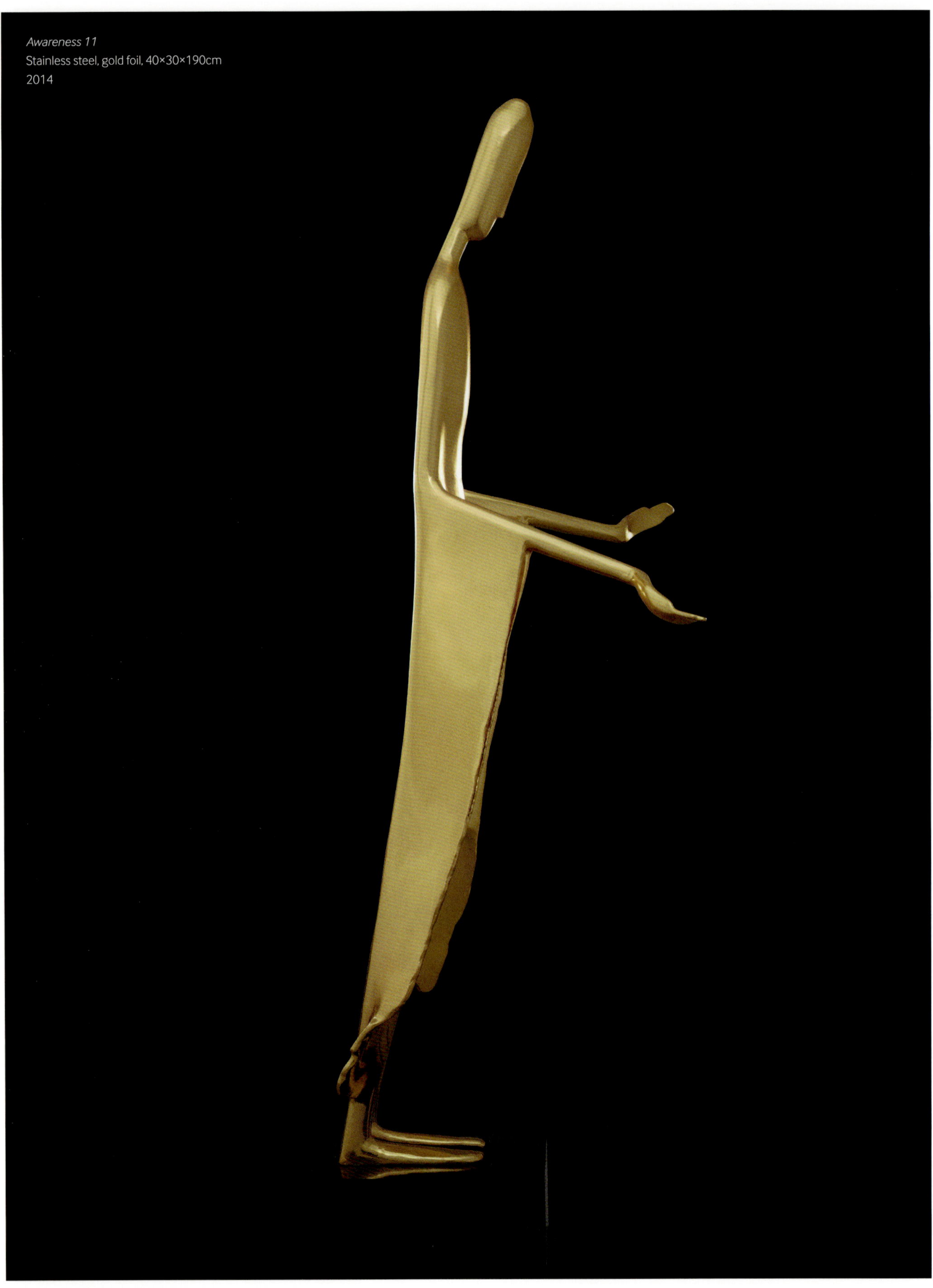

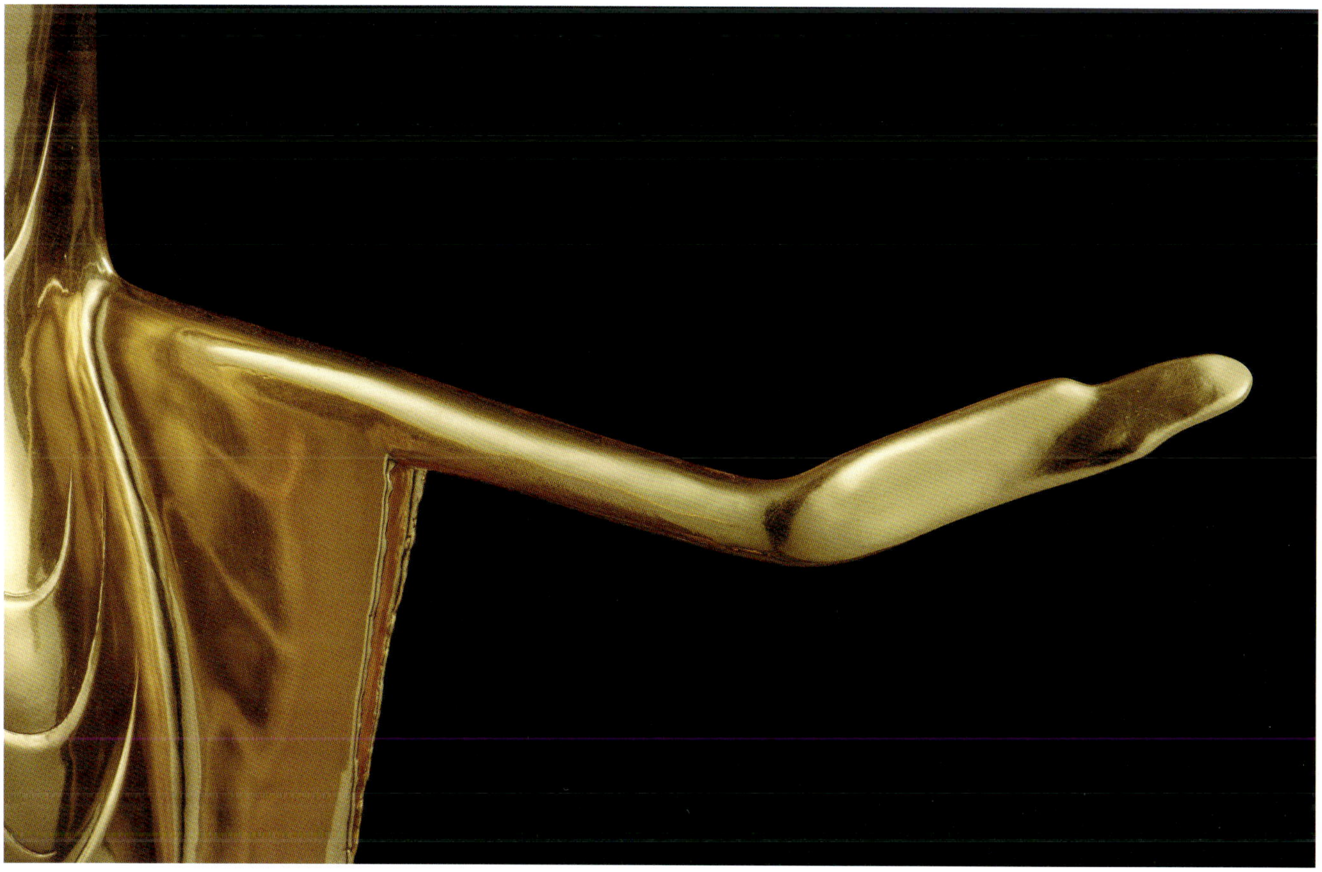

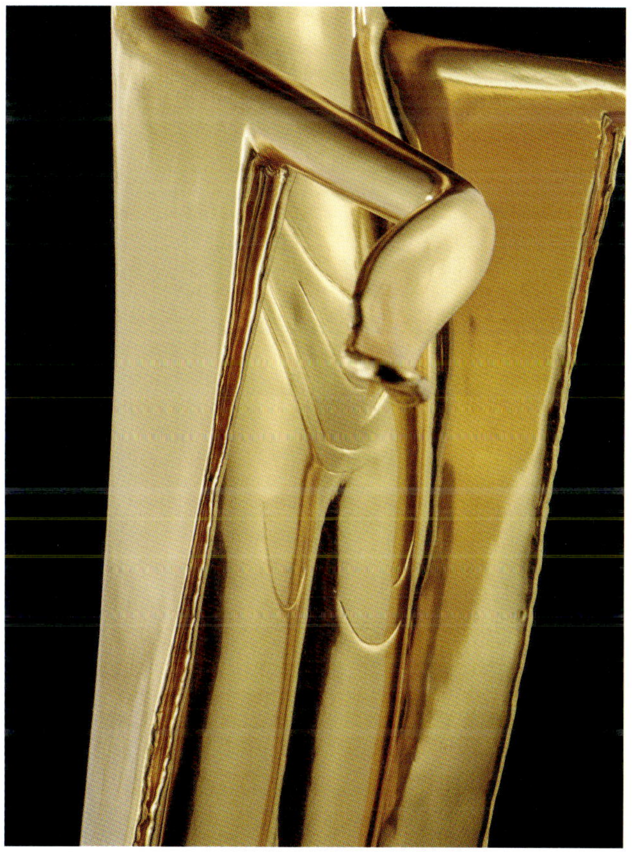

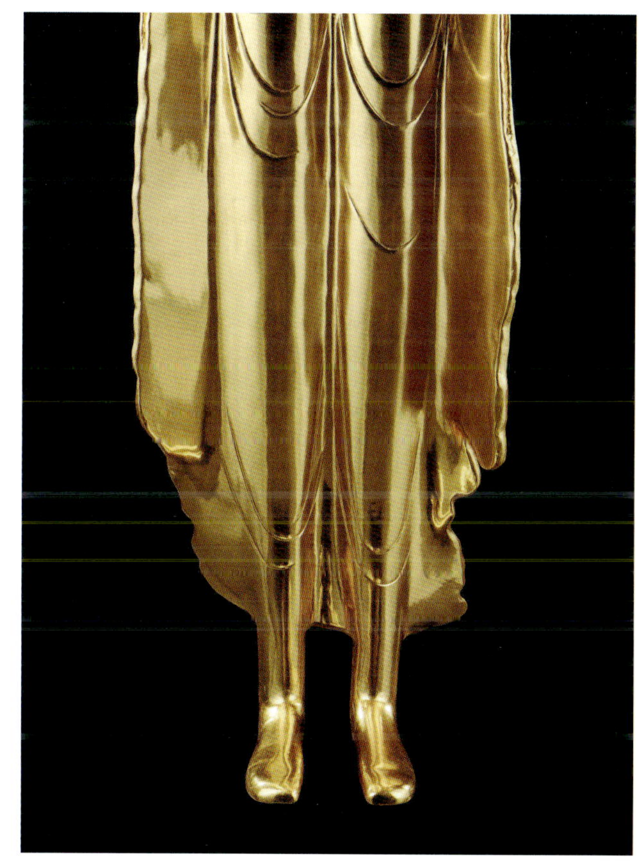

All phenomena are empty - they have no birth and no extinction, no defilement and no purity, no increase and no decrease.

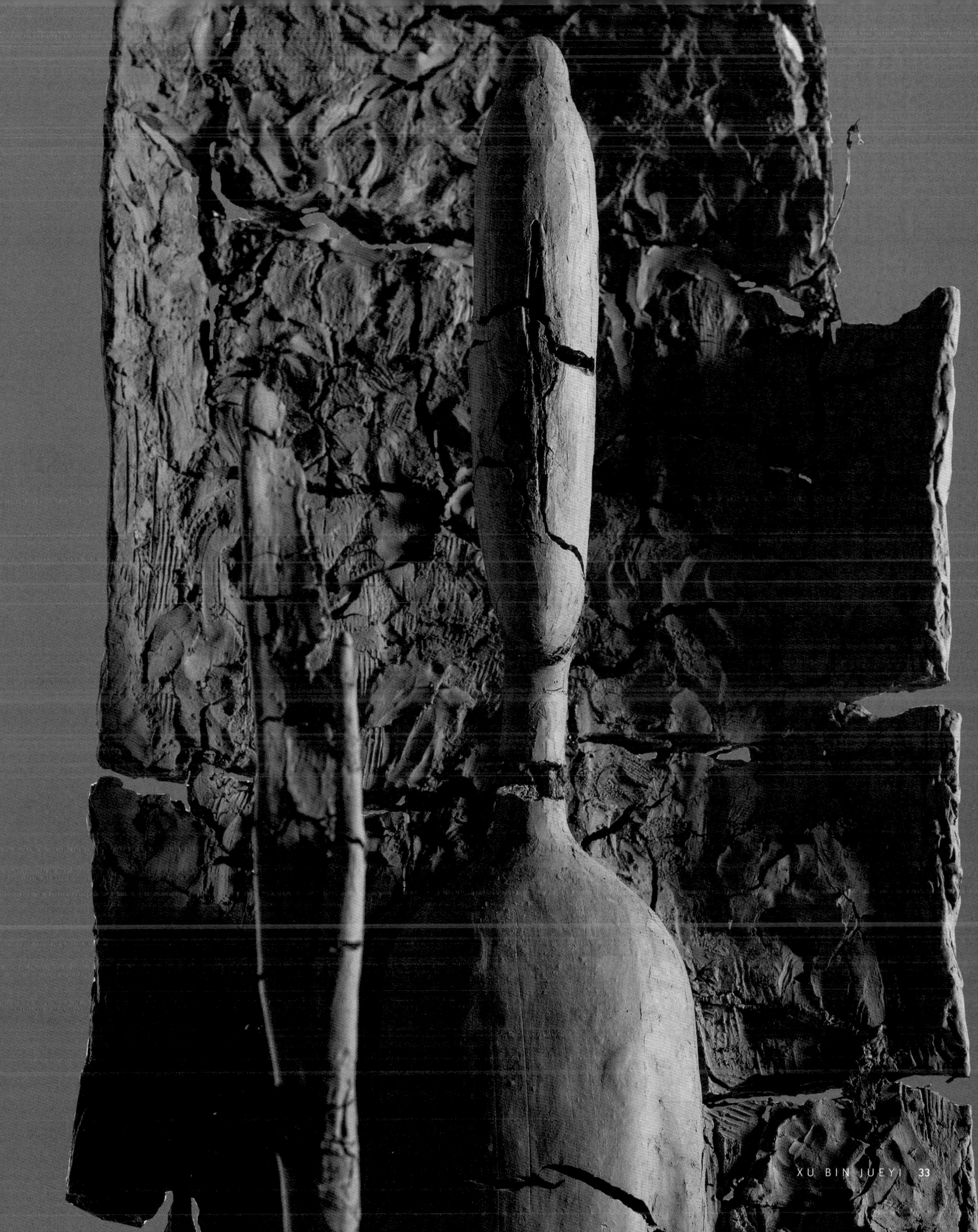

XU BIN JUEYI 33

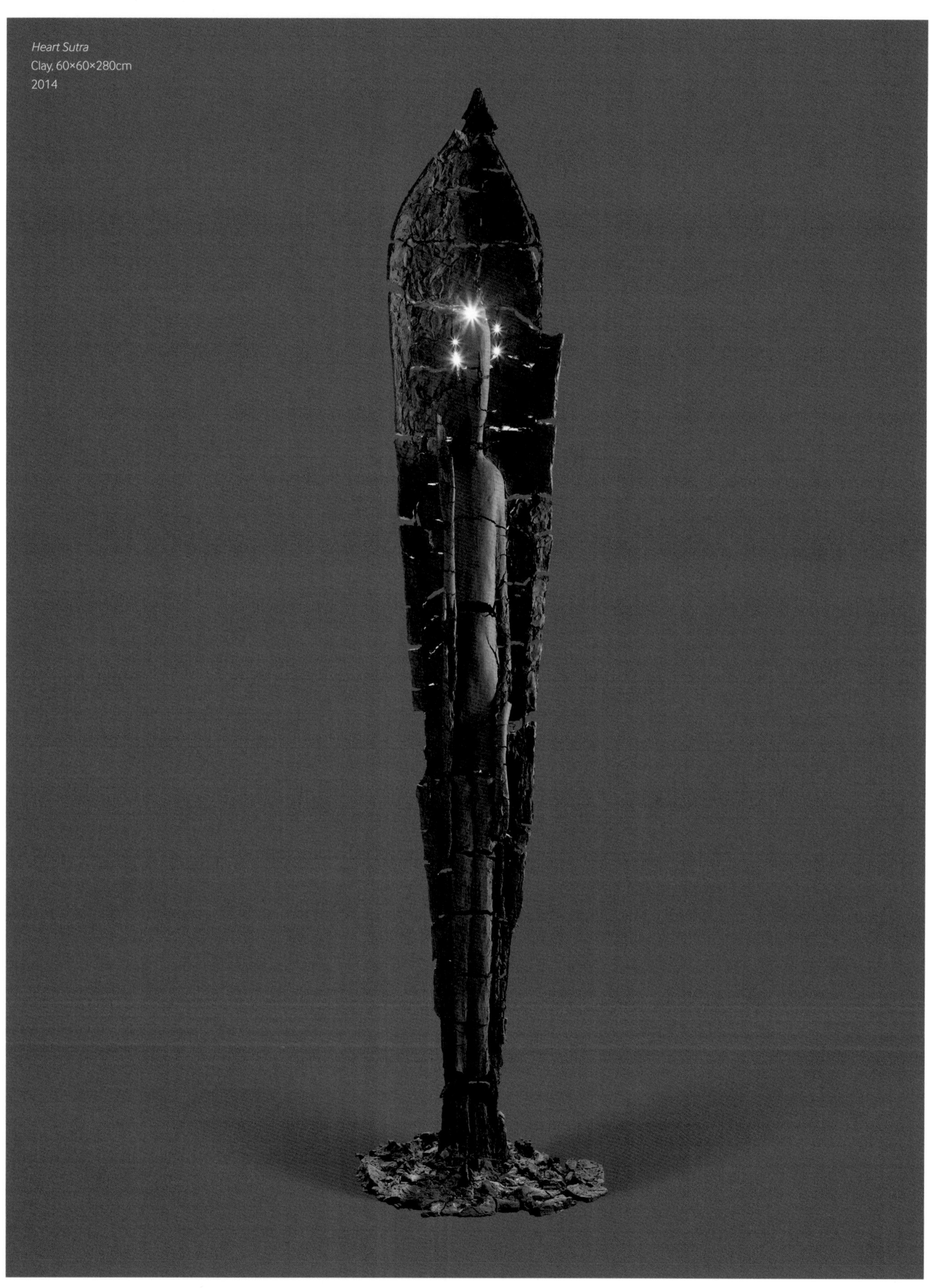

Heart Sutra
Clay, 60×60×280cm
2014

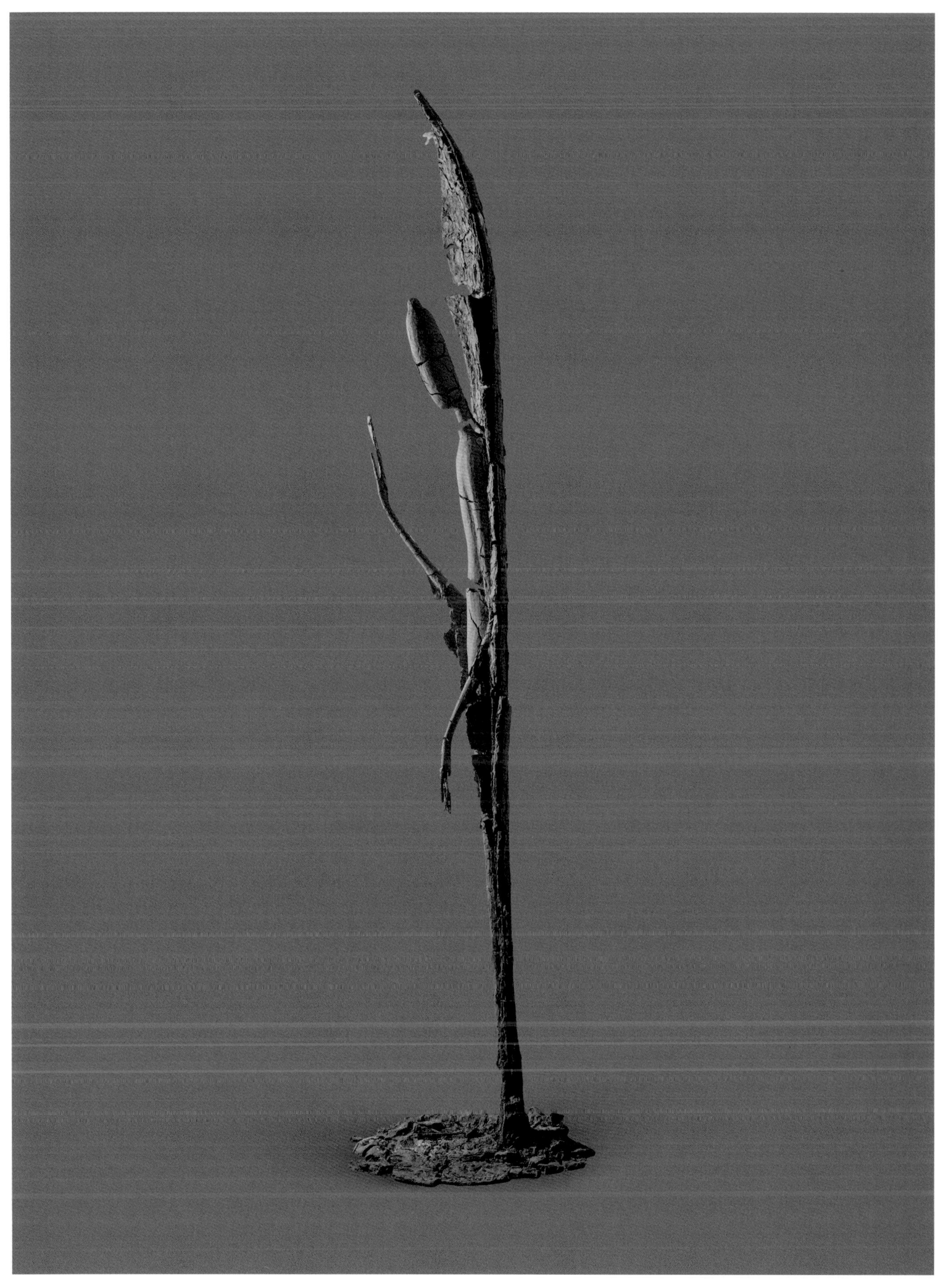

Diamond Sutra

From the back the work looks like an image of the Madonna, from
the front like the coffin of a pharaoh of Egypt, inside there is a
small statue of Buddha or Guanyin (Avalokiteshvara). When the
viewer stands inside the work, it is like being in the womb of the
Madonna; or you come to the realization that the experience of life
and death in the universe is only an instant, and that you should
not attach importance to gains and losses of the material world.
Everything is empty. As the Diamond Sutra says: 'All *sankhata*
dhamma are like illusory bubbles; if you see that all phenomena
are not phenomena, then you see the Tathagata Buddha ...
All phenomena are dream bubbles, like dew, like lightning,
and should be perceived as such.

Diamond Sutra
Stainless steel, 96×96×280cm
2015

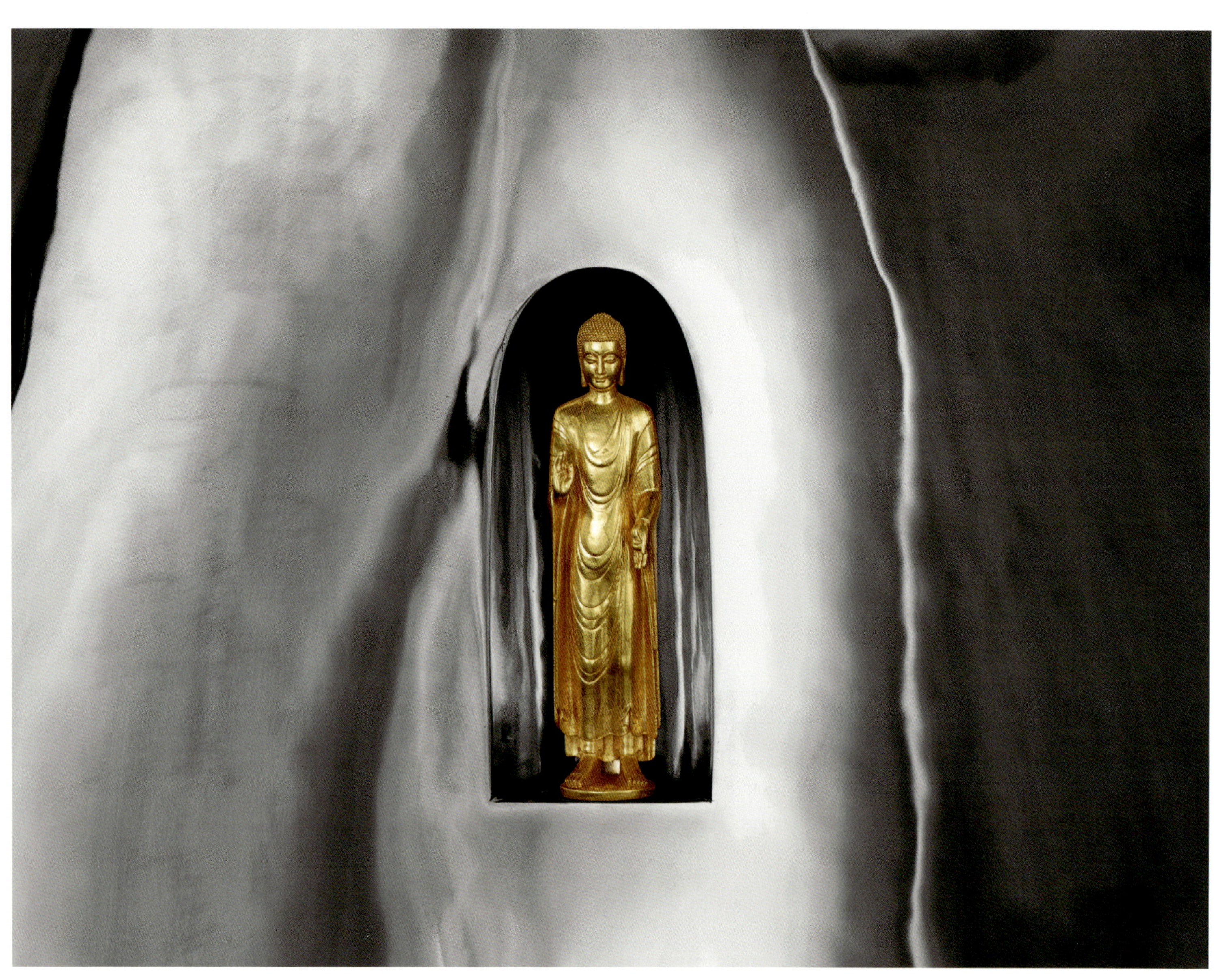

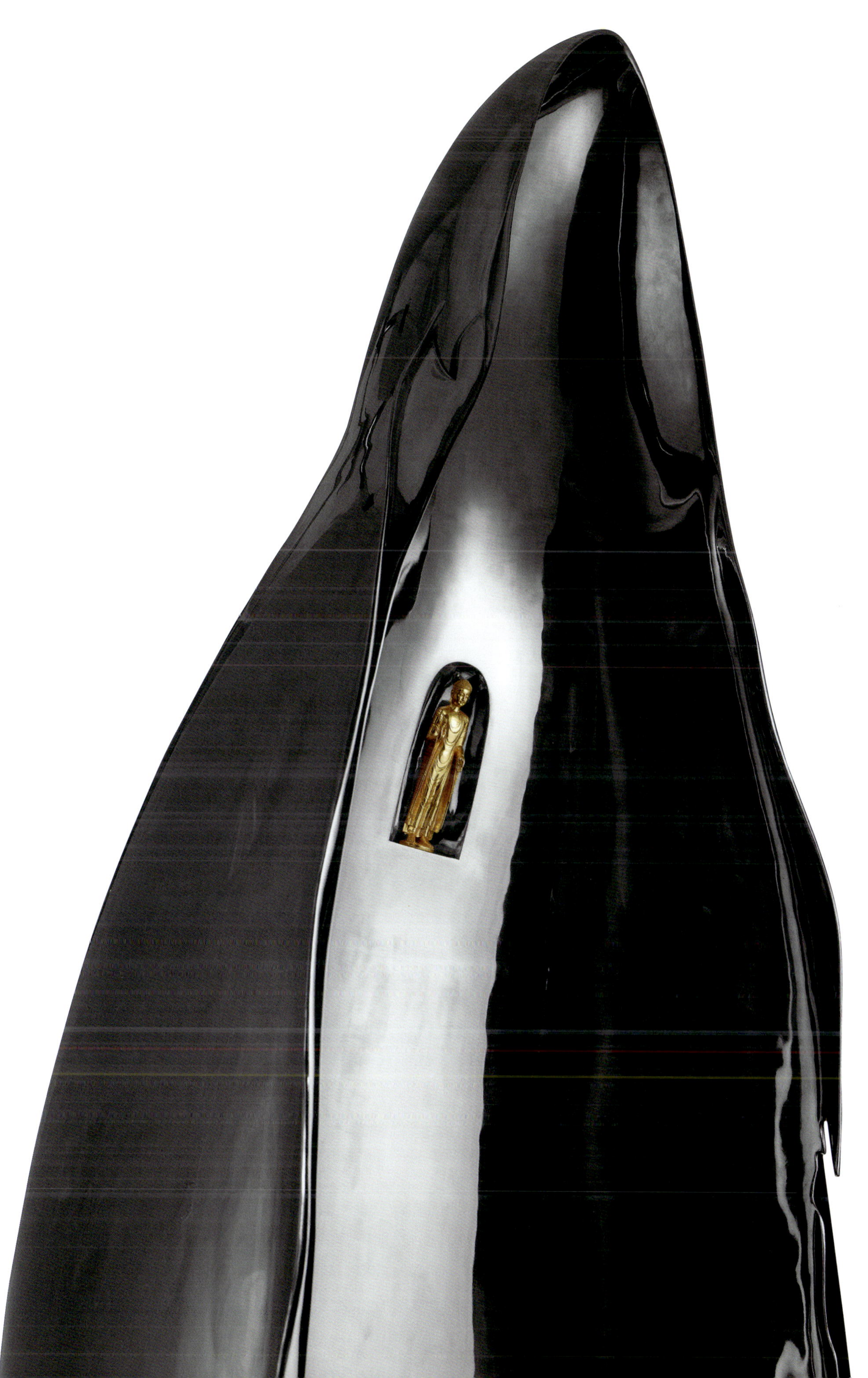

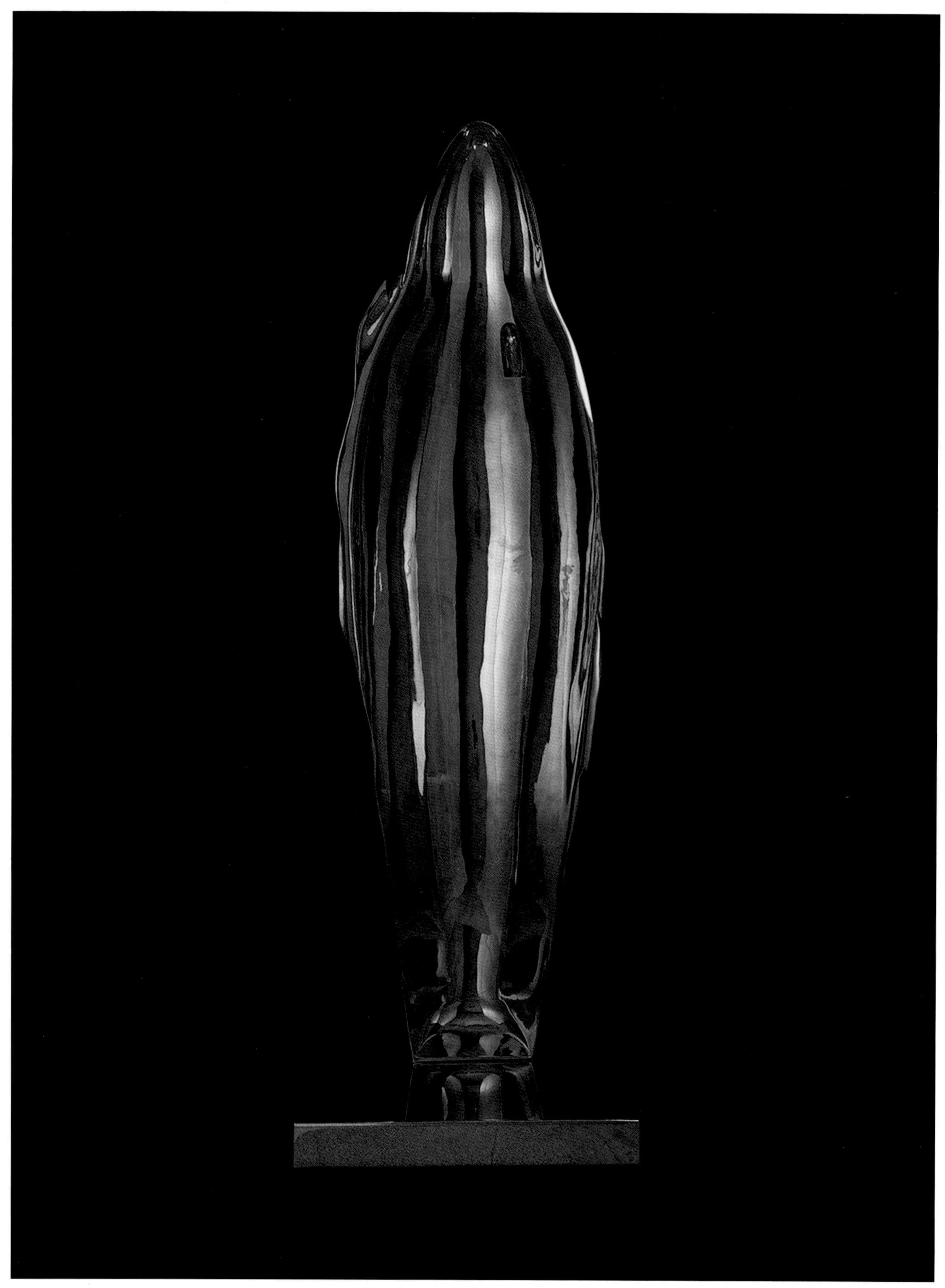

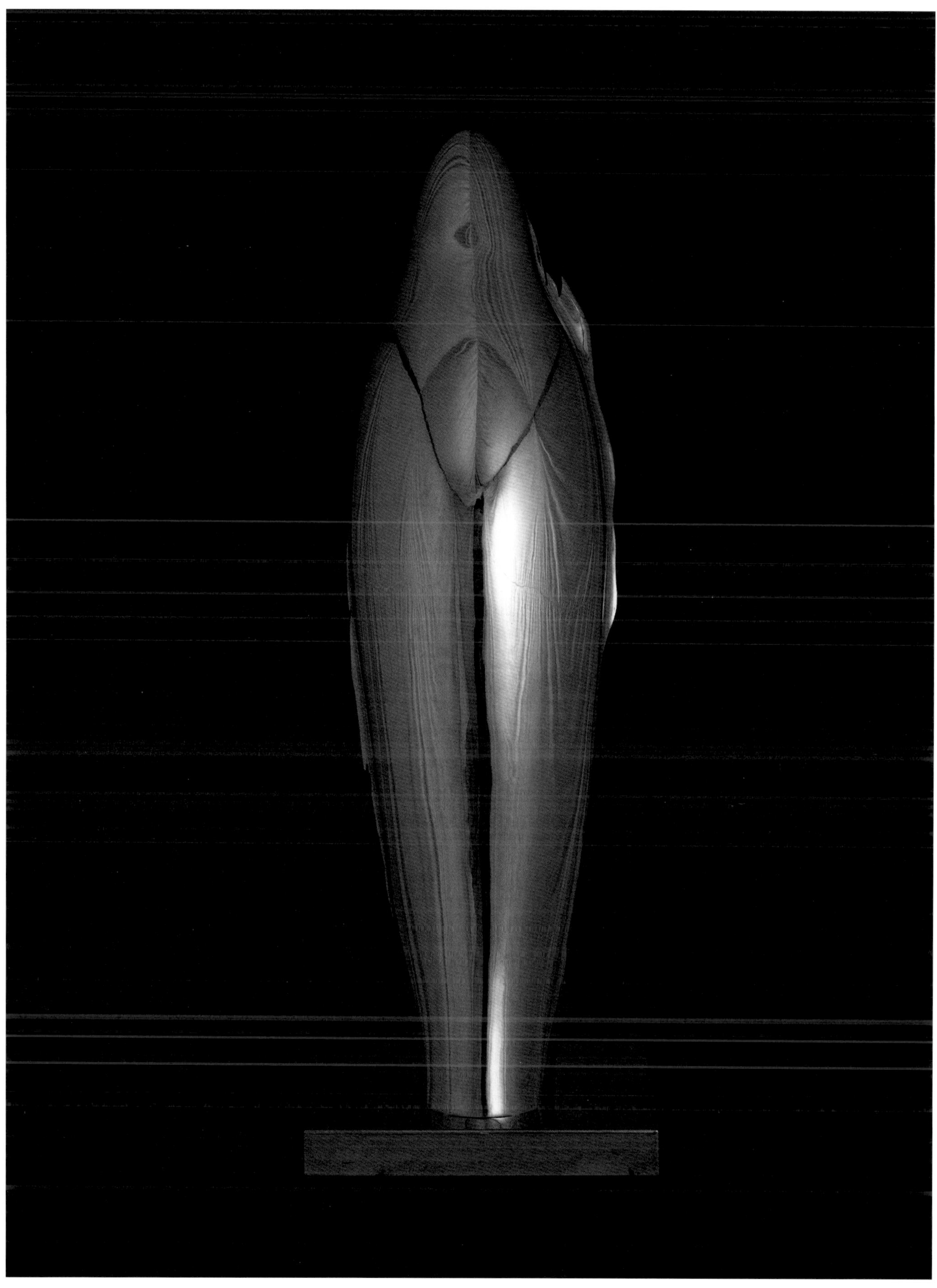

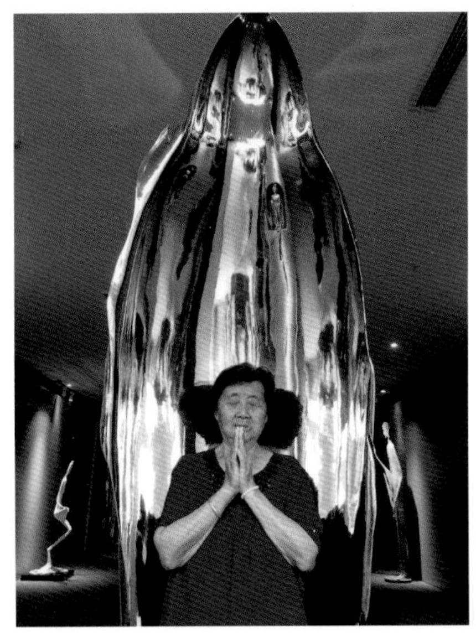
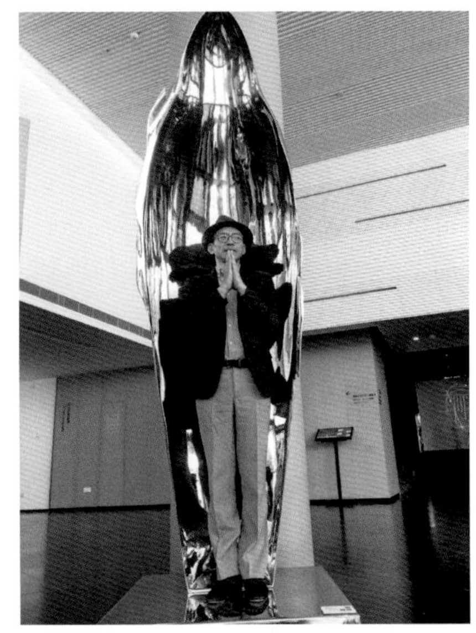
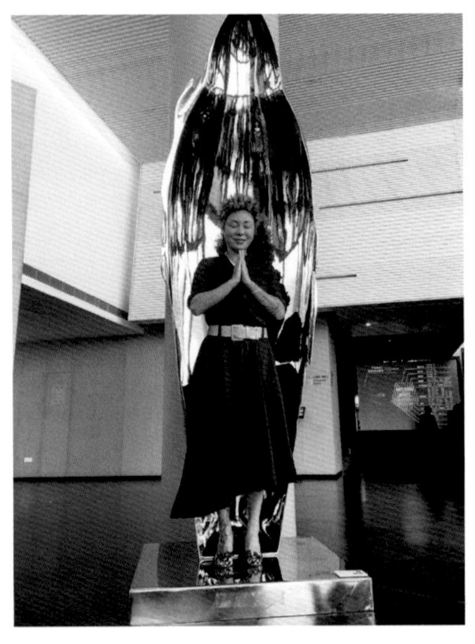
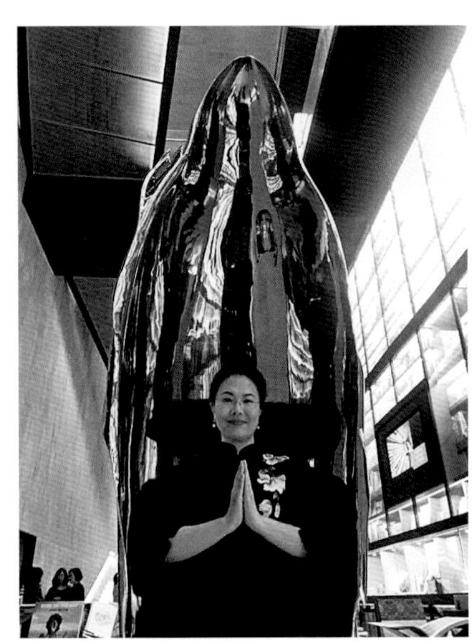
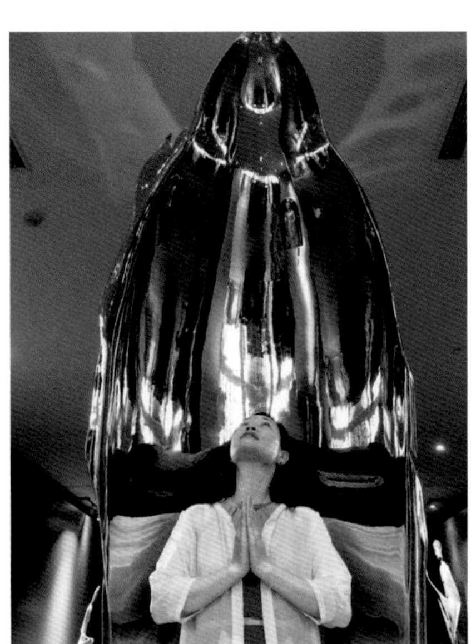
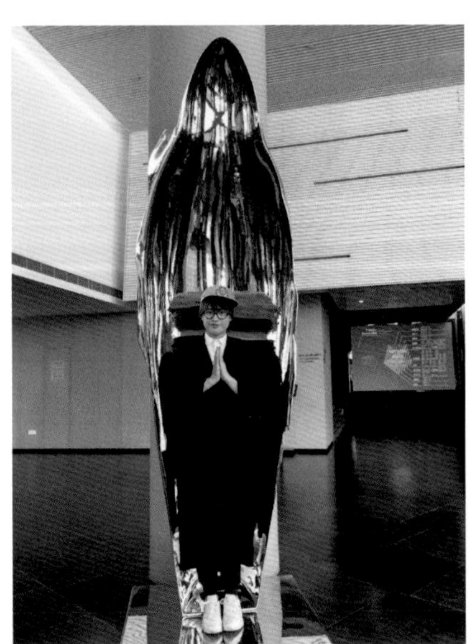
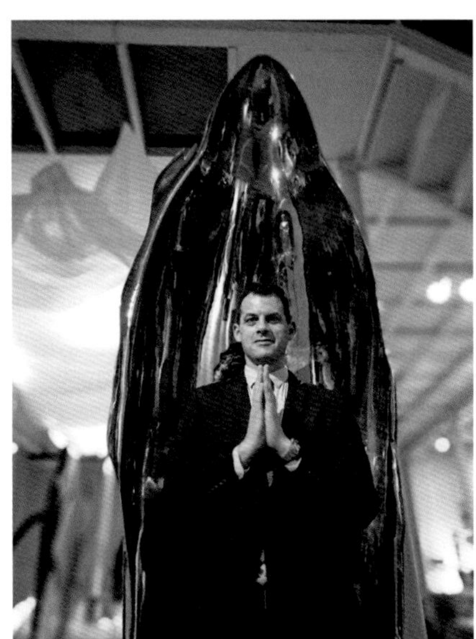

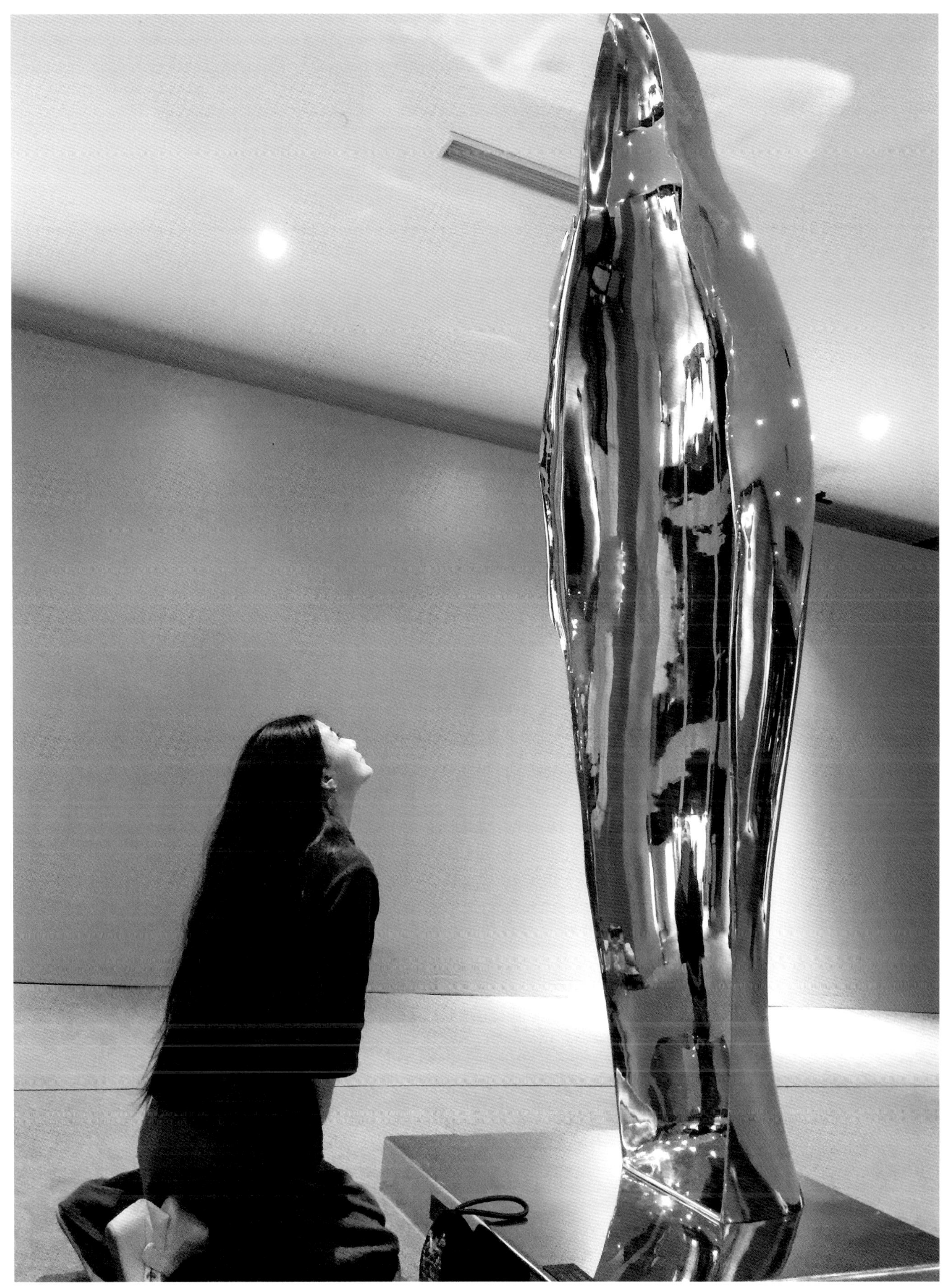

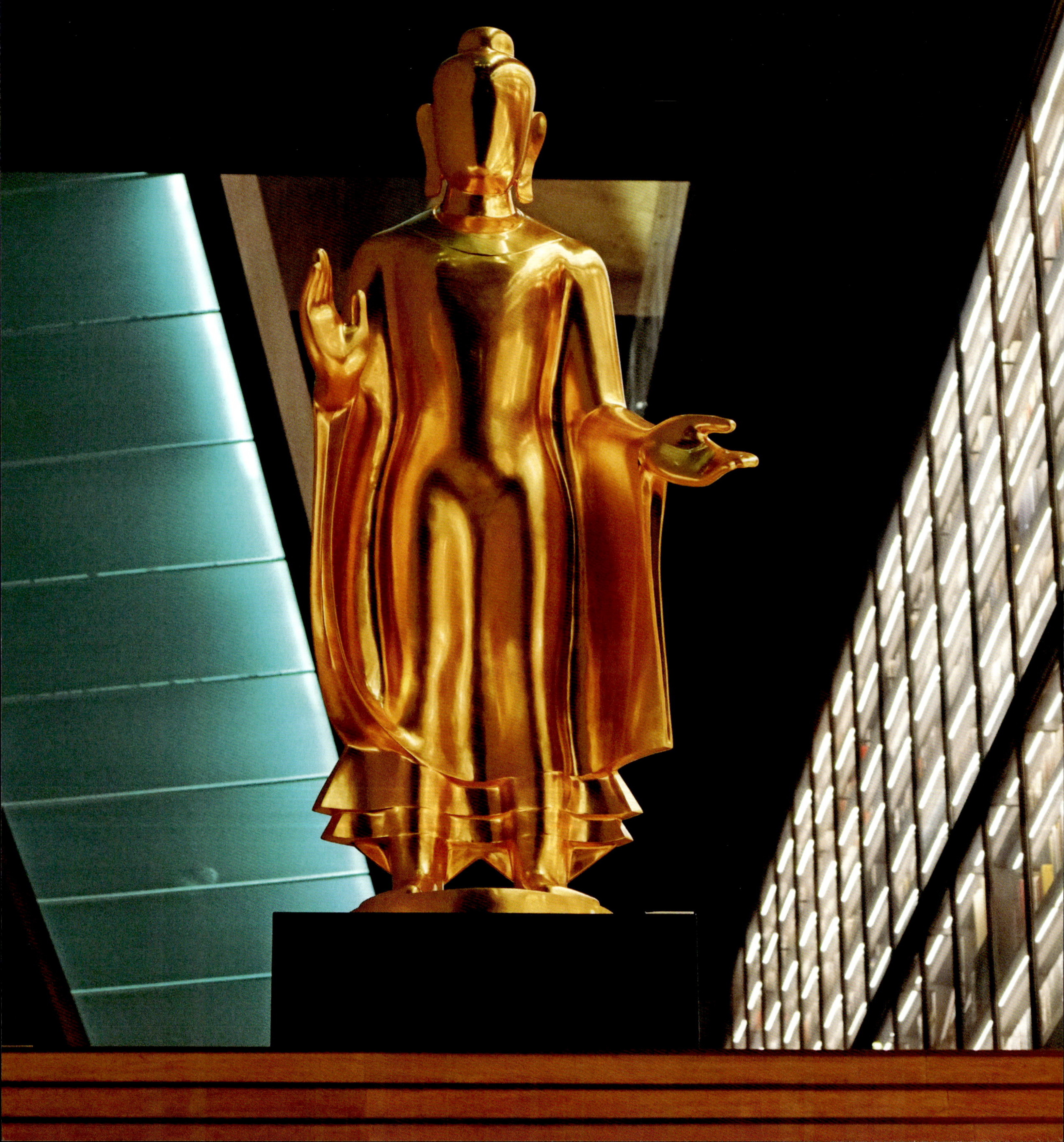

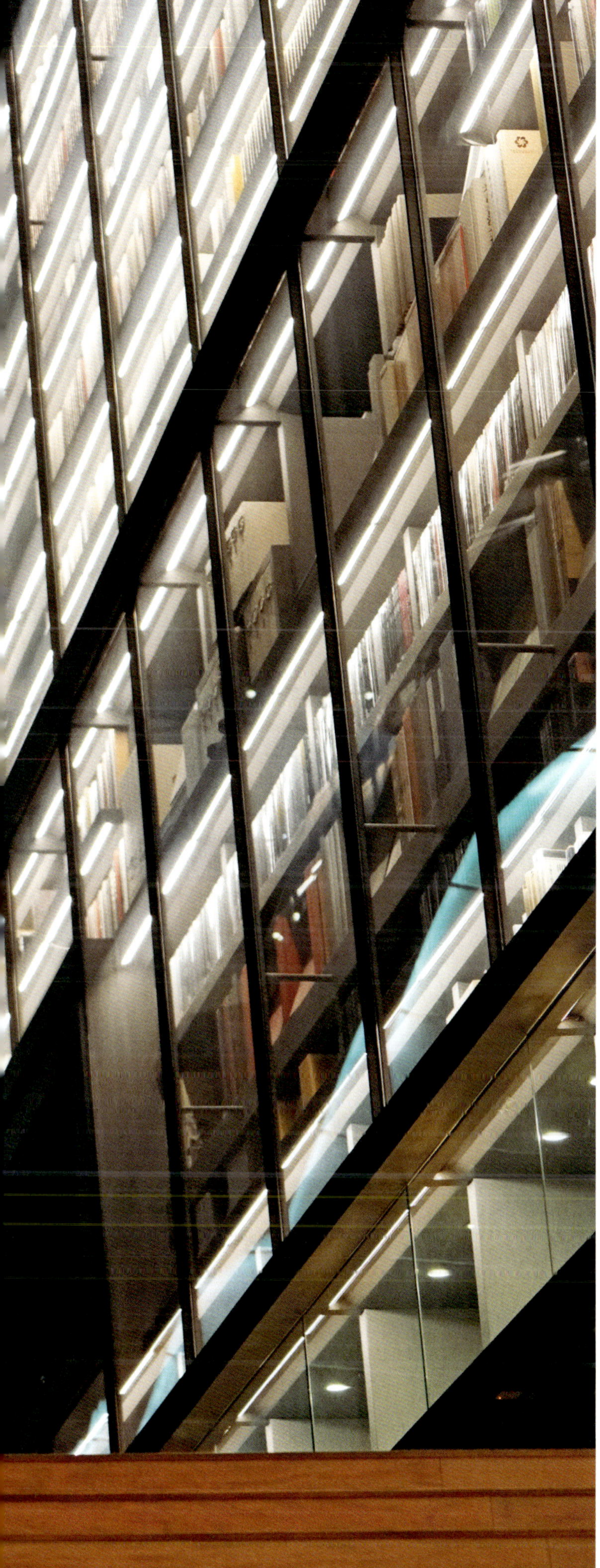

Bronze with gold foil,
99×55×369cm
2016

Installation

The installation consists of eaves of roof stilts forming a pyramid, bells, Bodhi door, cut-out vertical lines of diamonds and major religious elements to create a contemporary religious temple. It expresses boundless religious communion, peace and love.

The interior of the installation uses the concept of the Buddhist grotto. A series of small boxes made of steel planks create niches for buddhas, as in our present life state, like small rooms in a series of high-rise buildings. It puts the distance of indifference between people. The reflective surfaces of the pyramid create an illusion across space, representing humanity's exploration of the vast universe.

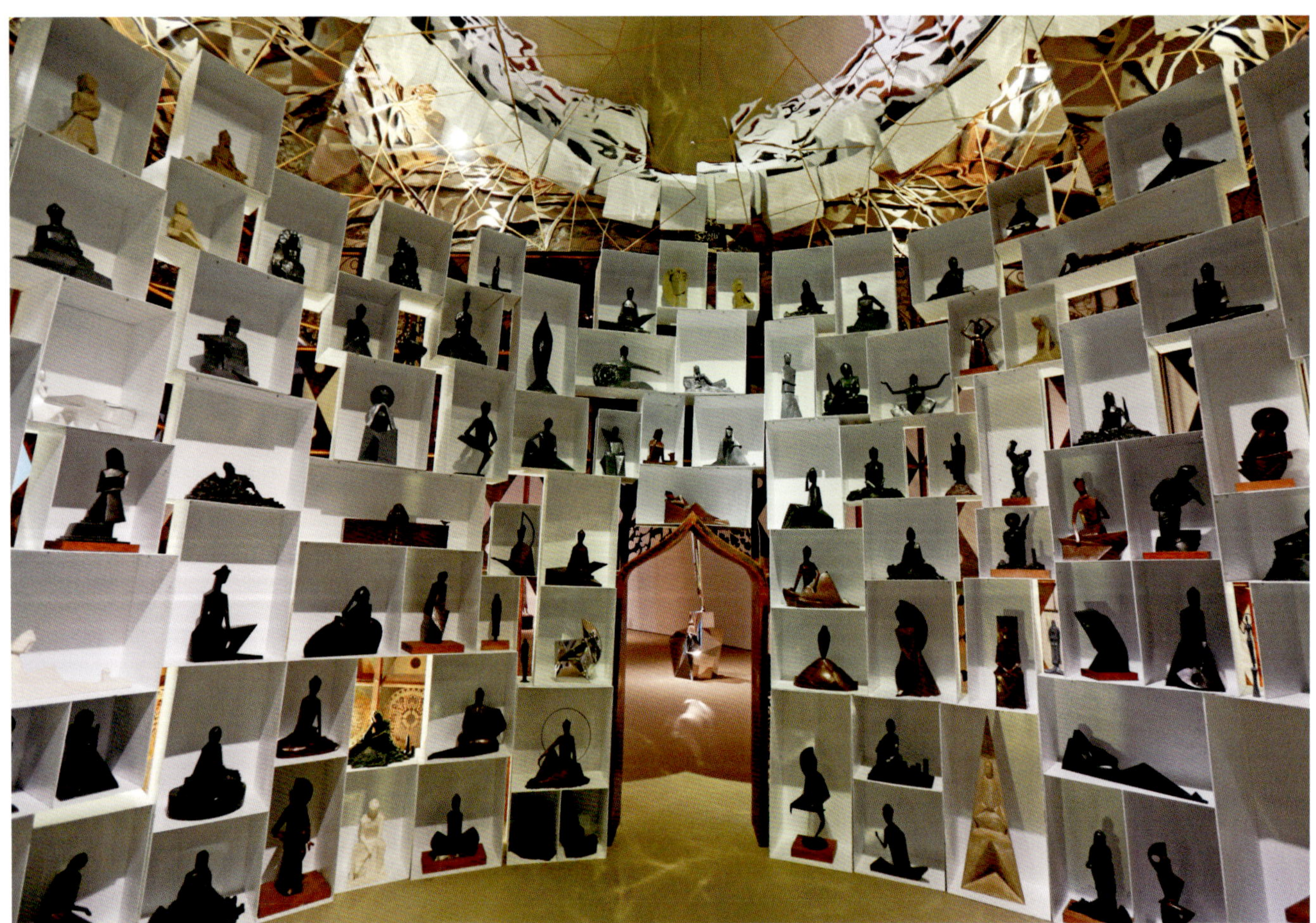

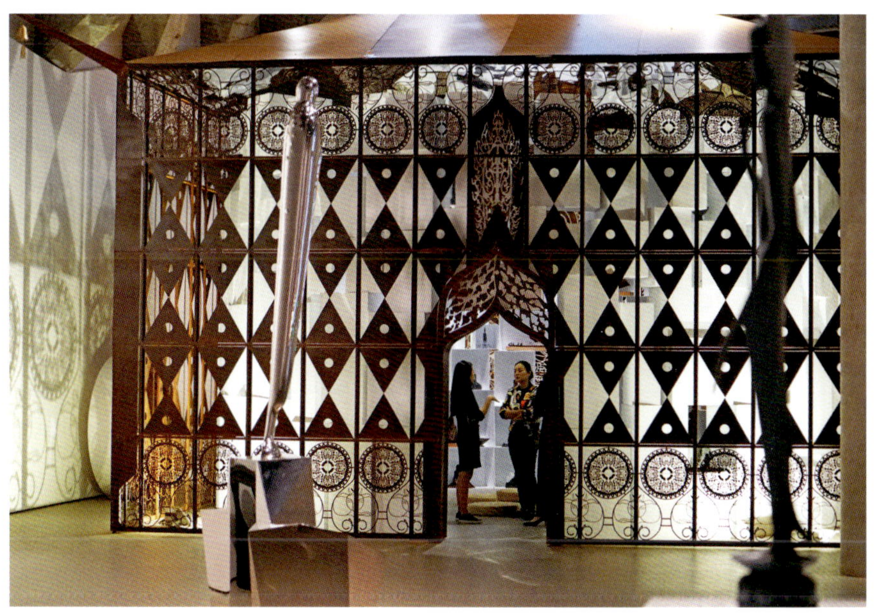

Universe
Steel, 700×700cm
2013

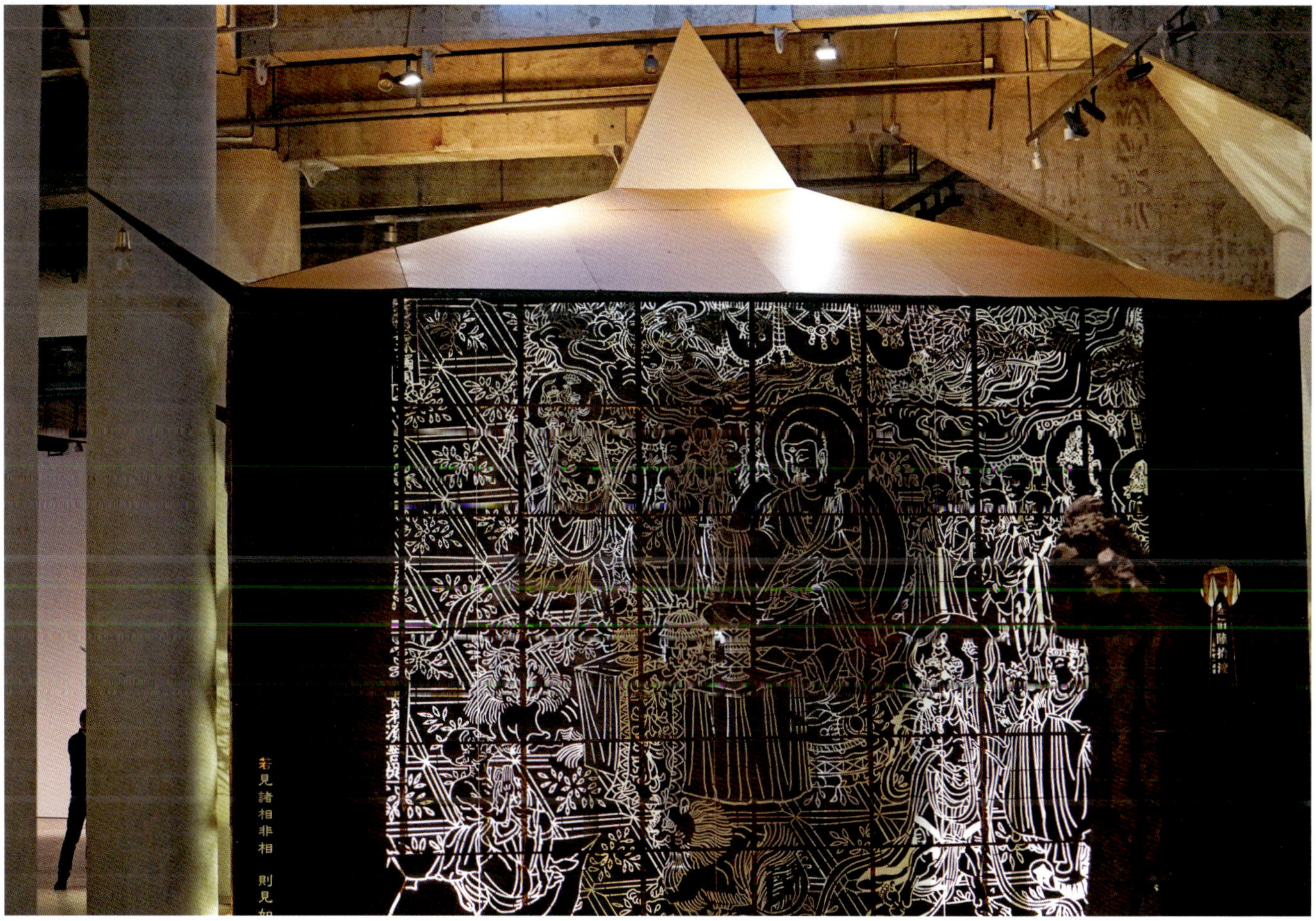

Compassion

If the world is at peace,
how does a triumphal arch
come about?

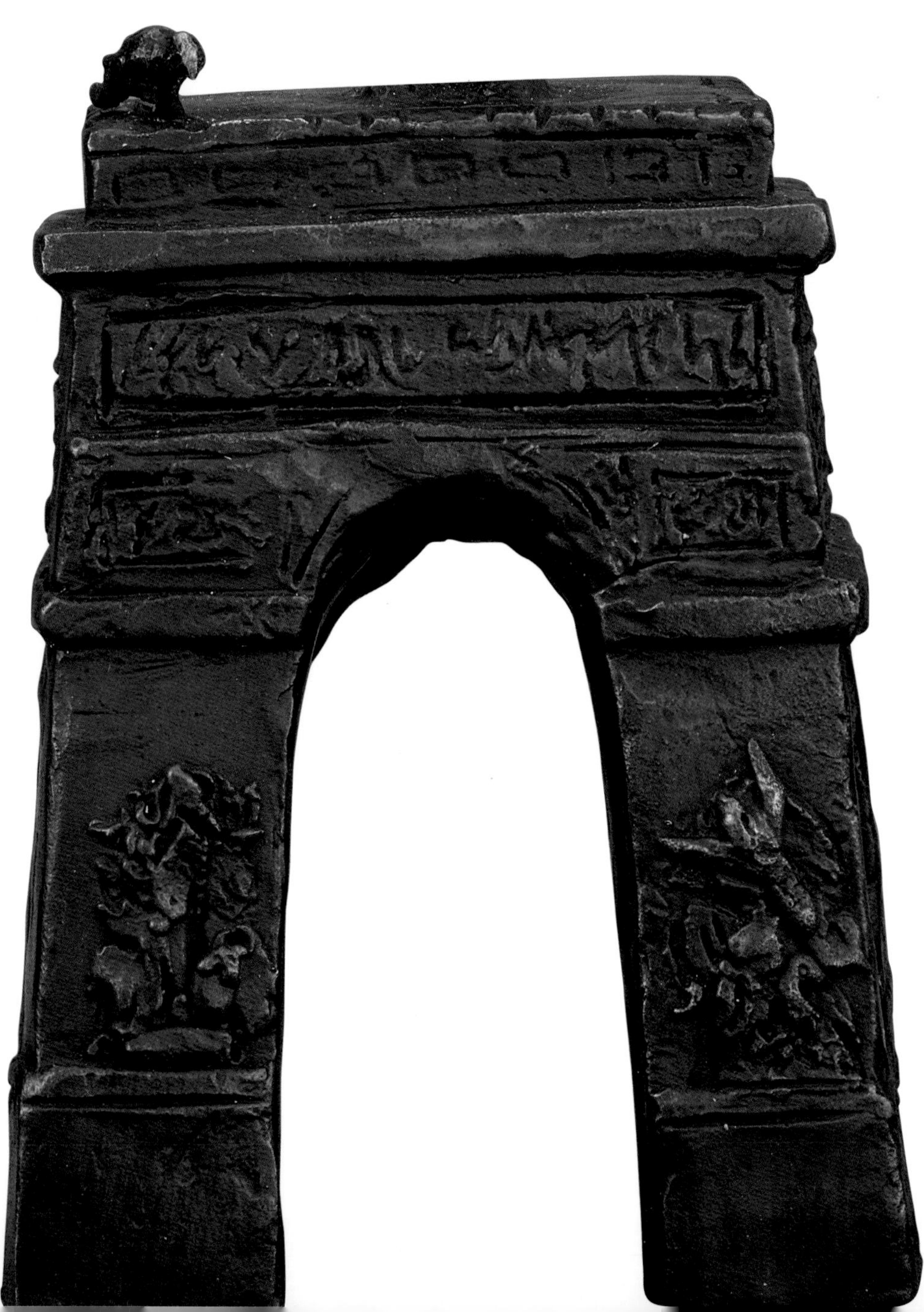

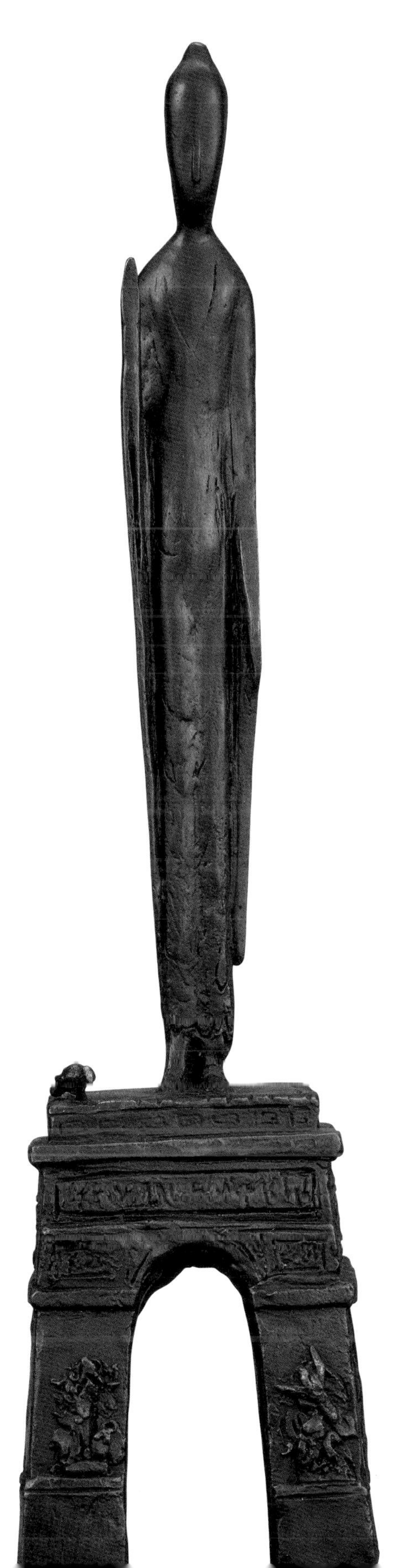

Triumphal Arch
Beauty of Compassion
Bronze, 8×7×35 cm
2014

Psychic Power Can Penetrate The Universe
- *Jiang Ning*

A chance opportunity enabled me to participate in the Xu Bin Jueyi Myriad Buddha Programme. When I encountered the programme, my first response was, this is fantastic — this is what contemporary art should look like.

It is a great contemporary art project: its greatness lies not only in that it fills a gap in contemporary art, but also in that, from the human point of view, it lets art into the homes of ordinary people. The programme is not just about artistic creation. Instead, it is essentially an activity: an activity that, through the form of contemporary art, through a dialogue between the created Buddhas and Xu Bin Jueyi, records a discovery, an abstract generalized refinement of the story and psychic power of each person. This activity, called the 'Myriad Buddha Programme', reveals the beauty of compassion.

Art and human understanding of the world complement each other

In primitive society, humanity feared the unknown, feared the mysterious force of the universe, feared God and spirits. By the period of early and mid-feudal society, a small number of people took on the role of representatives for God and the spirits, causing many people to be in awe of, and worship, them.

And by the Renaissance, or the late feudal period, with the rise of science and start of the Industrial Revolution, people became self-aware and started to become human-oriented. They denied God and the spirits, and those who set themselves up as their representatives. By the time of the 18th and 19th centuries, humanity had achieved some success in the contest with nature, developed inflated ambitions to conquer everything, and, with superstitious faith, put the self at the centre. Art was raised to the same level as philosophy, and started to be revered at the altar.

In discussions of modern art, creative pieces of art are generally seen as superior to ordinary ones, so the work of the artist, and the art itself, is distant from most of us ordinary people.

Today, contemporary art is booming, so we return from the lofty heights of art theory to reality. And Xu Bin Jueyi's Myriad Buddha Programme gradually dissolves that feeling of art being distant. This is a very valuable artistic practice the artist offers.

The peak of the development of modernist aesthetics is the theory of human self at the centre. To look at things more philosophically, at the time of the Renaissance, putting humanity at the centre had a certain basis, because there was a desire to get rid of God. And it touches on the ideas of classical philosophy: where do people come from, where are we going, who am I?

This represented a big step for human civilization and thinking, but reality has shown that the thinking of that time was still very limited.

Today's emphasis on science represents only a limited part of the observation and perception of the real world — on this point most people now agree. This means that logical thinking has its limitations. Therefore, we should return to an outlook not centred on the human self. We cannot address the vastness of the universe with an approach that implies if something has not been perceived it should not be acknowledged. Because the vast universe, has always run in its own way, and with its own will, not changed by the will of individual people. Instead, each person's will exists in its own way within the universe, as a part of the universe, co-existing and intertwined with opposing entities, interacting, in phases of mutual productivity and resistance.

Macro and micro perspectives fuse in the 'Myriad Buddha Programme'

So now we see that, taking the imposing universe as a macro description of direction, if we strive to have a little more understanding of it, we should return to a theory that is not based on the human self at the centre — we cannot address the vastness of the universe with an approach that implies if something has not been perceived it should not be acknowledged. In my understanding, the macro perspective of the Myriad Buddha Programme is: Stand on the highpoint of civilization to look at the vast boundless universe. If you want to use a word to express this, it is 'Buddha'.

The 'Myriad Buddha Programme' represents the artist, taking many small artistic observations, or observations on people's inner selves, to build a vastness, a spectacular panorama like big data. The beauty of human nature and the search for the vastness of the universe can be called 'Buddha', and our every micro inner perception and introspection can be called 'myriad'. From this perspective, every ordinary person who participates in the Myriad Buddha Programme, their every thought, belongs to his (the Buddha's) thought and will; their will cannot change the way the universe works, but their thoughts exist in the universe in a variety of ways. Or, they are also part of the vast universe in the form of oppositional forms of interaction. Thus, the 'Buddha' and 'myriad' of the 'Myriad Buddha Programme', reflect on the human self and human culture, and so reveal their far-reaching significance.

Xu Bin Jueyi's forward-looking artistic practice

Contemporary art in the fast-moving world of today, represents the progress of the whole of humanity's thinking and the main direction of thinking. Now, if we return to our awe of the universe, admit our ignorance, and acknowledge that we cannot perceive the breadth of the universe, this is itself a kind of progress.

Through an artistic practice, or, you could say, a way of reflecting on civilization, completely divorced from modernist aesthetics, Xu Bin Jueyi expresses his observations, and brings us a completely new perspective on the self and the universe.

And then, if we reflect on the modernist theory of aesthetics, the artist's thinking on art is in contrast in keeping with the high point of classical philosophical thought. The modernists do not allow ordinary people to participate in the artist's practice; they put it on a pedestal and do not let people participate. But Xu Bin Jueyi invites the general public to participate in introspection. The artist simply records and summarizes this 'introspection'. He uses sculpture to express their thoughts. This is a characteristic that distinguishes contemporary art from the modernist aesthetics of the last century. And his is an unprecedented practice. His achievements cannot be summed up in terms of the generality of artistic creation – there is a common participation and reflection process between him and the participants in the creation, so it is a very constructive practice.

Making Buddhas so that everyone sees the beauty of the self

Having invited more than a thousand self-conscious, introspective art-practice participants as partners in the creation of themselves, Xu Bin Jueyi faithfully discusses with them ideas of their own inner selves and then expresses these ideas through sculpture, that is in the array of myriad Buddhas we see today. Here, it is worth emphasizing that, in Xu Bin Jueyi's 'Myriad Buddha Programme', there is no underlying logic. In making each sculpture, he does not think about how to

create or what materials to use. Often it is only once he has taken up his pen or is about to start sculpting that the inspiration comes. It could be said that he refuses to be trapped in a theoretical system, that in his thinking about culture he breaks the shackles of modern aesthetics. This is a kind of aesthetic practice, and I feel honoured to have participated in this practice.

Furthermore, let me double my gratitude to him in respect of a certain point, that is for the moment when, in creating the Buddha, he reveals the Buddha nature, and discovers the beauty of human nature. We live in a world full of conflict, and our inner selves have long been hardened over with a layer of calluses. We are so afraid of being hurt, of being spied on, afraid to reveal ourselves, that we lock up our hearts, and rarely enjoy soft things. But he is somehow able to uncover that inner fresh, soft and brilliant shining part of our human nature, and make people reflect on themselves. I think this is psychic power.

In the process of the creation of my Buddha, I found that some of the people who participated in the creation of their Buddhas with me were cold and rather terrifying, the sort of people to be wary of. But, during the project, they were somehow broken down, and I saw each person's compassion and their good thoughts. The moment when those who were made Buddha revealed their Buddha nature was recorded, and written into short accounts of a thousand words; readers of these accounts often burst into tears. Xu Bin Jueyi now wants to collect these accounts and assemble them into a small book (see note), and present it to us as part of the programme. This book represents a dialogue of artistic creation, a spiritual dialogue.

Perhaps, when you see this book or appreciate these works, you will feel the greatness of this programme, and experience the deep beauty of human nature.

We see that kind of compassion in the people around us, those sorts of good thoughts, converging today on the programme. It is not limited to artistic creation; the programme itself is an activity. This activity, through the medium of contemporary art, through the dialogues of a myriad people with Xu Bin Jueyi records a discovery, an abstract generalized refinement of the story and psychic power of each person. This activity, called the 'Myriad Buddha Programme', reveals the Beauty of Compassion.

(Note: The book mentioned by the author refers to the one about the artist Xu Bin Jueyi planned and published in November 2016 by the Chinese publisher Zhang Dong: 'Myriad Buddha Programme' Beauty of Compassion.)

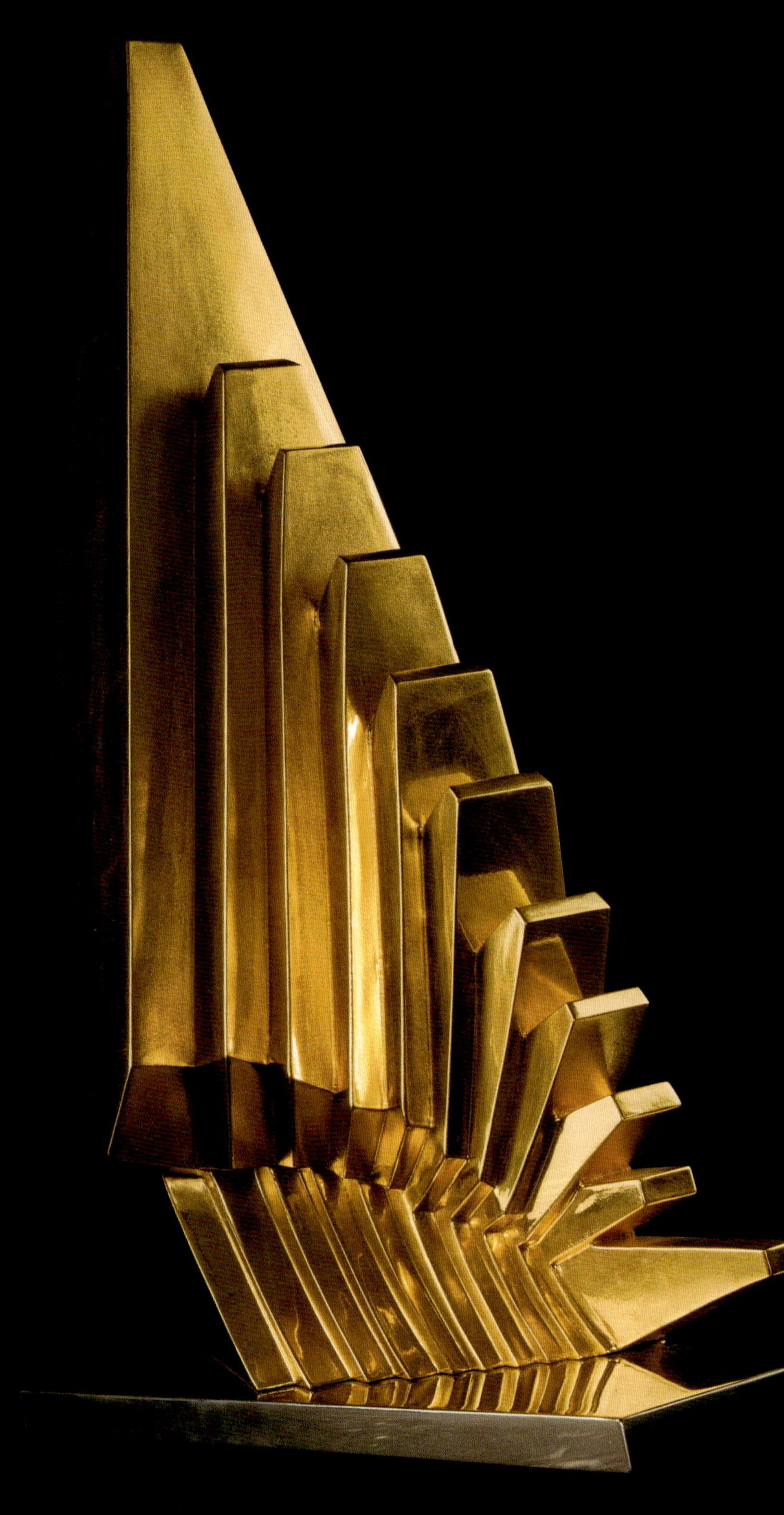

Beauty is Strength

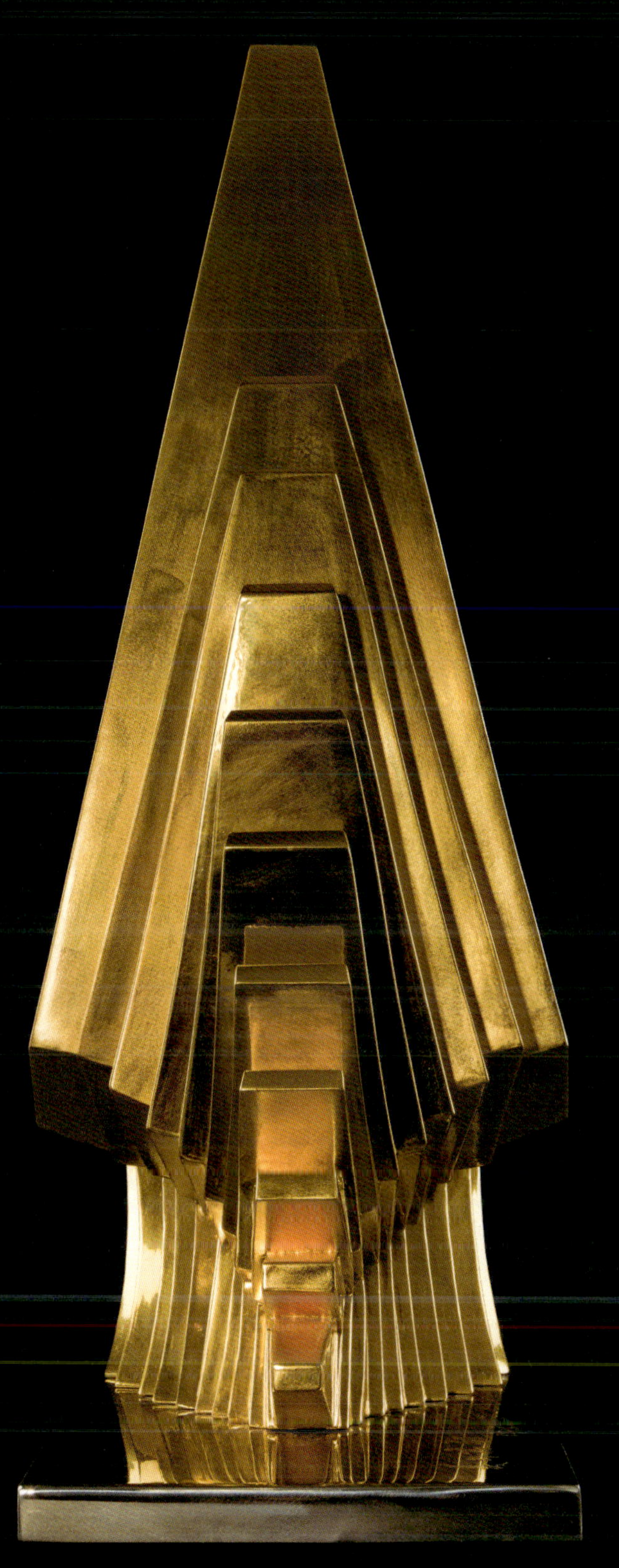

Flight of Beauty
Bronze with gold foil,
51×23×70cm
2016

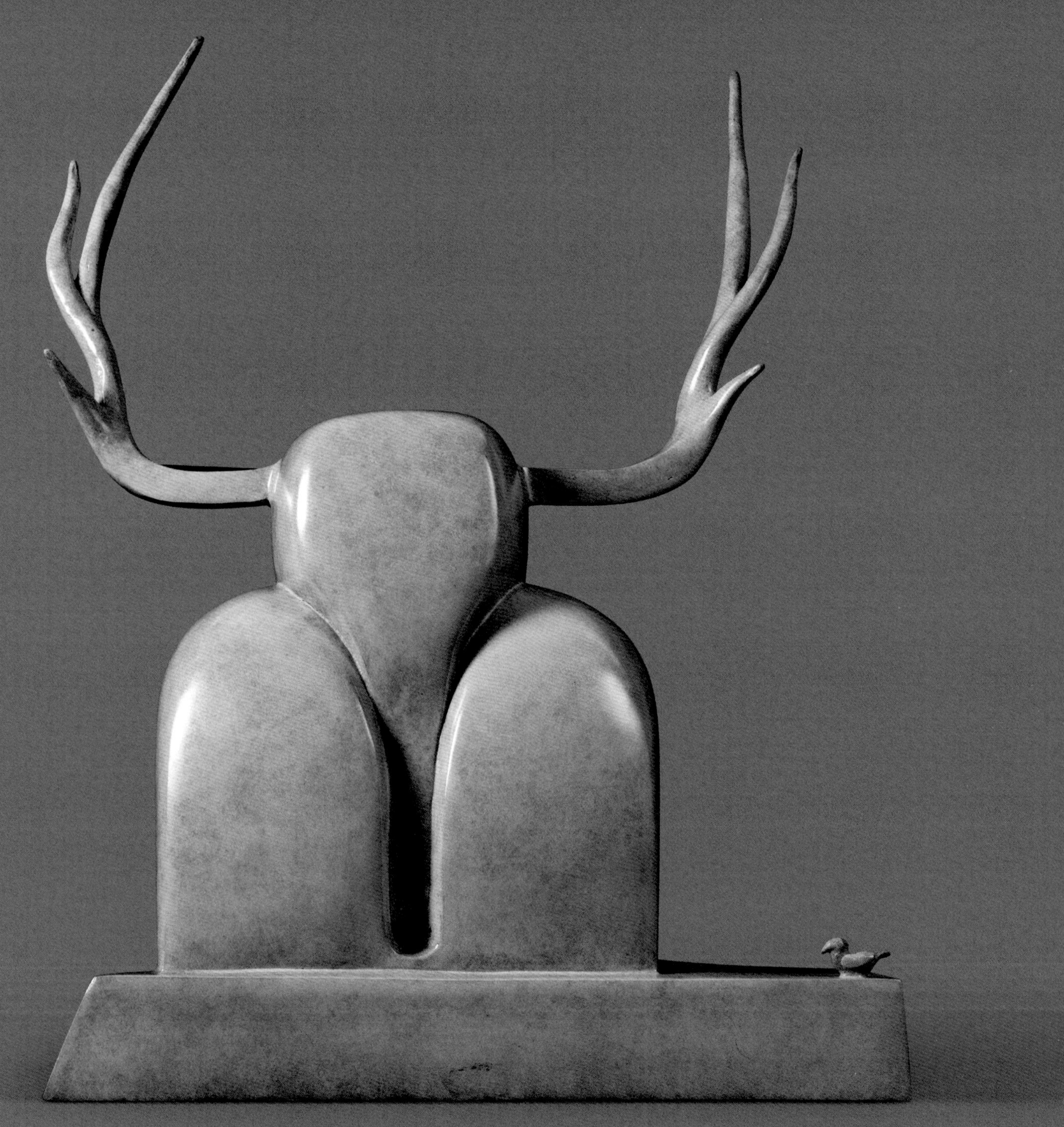

'Shakyamuni offers himself to the tiger, and is compassionate. The
Deer Park (Sarnath) is the place where Shakyamuni Buddha started to
practise Buddhist teaching. The ancient king of India was addicted to
hunting deer. The deer-king had the herd cast in lots. The king hunted
down one deer each day. One day the king saw a noble deer appear,
and approached it curiously. The deer spoke in human language, and
said there was a pregnant doe, that it would be unjust to replace it
with another deer, so it had come itself instead. The king was greatly
moved, and after this no longer hunted deer. This deer-king is the
Buddha in his past life.

Deer King Compassion
Beauty of Compassion
Bronze, 35×19×48cm
2015

Buddha's Light Shines
Beauty of Compassion
Bronze with gold foil,
39X23x57cm
2014

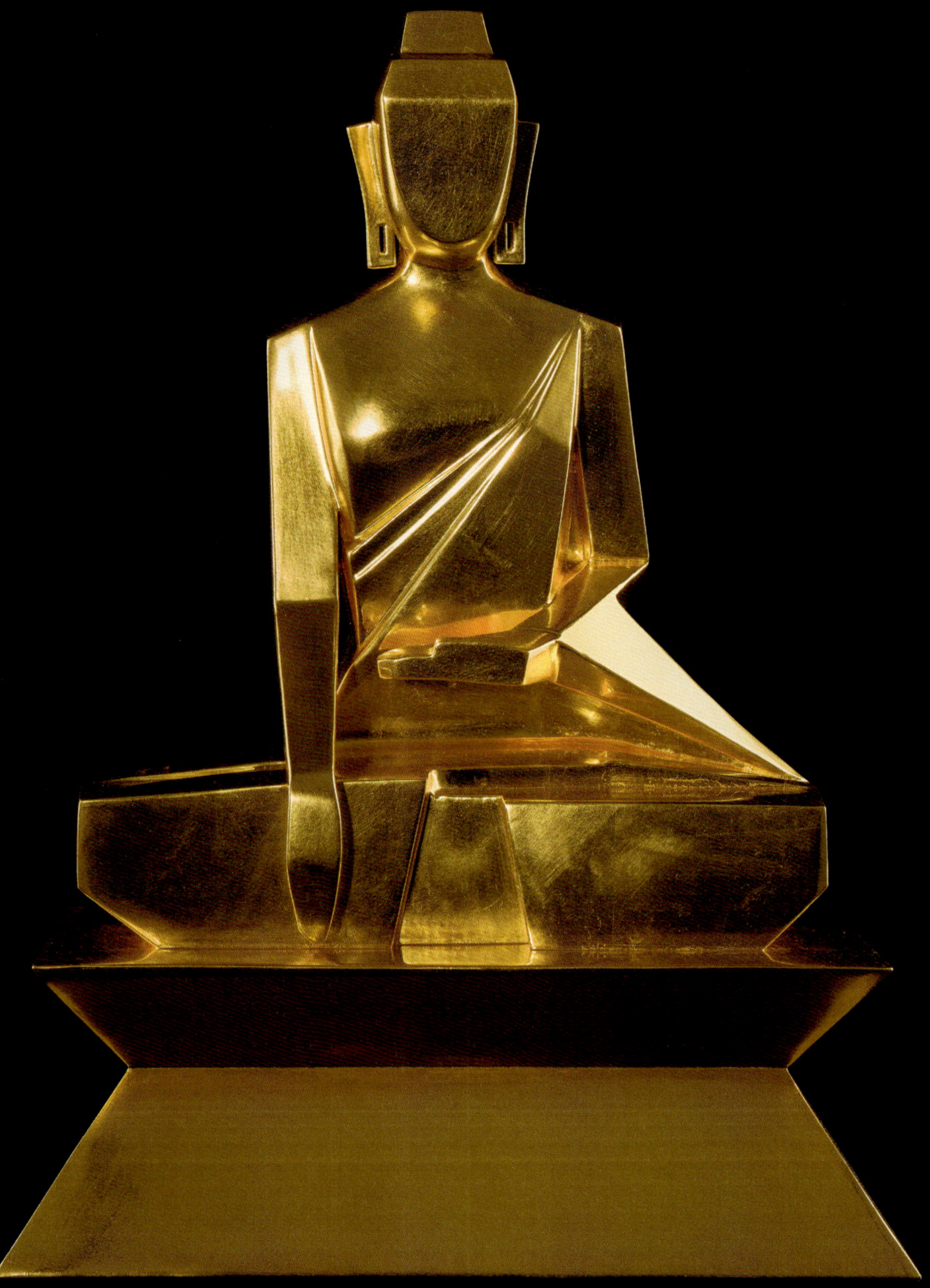

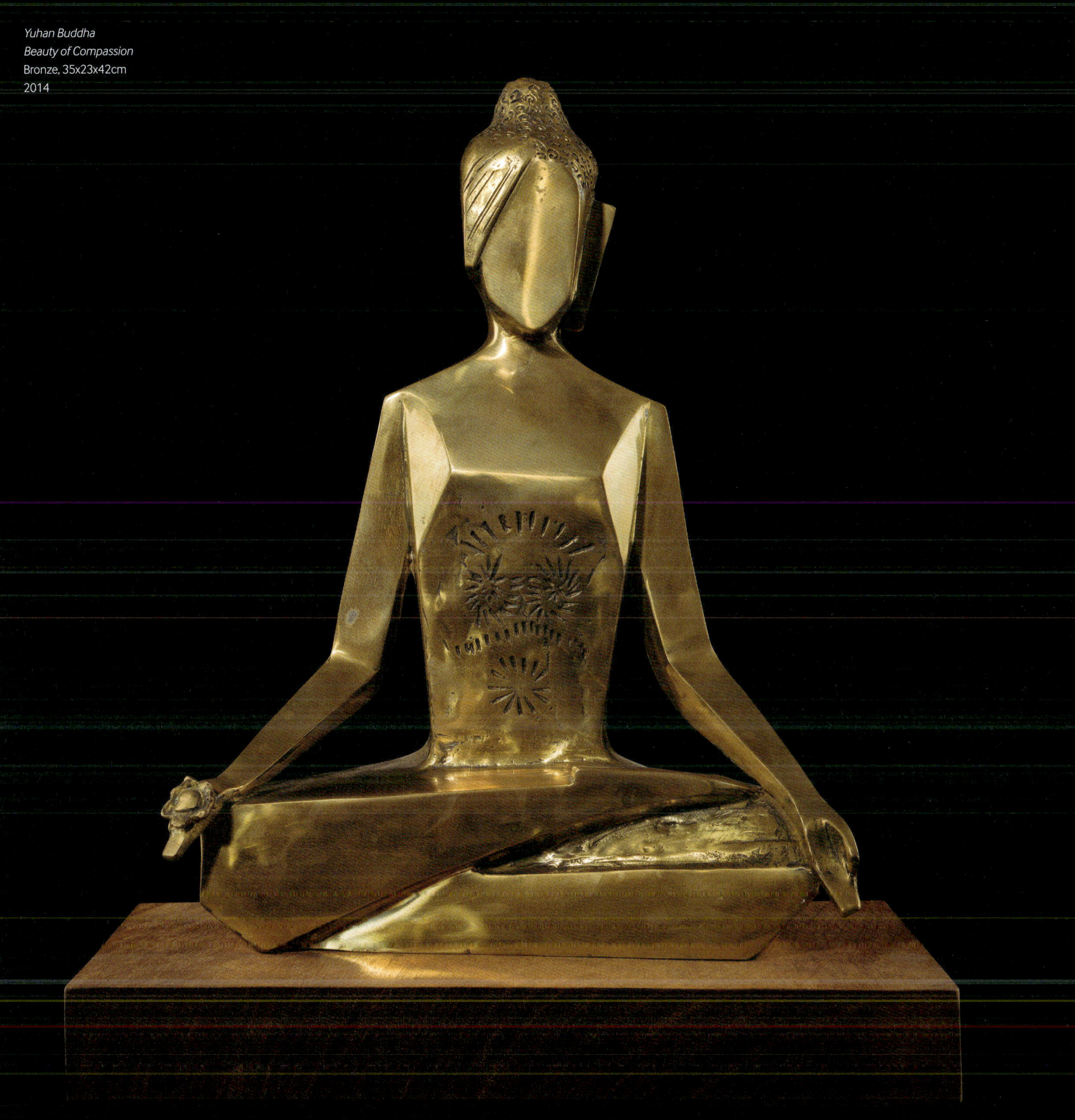

Yuhan Buddha
Beauty of Compassion
Bronze, 35x23x42cm
2014

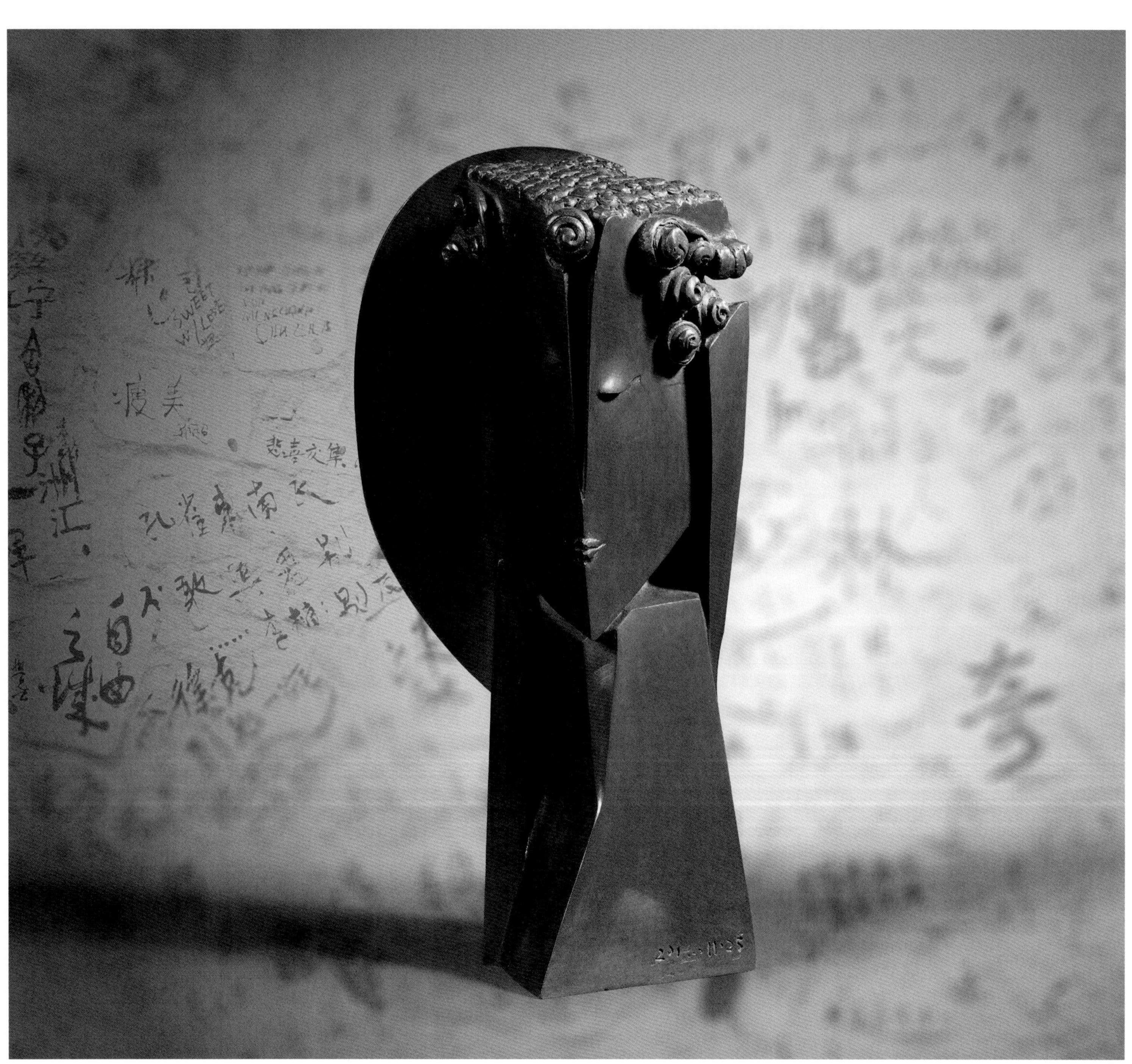

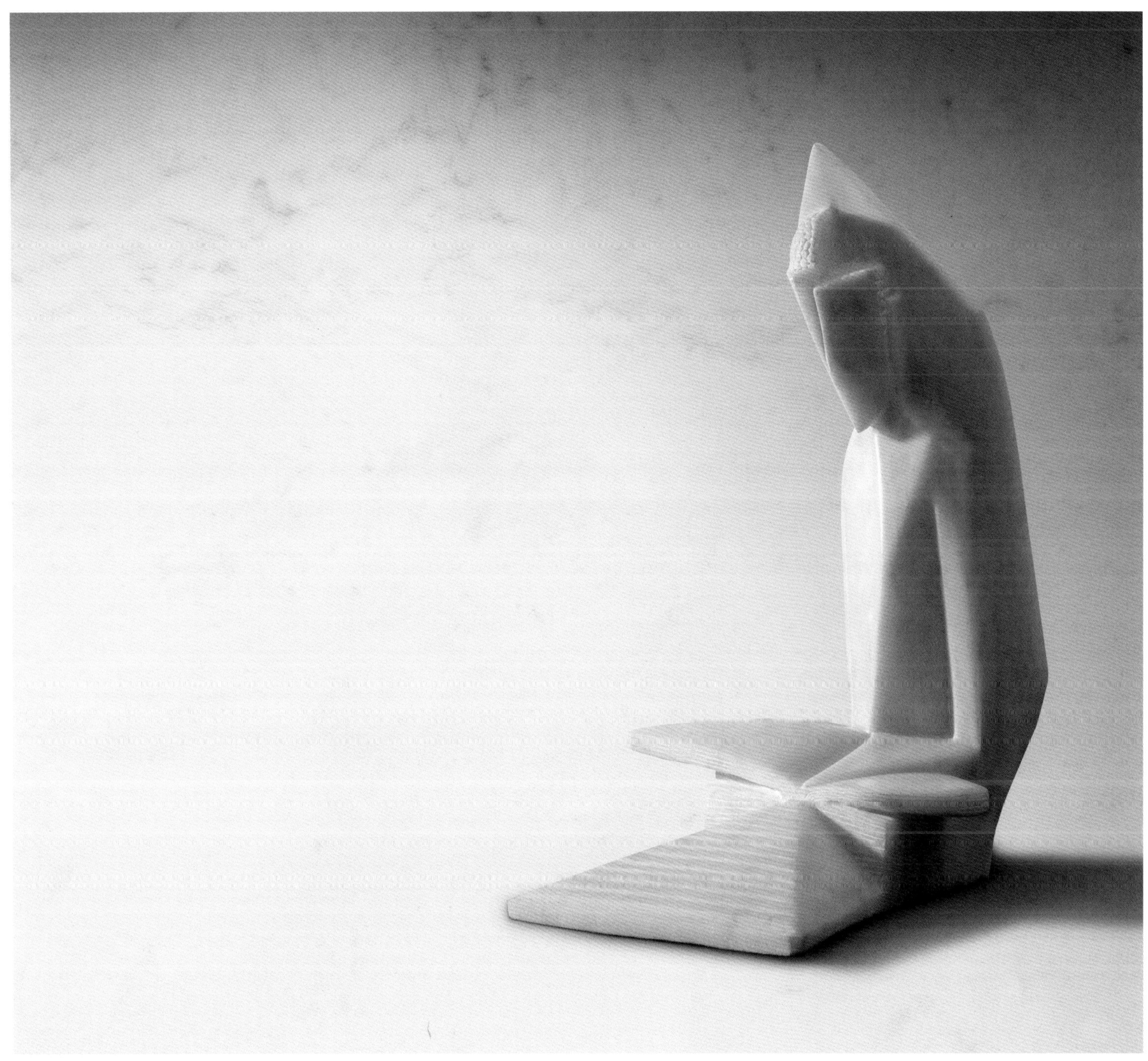

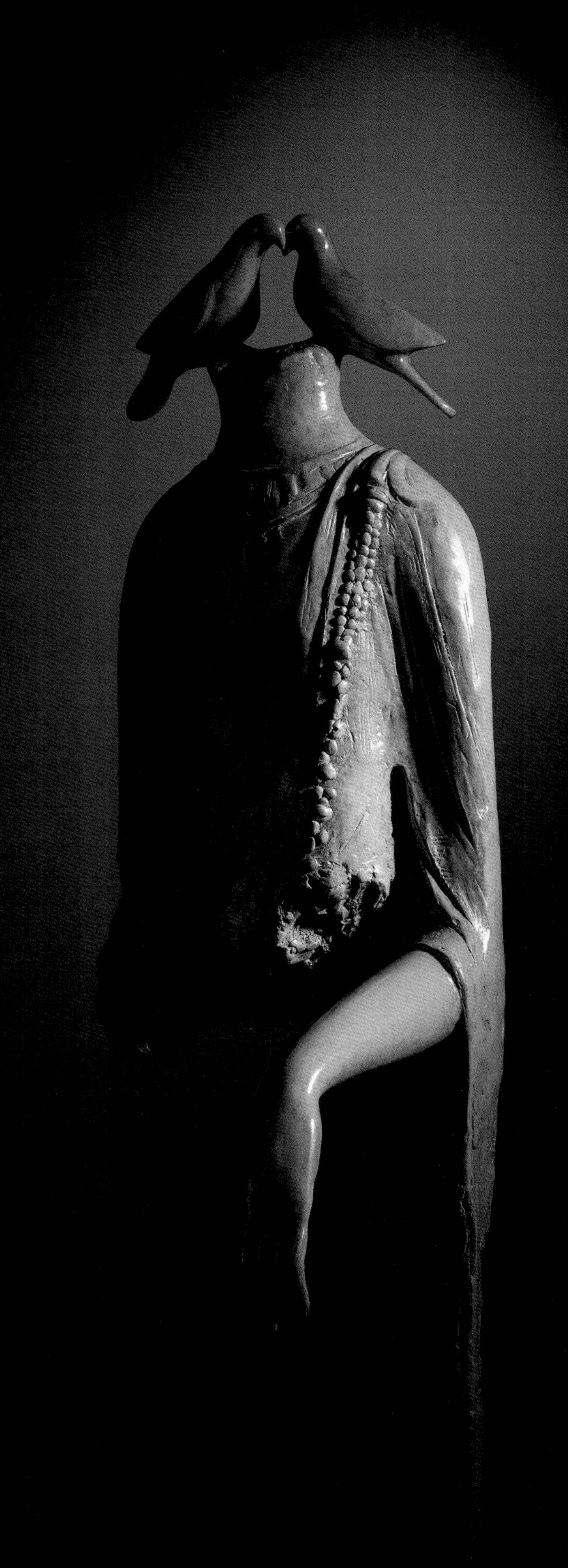

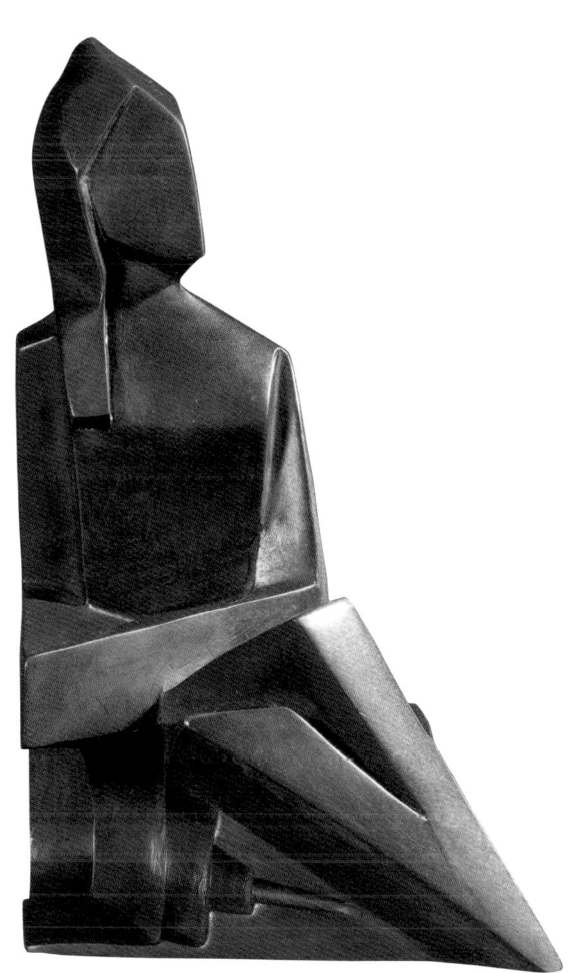

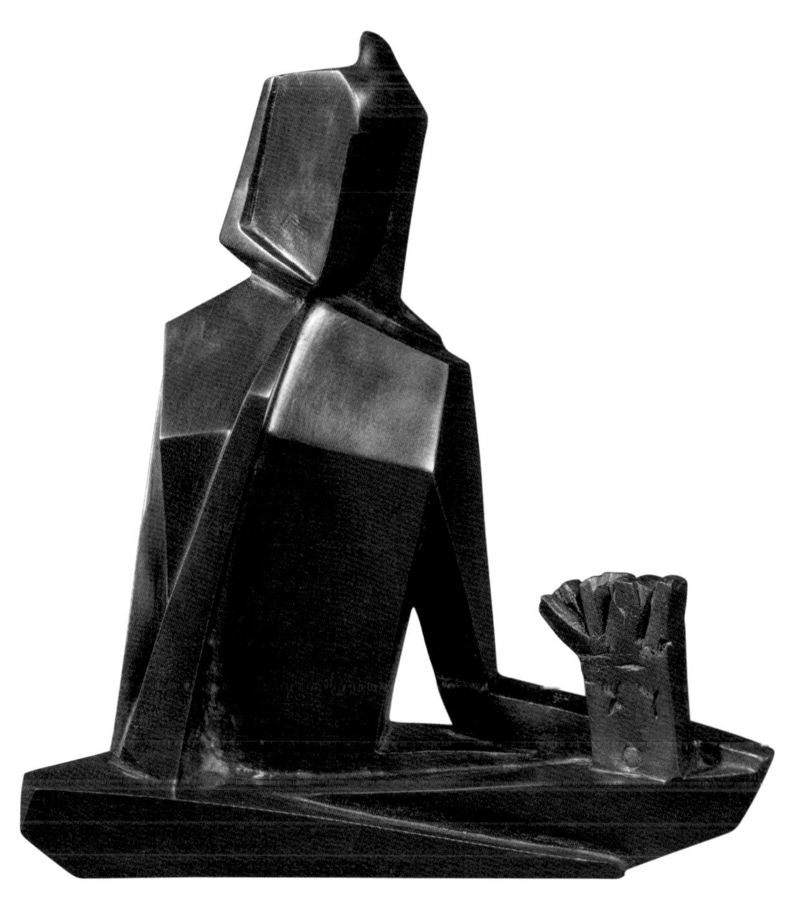

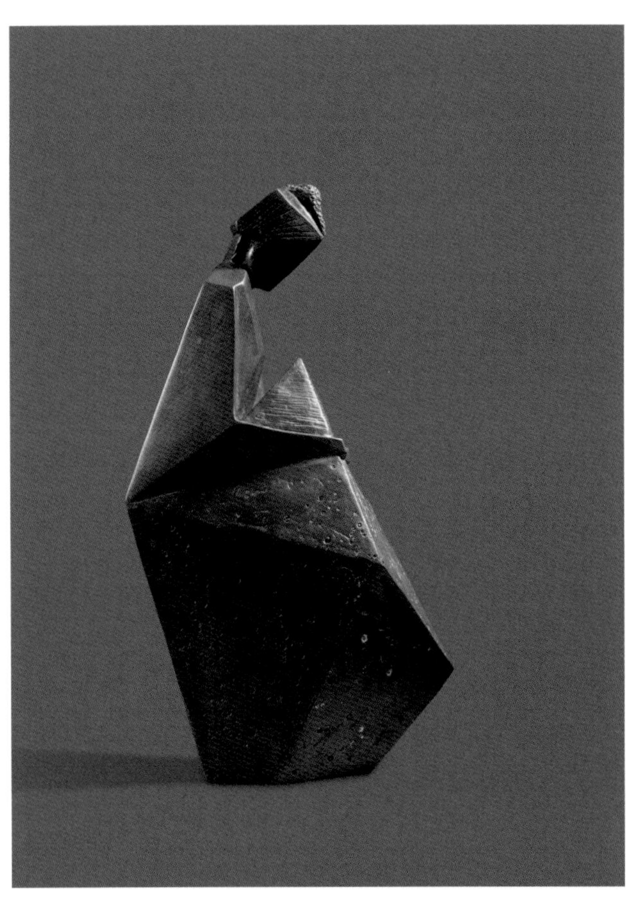
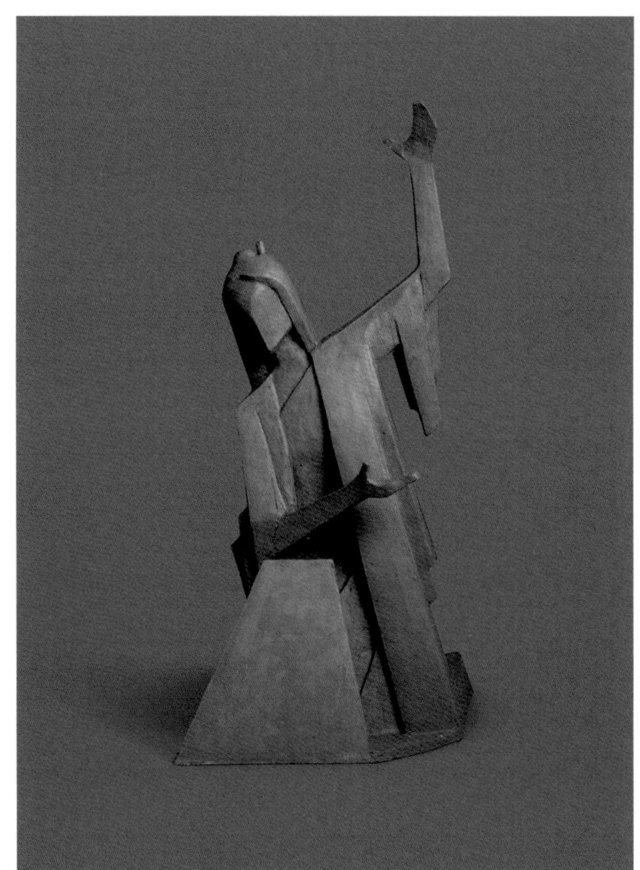
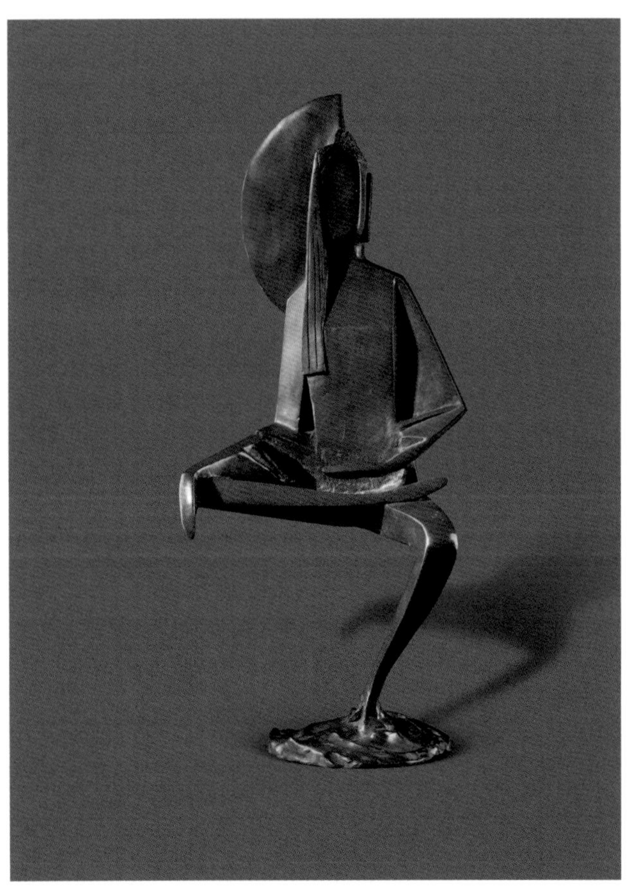
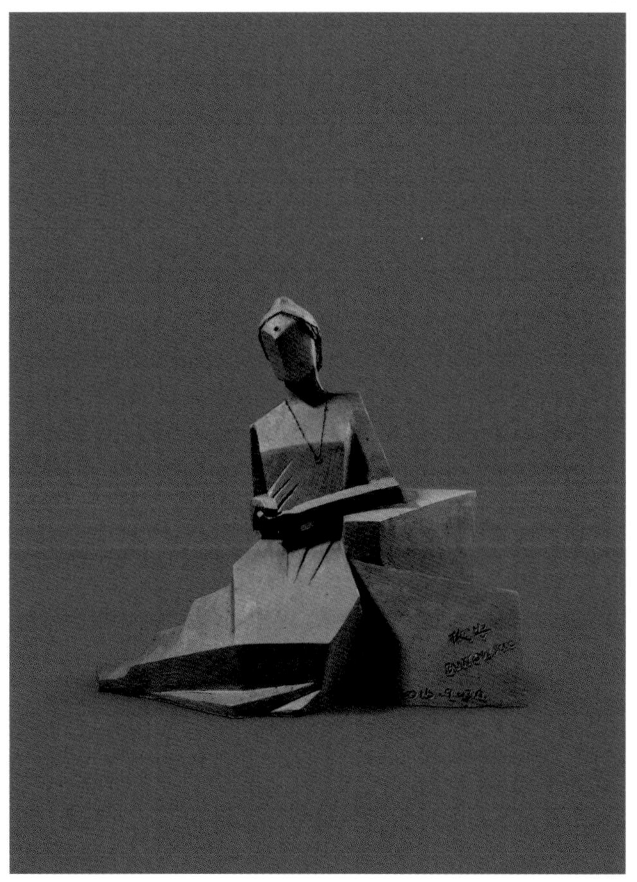

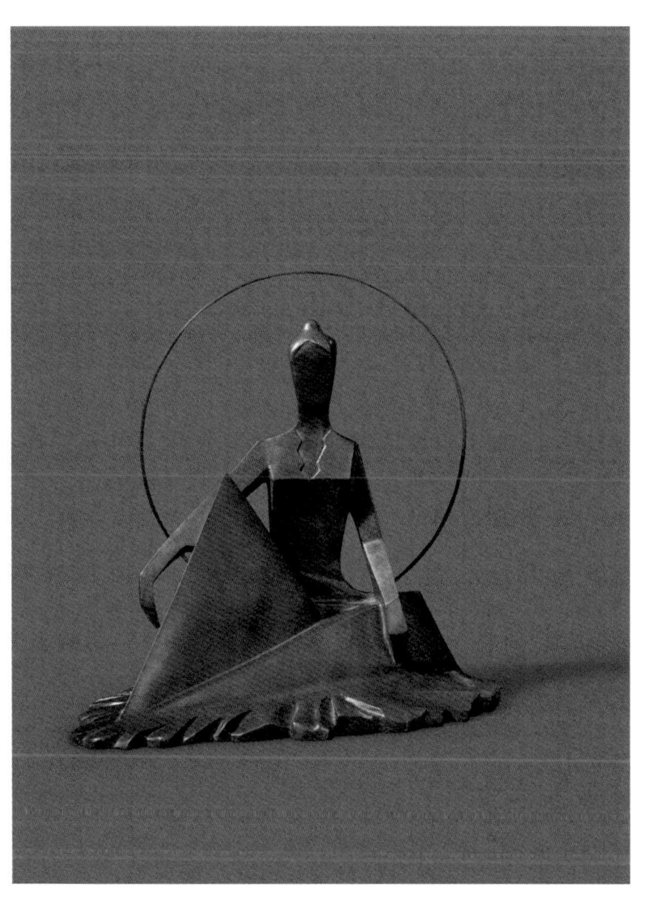

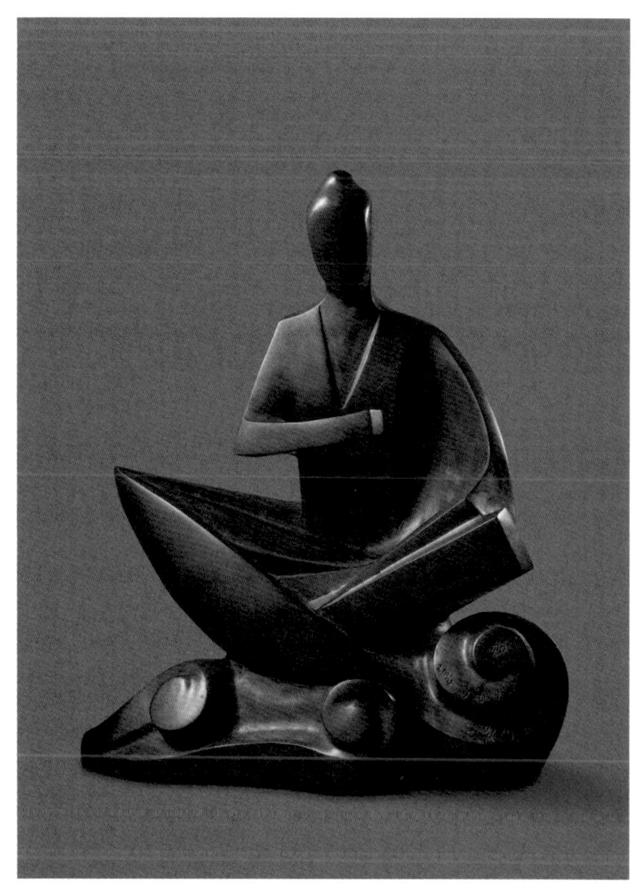

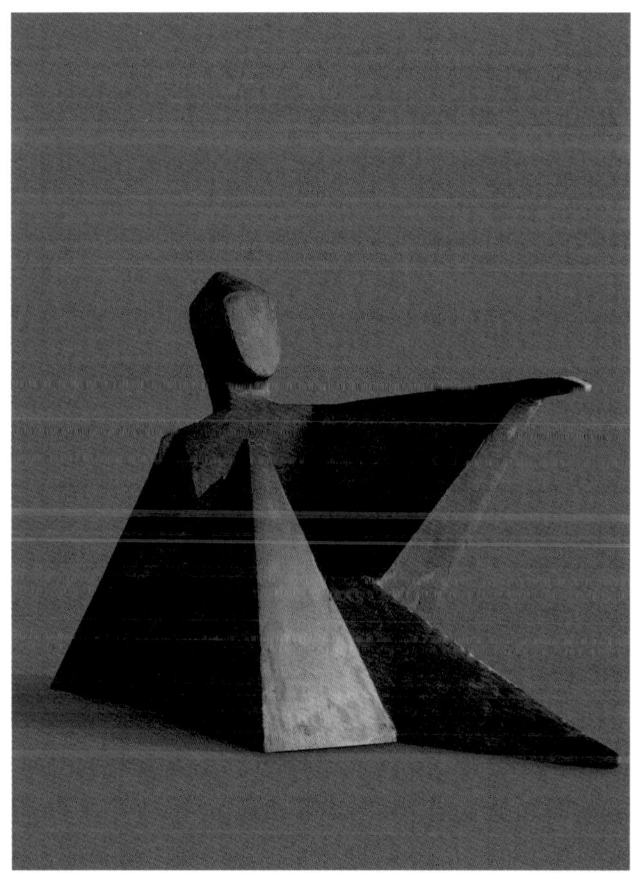

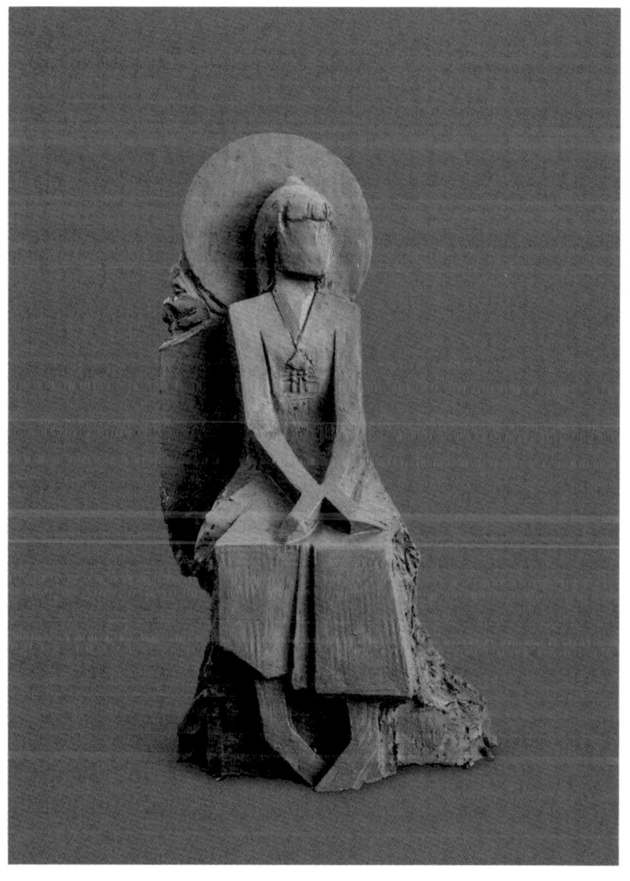

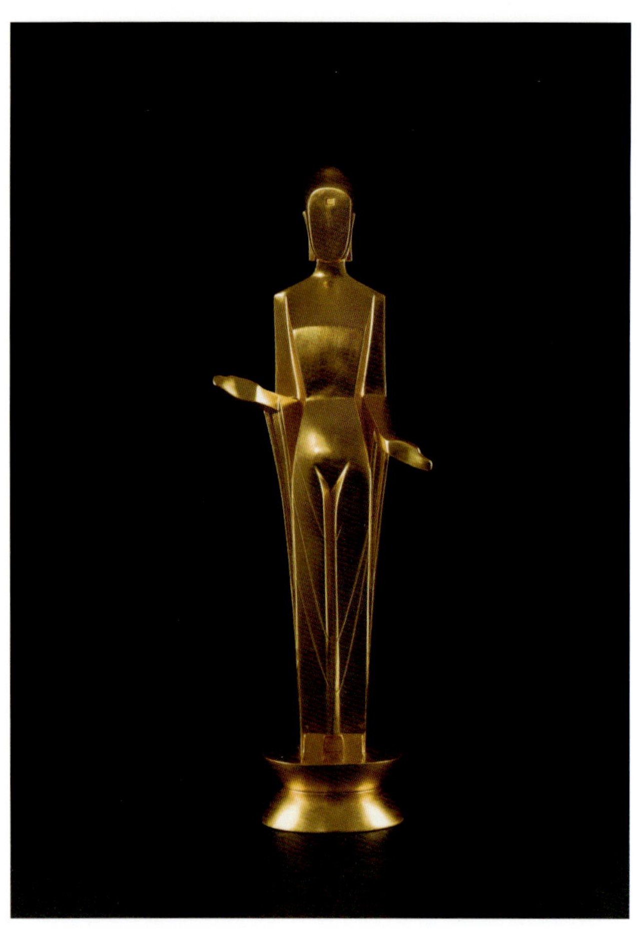

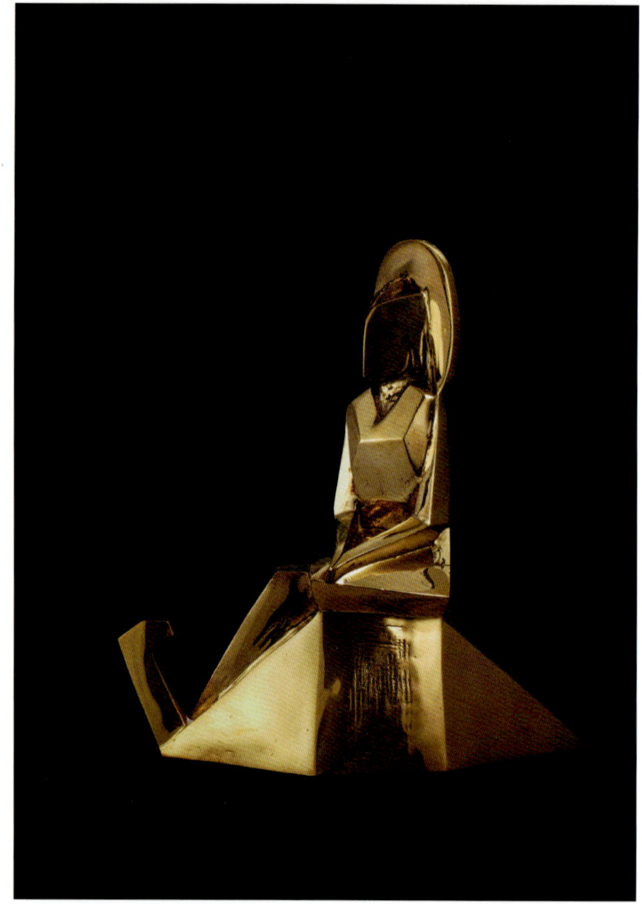

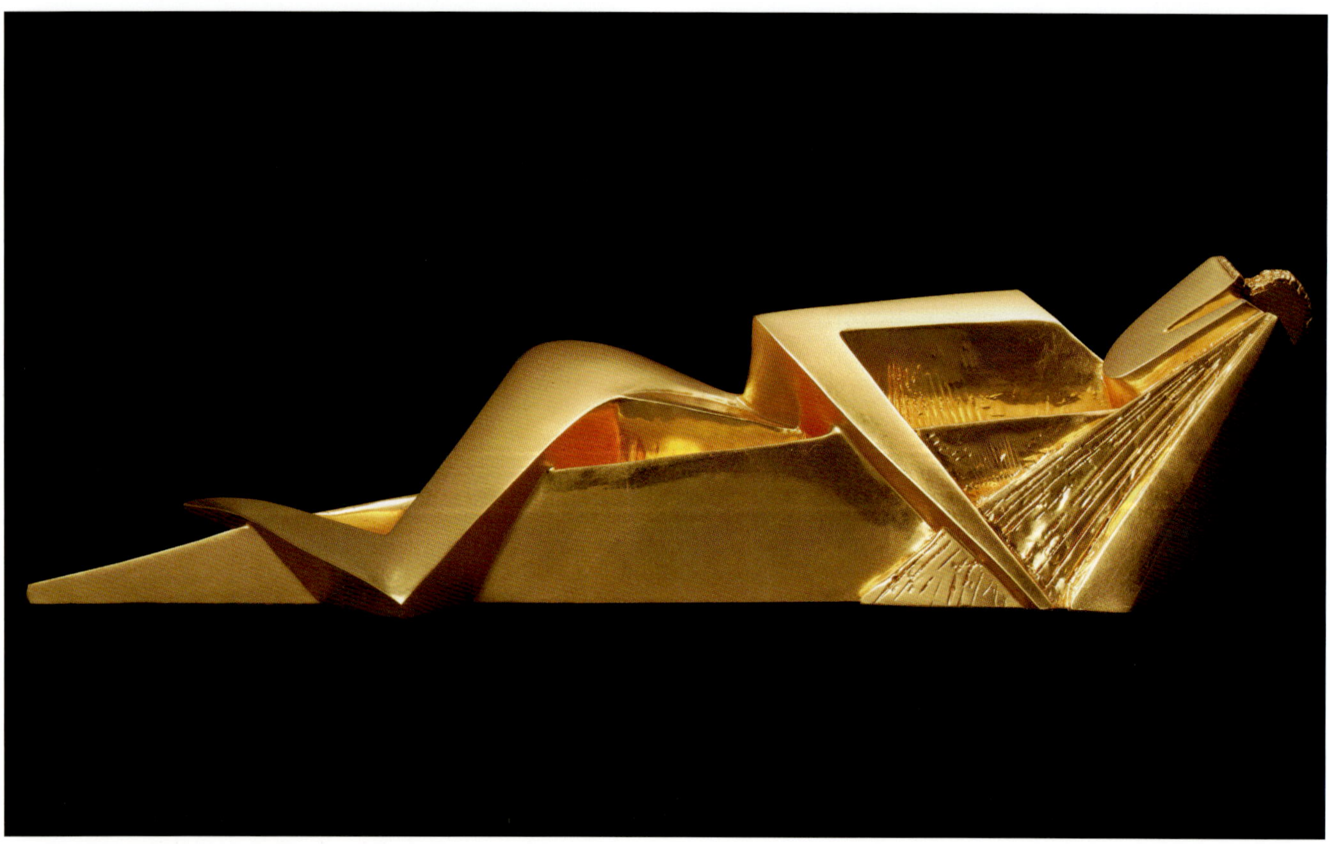

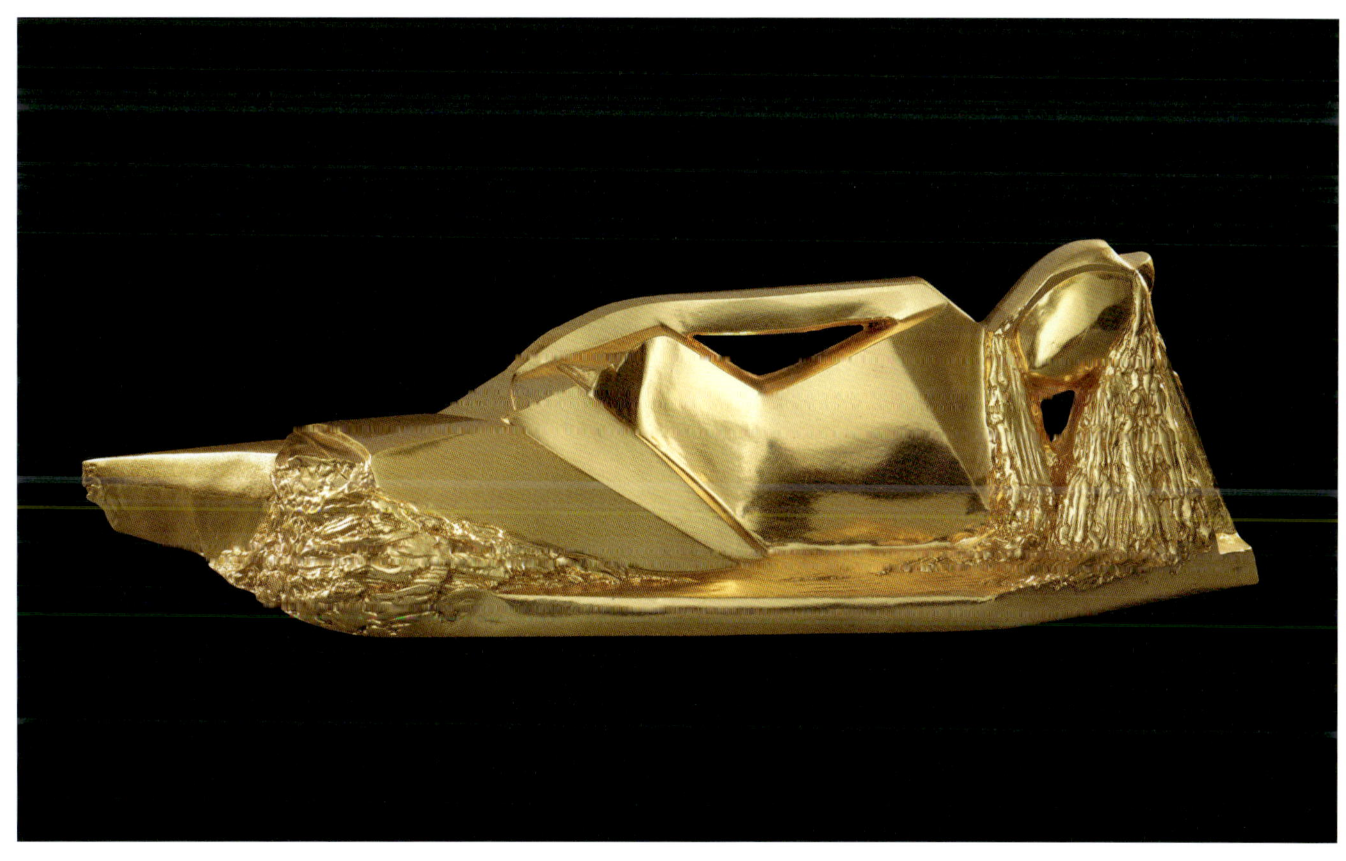

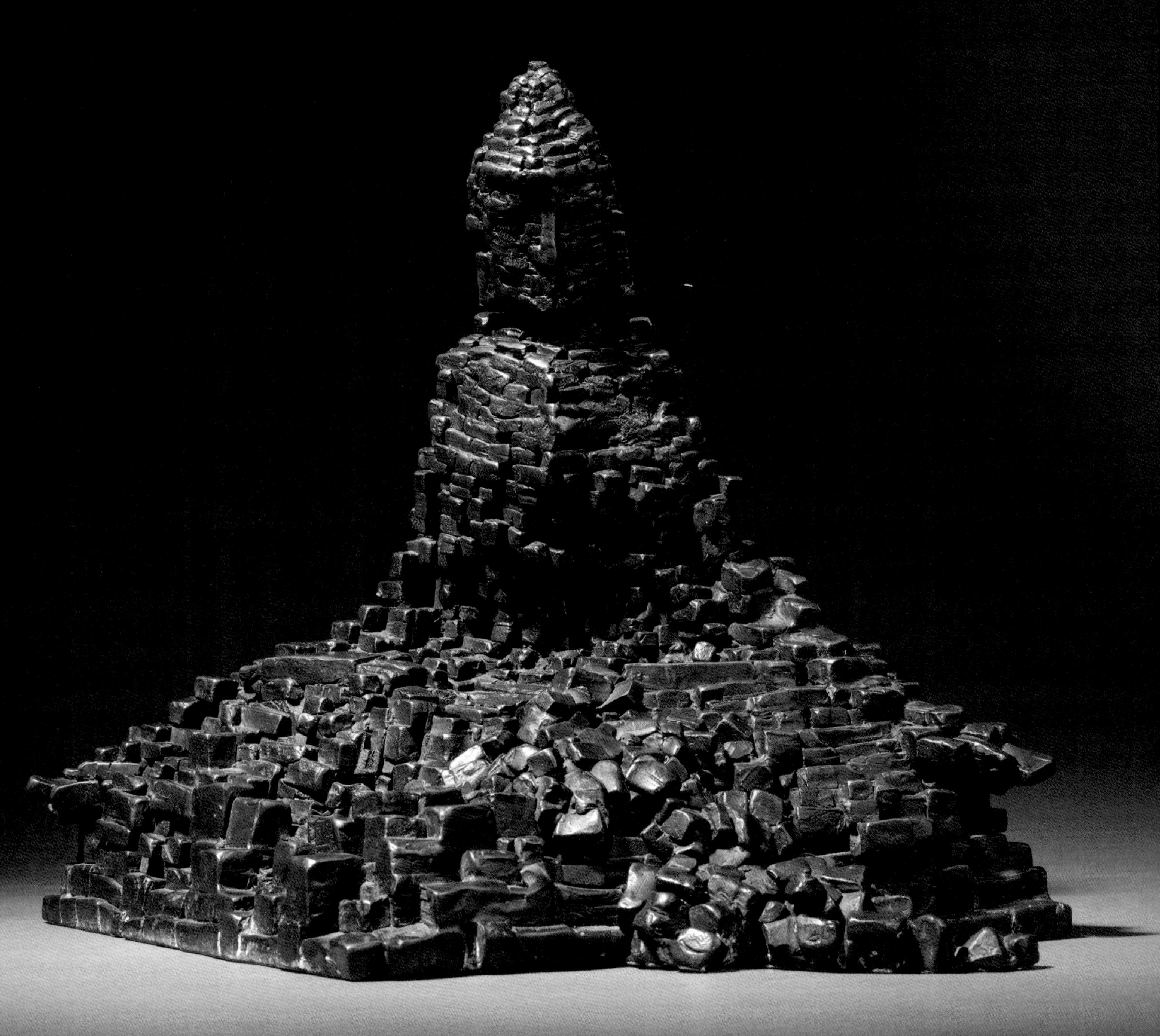

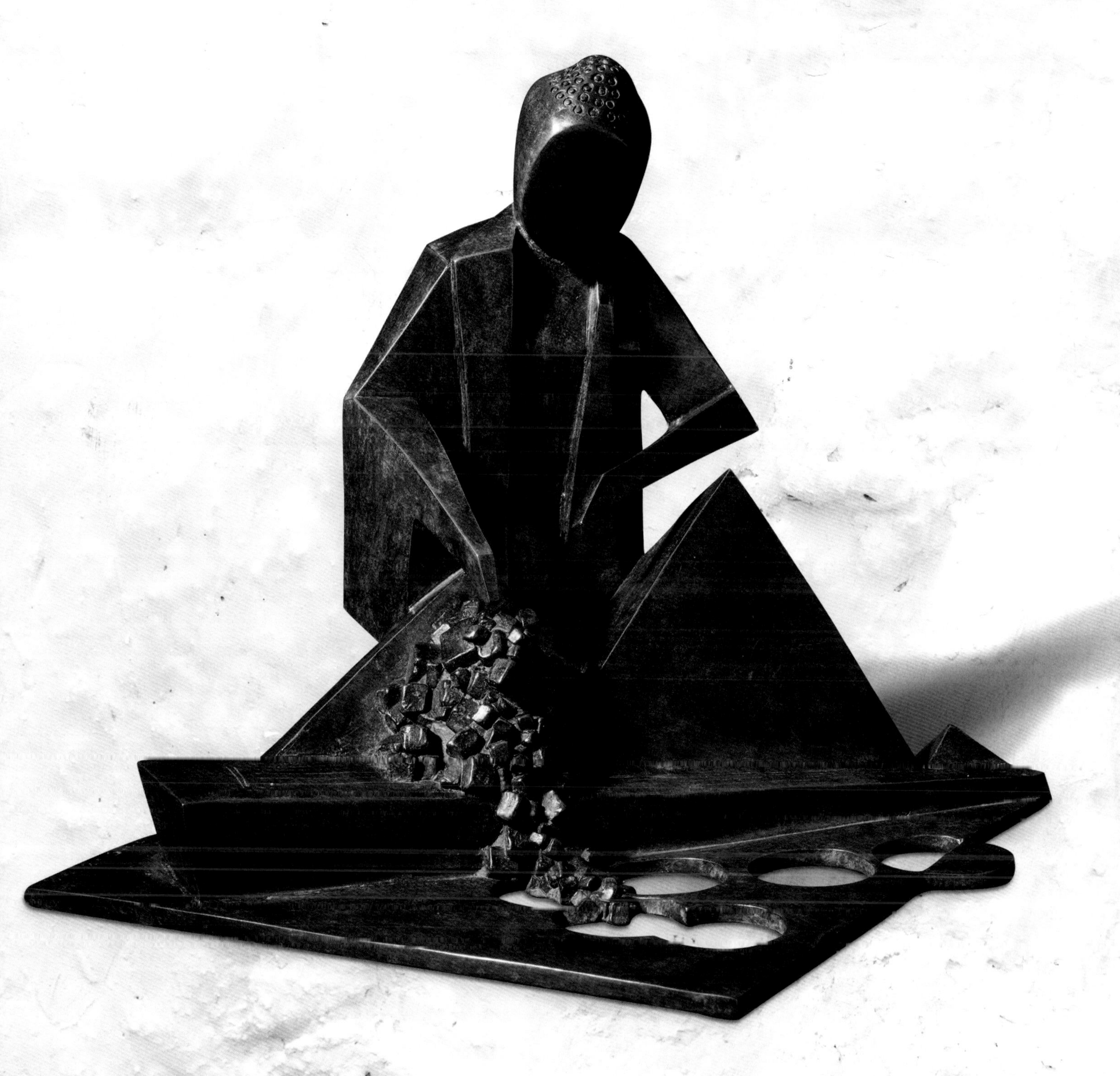

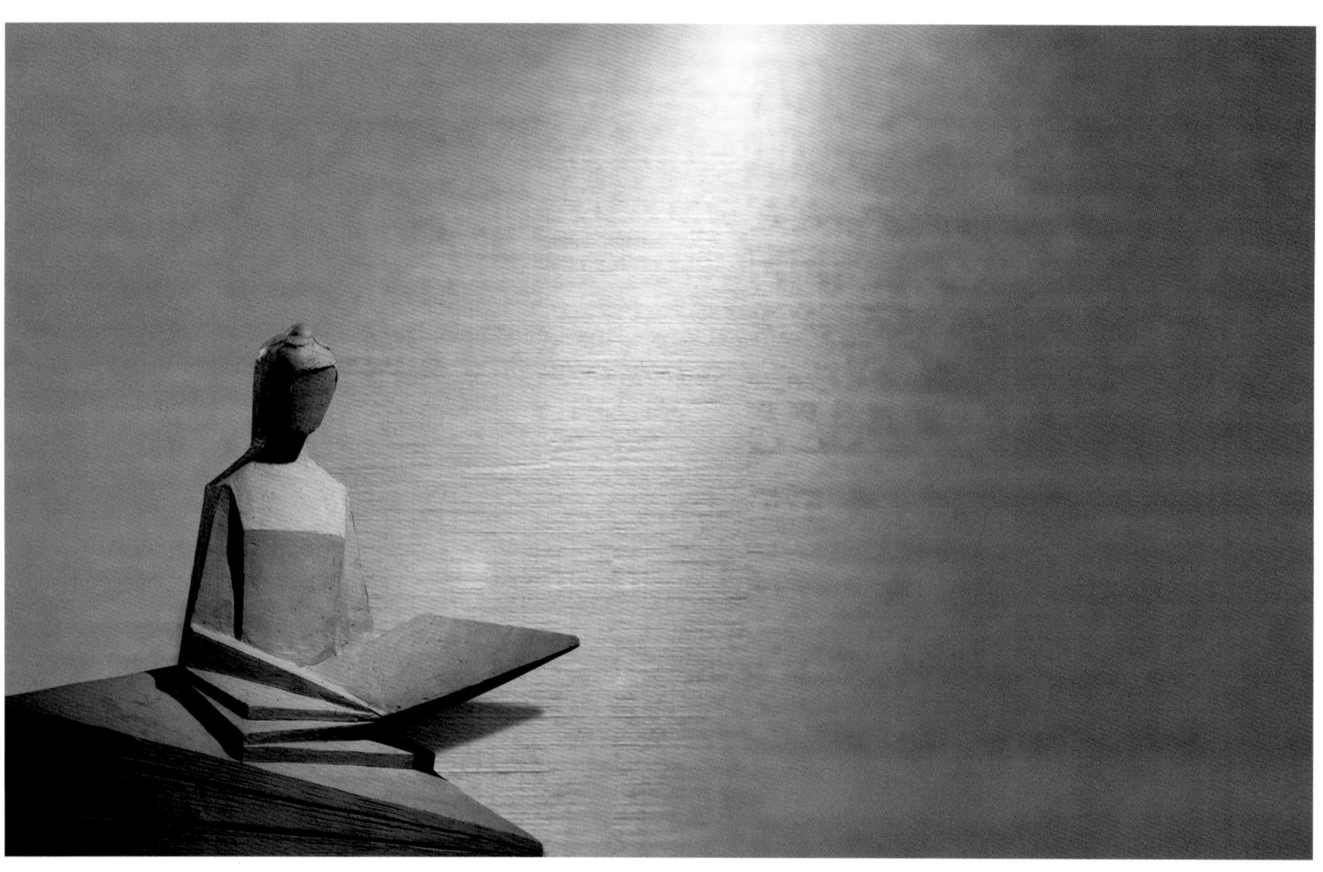

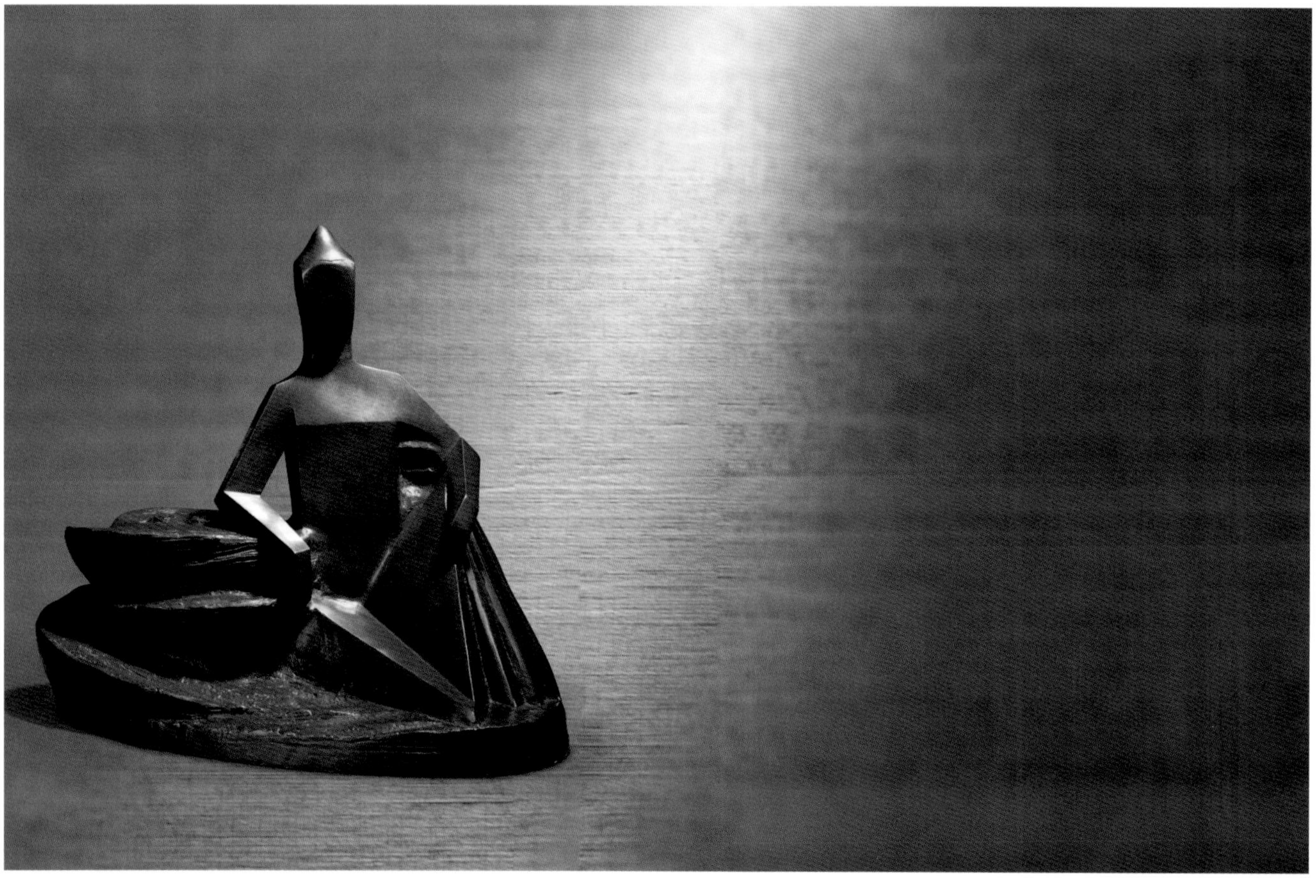

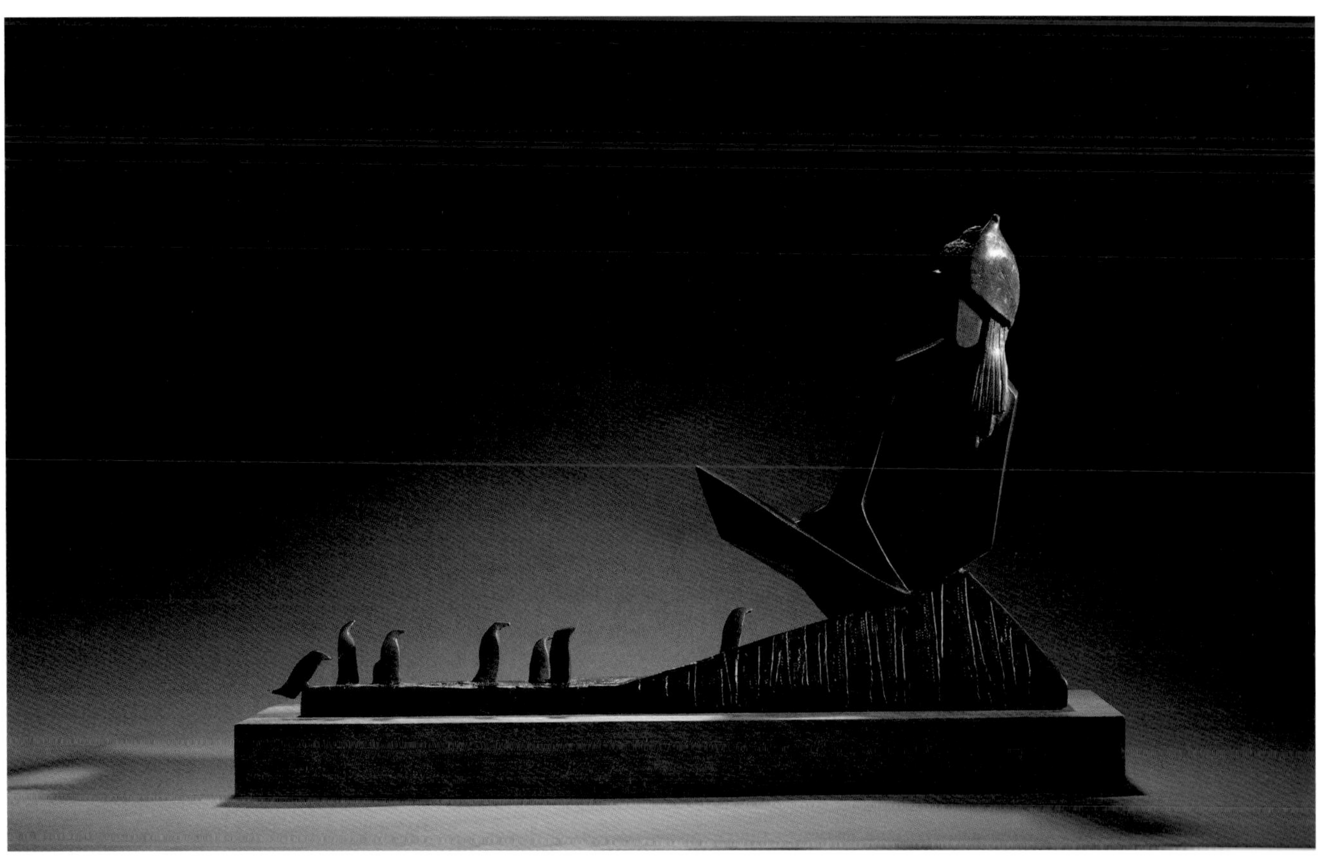

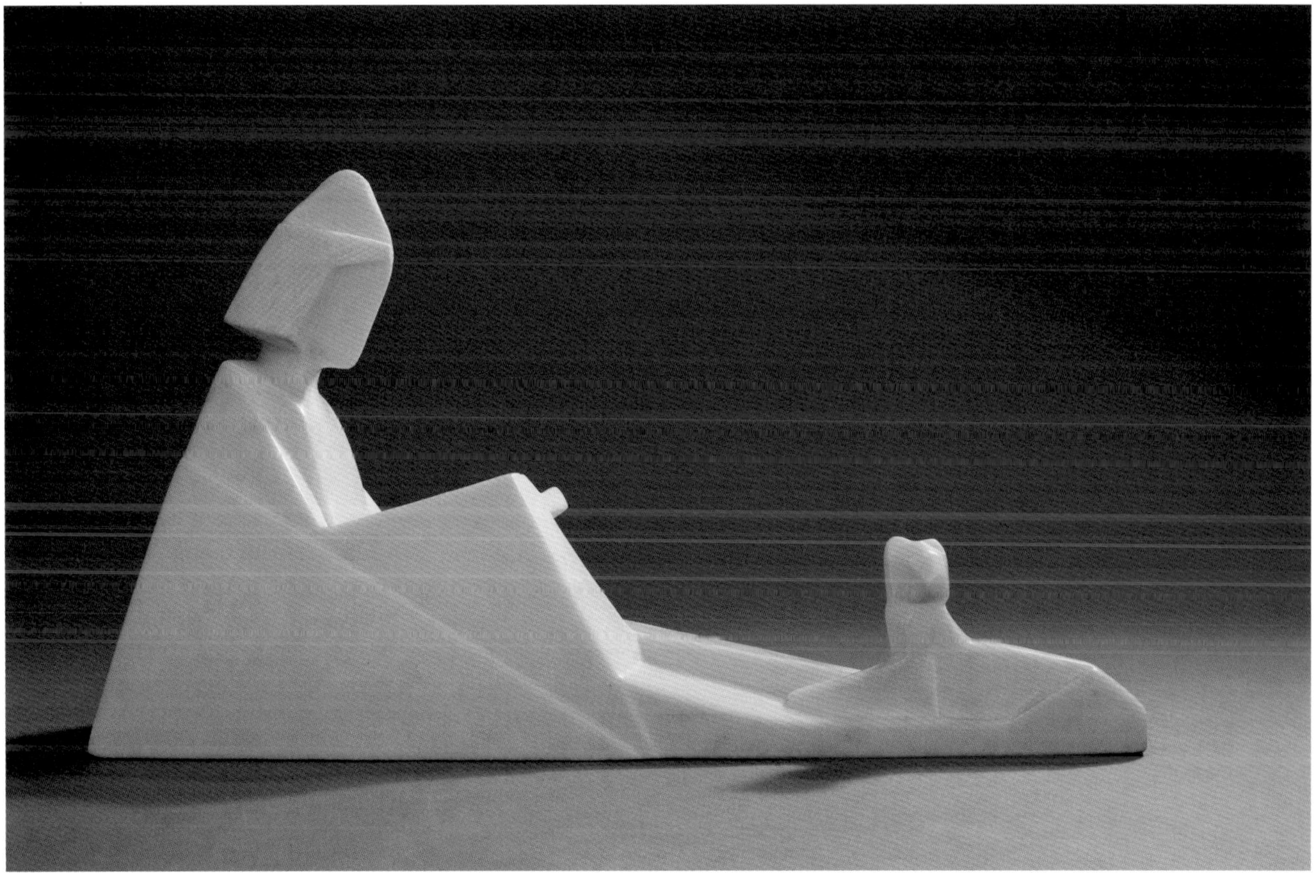

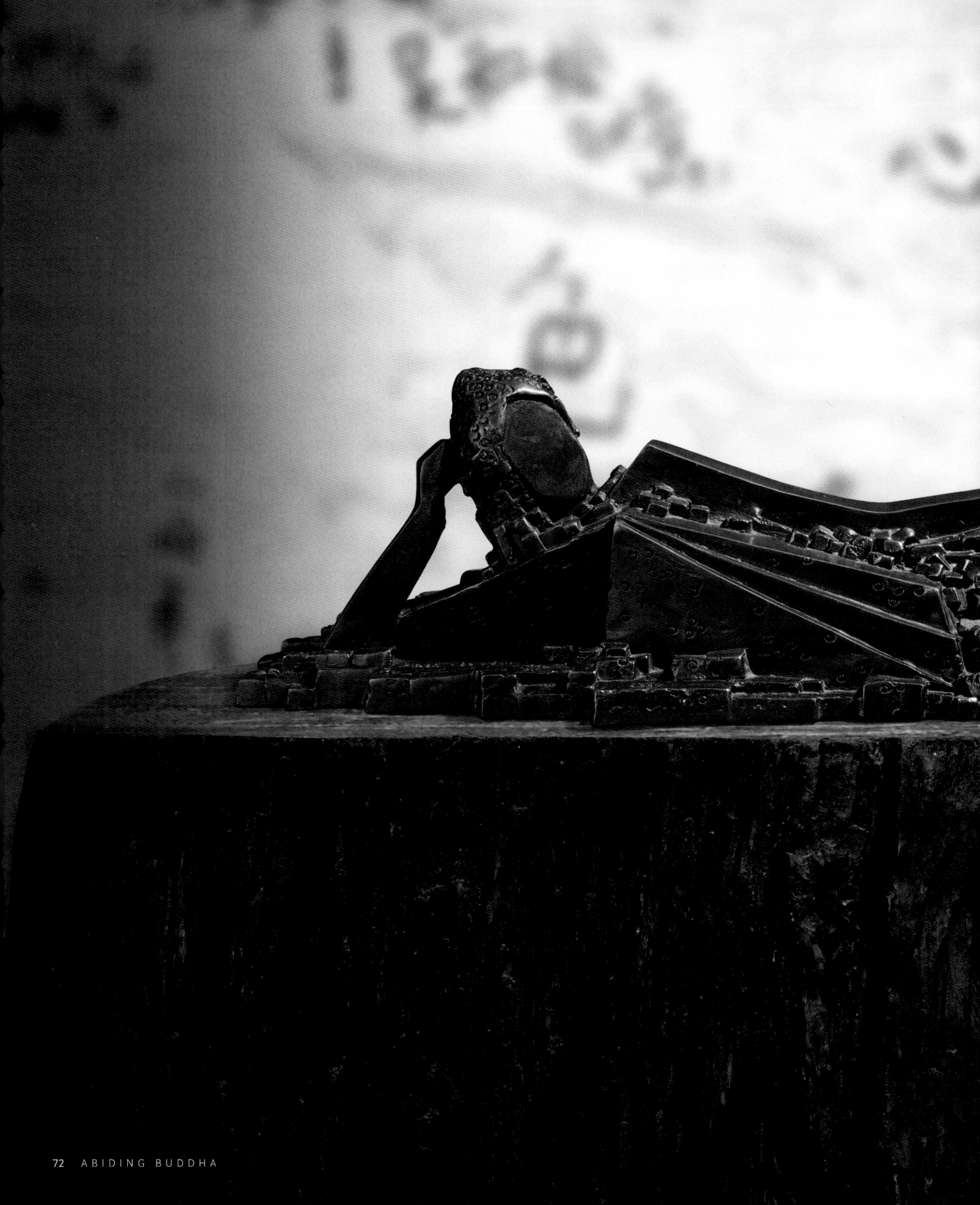

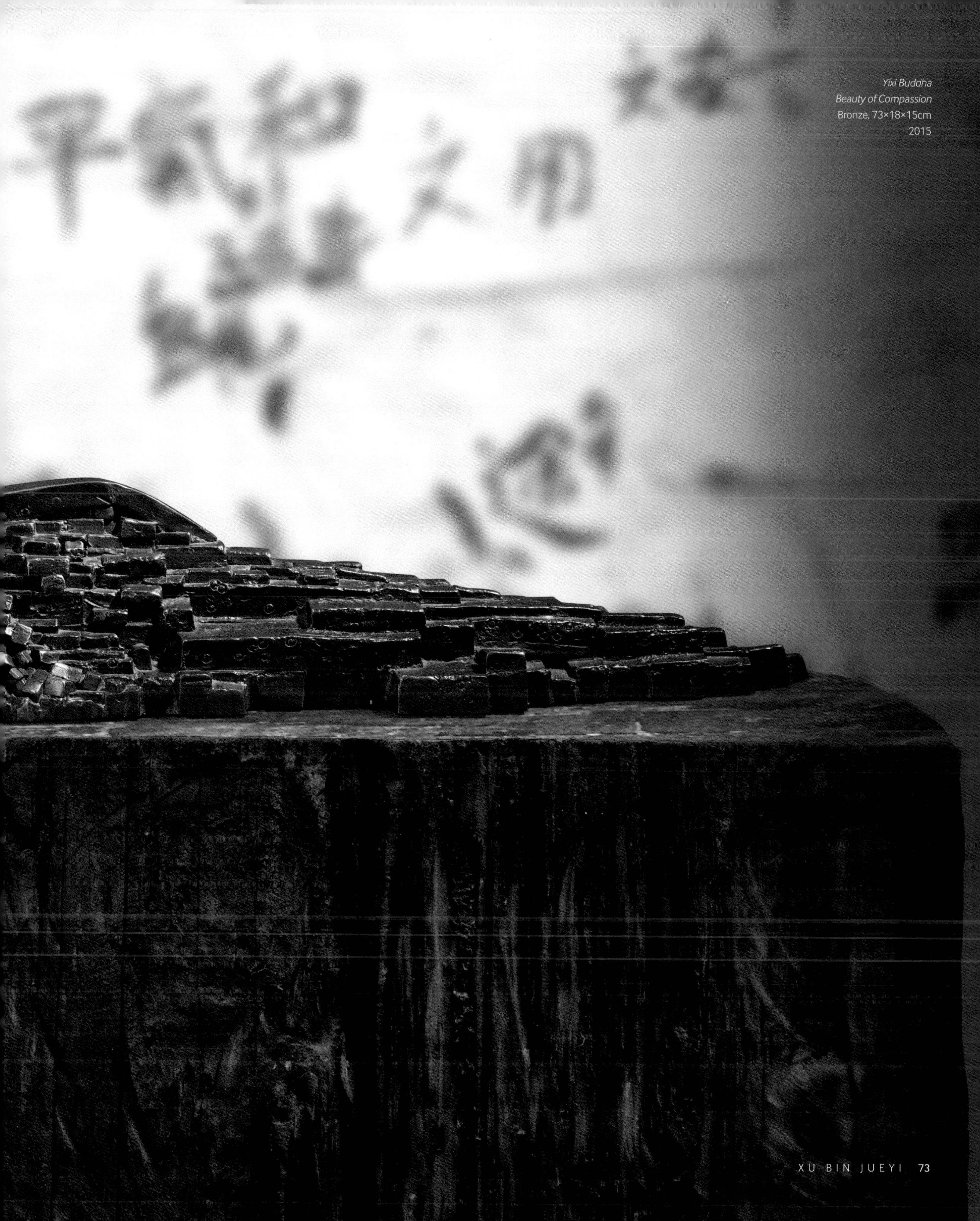

Yixi Buddha
Beauty of Compassion
Bronze, 73×18×15cm
2015

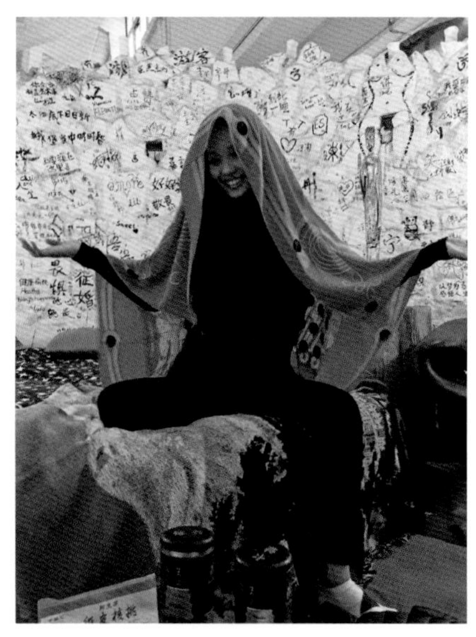
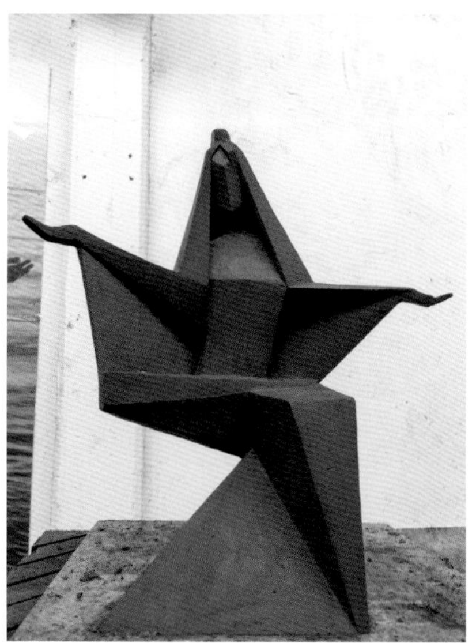
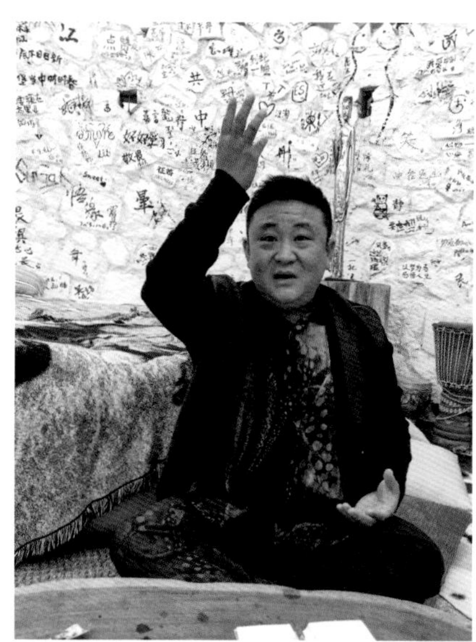
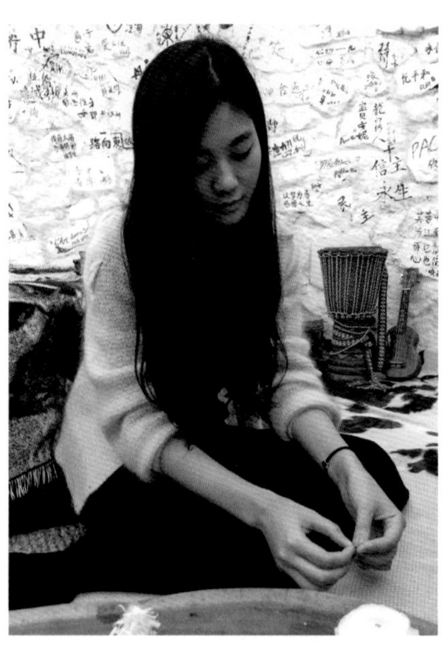
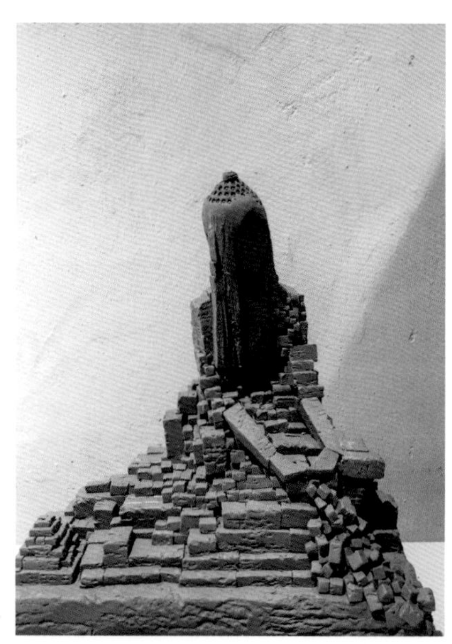
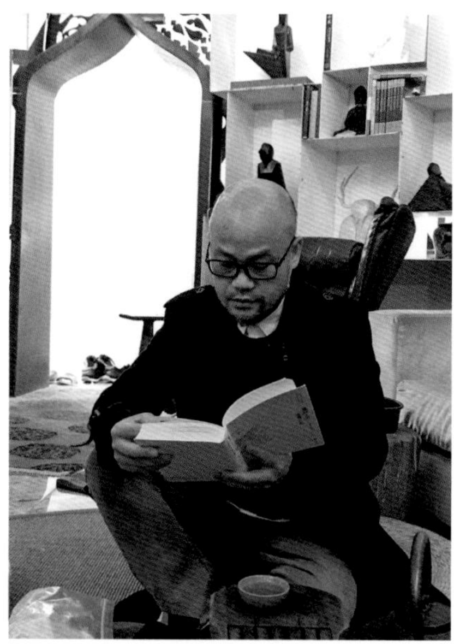
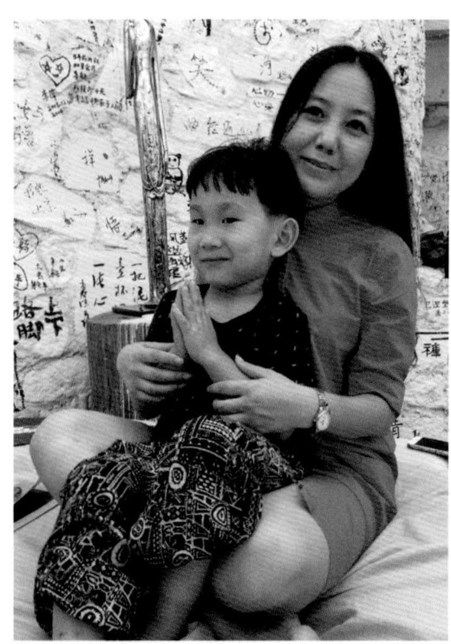
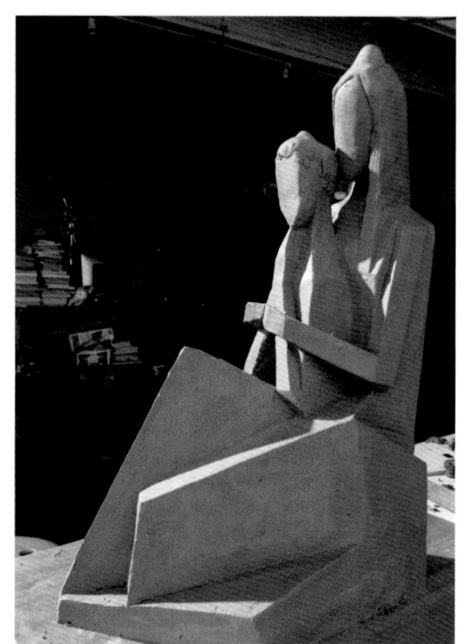
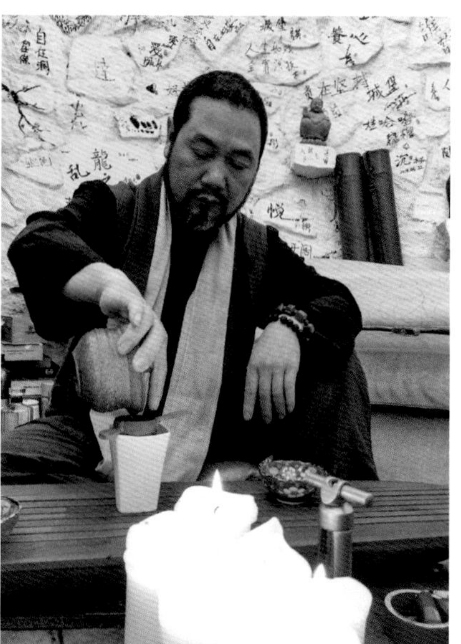

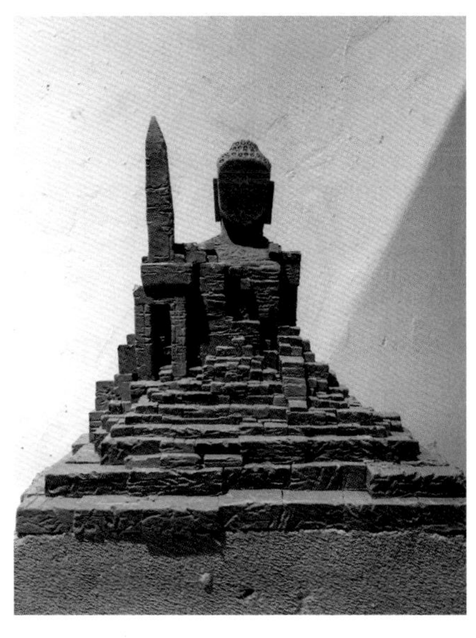
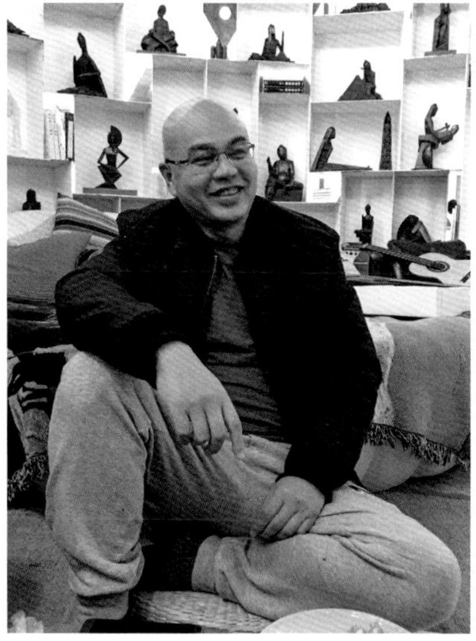
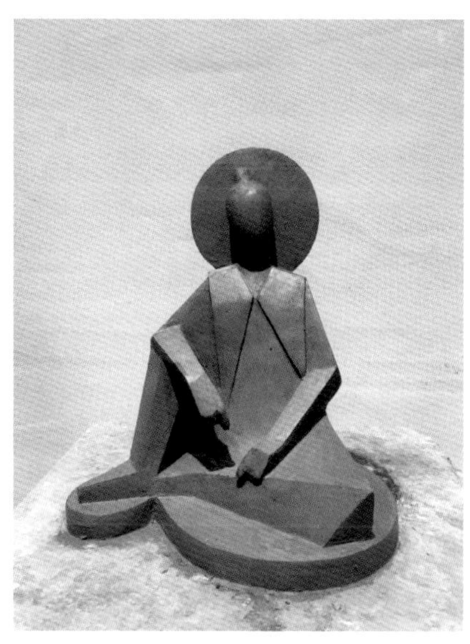
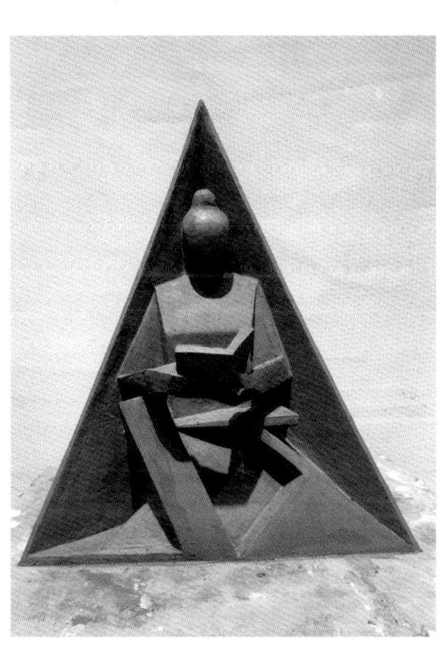
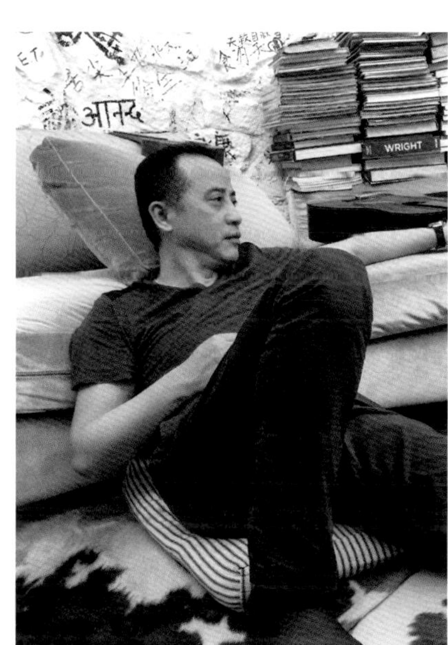
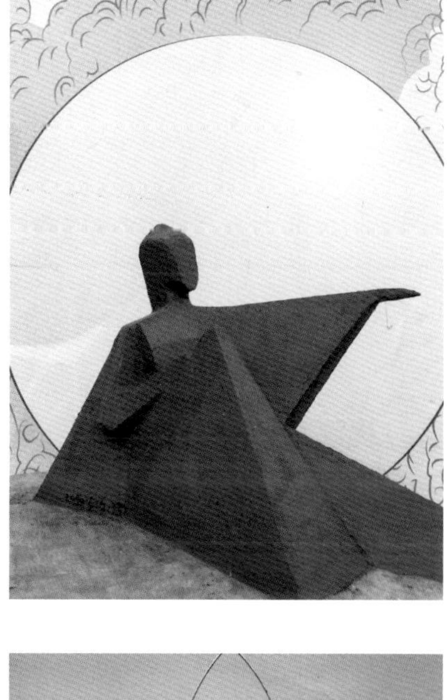
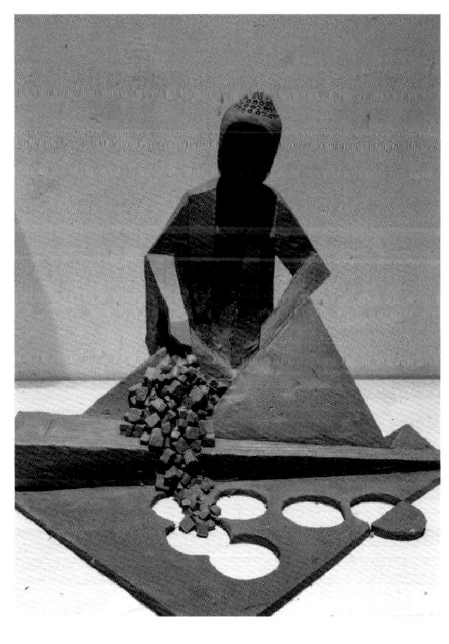
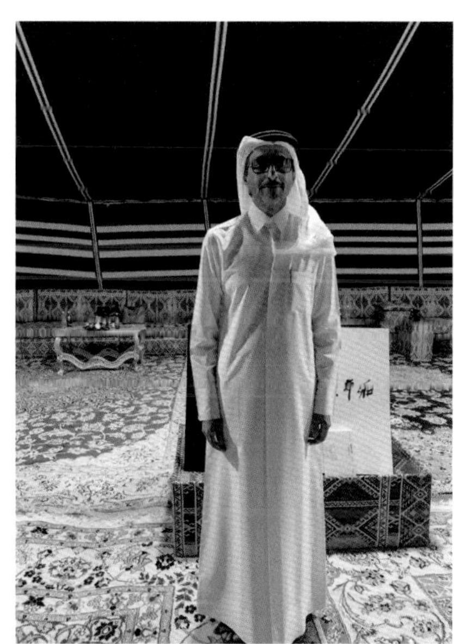
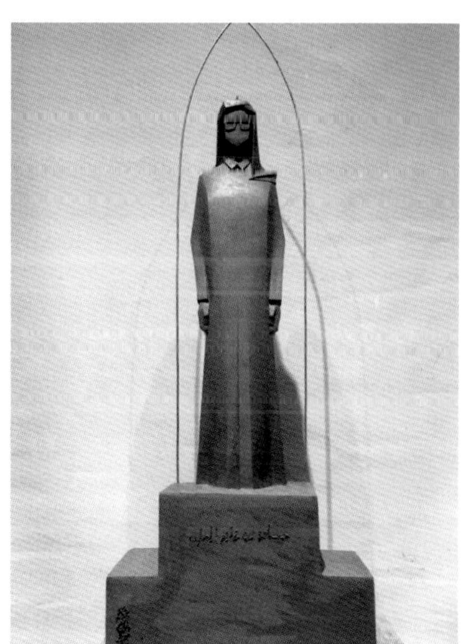

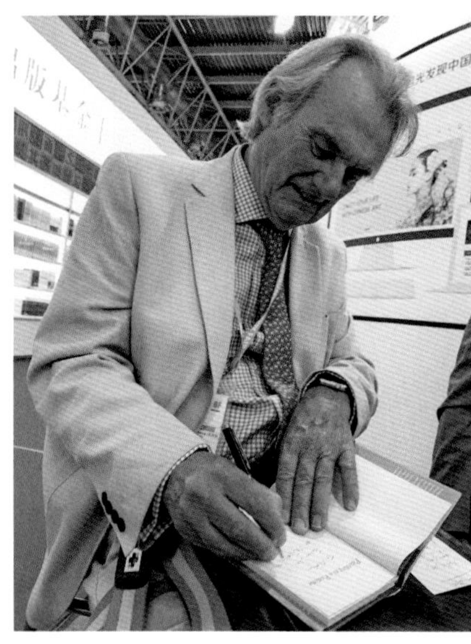
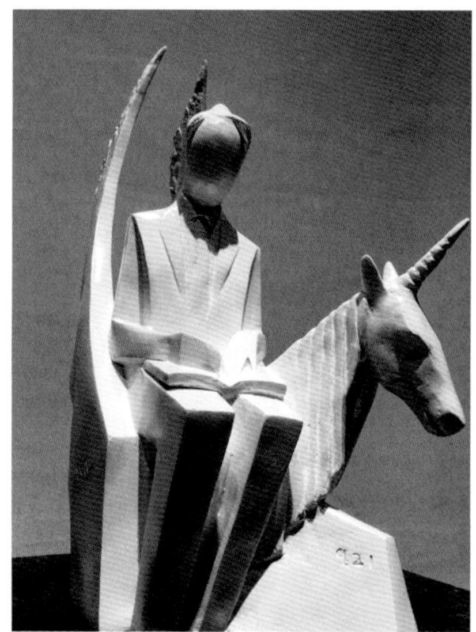
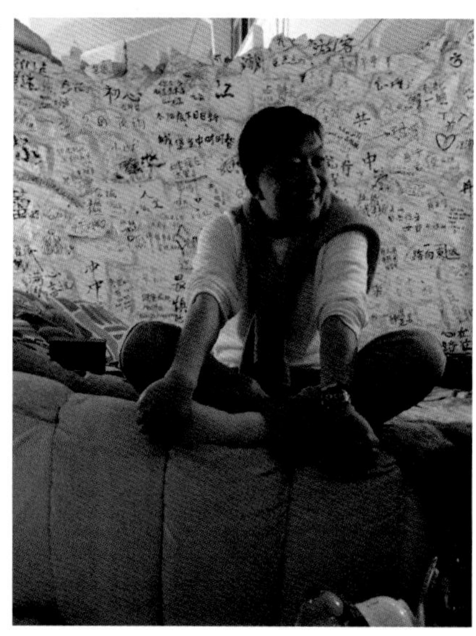
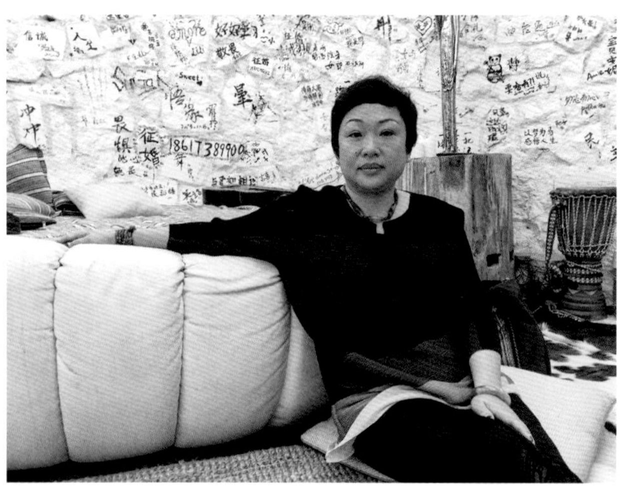
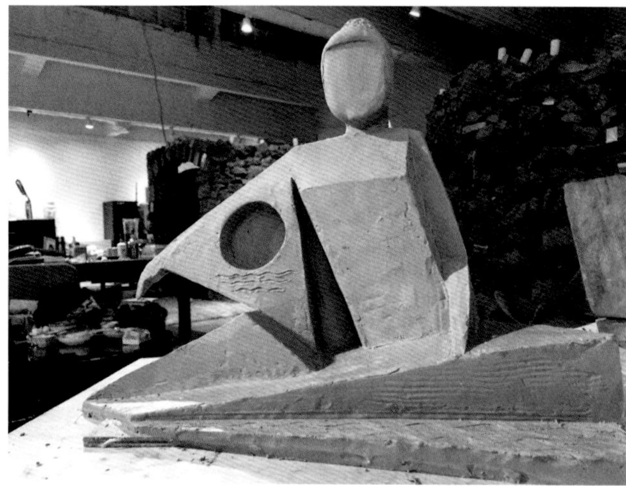
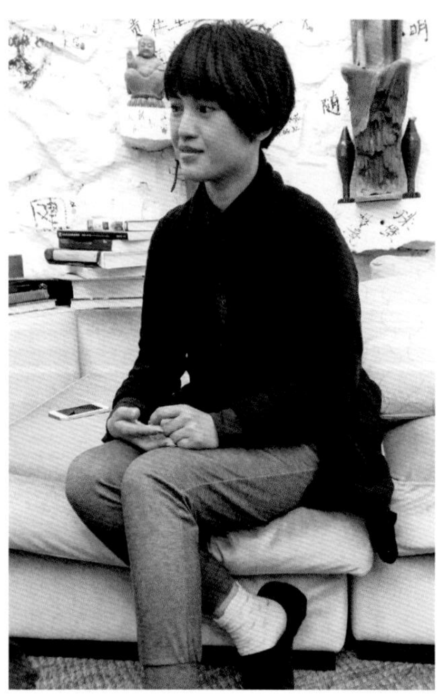
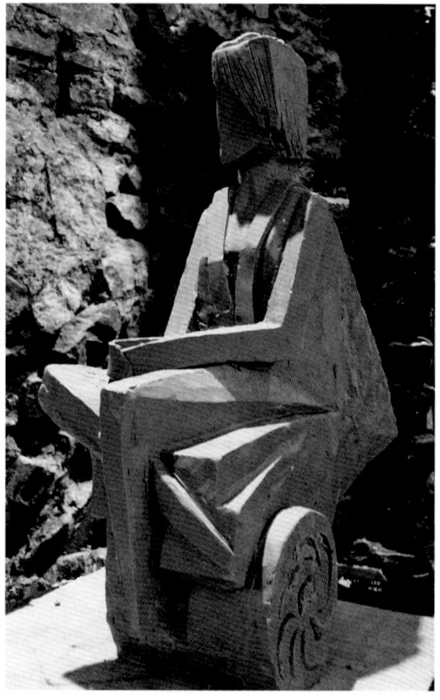
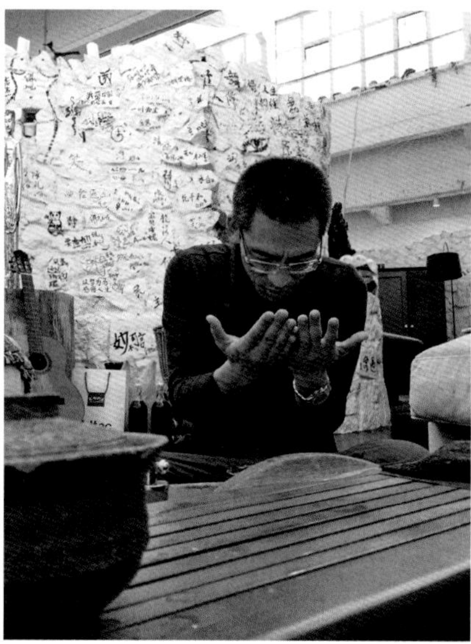

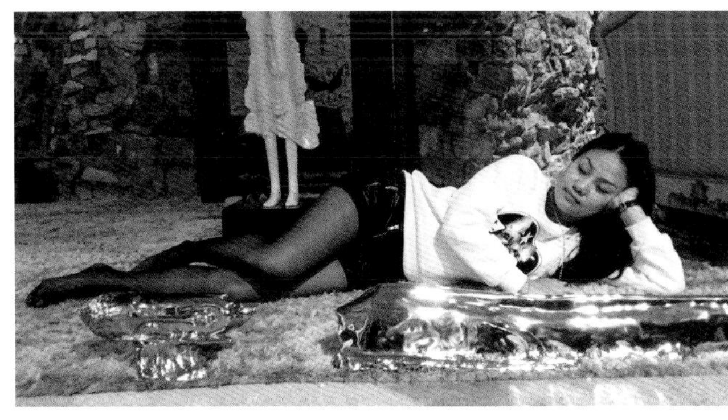
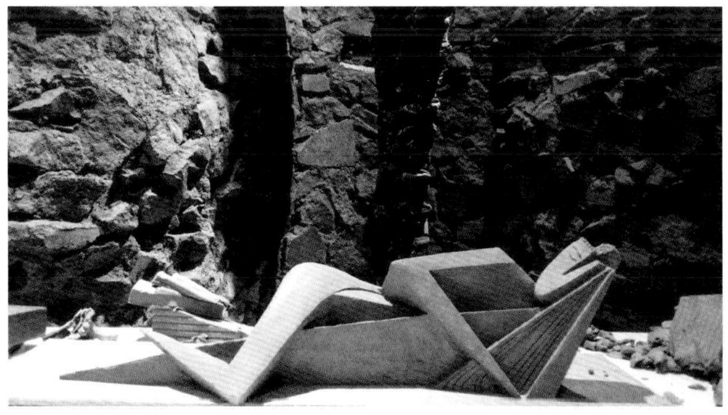
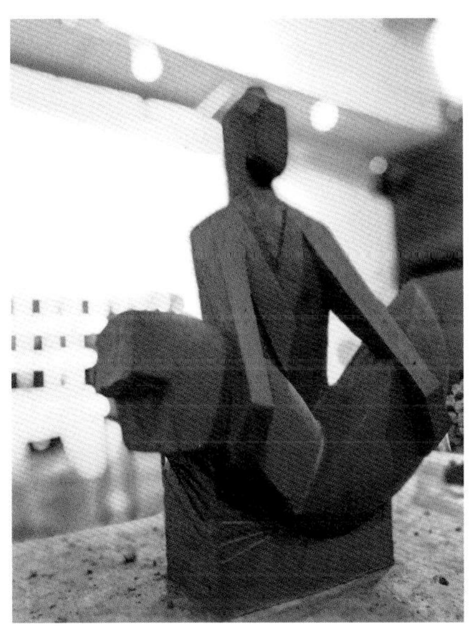
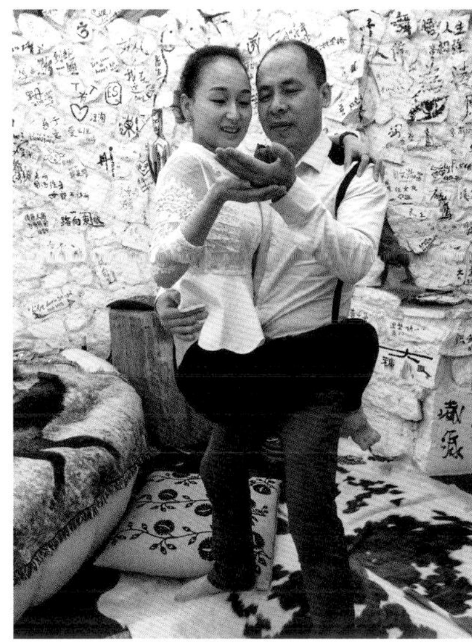
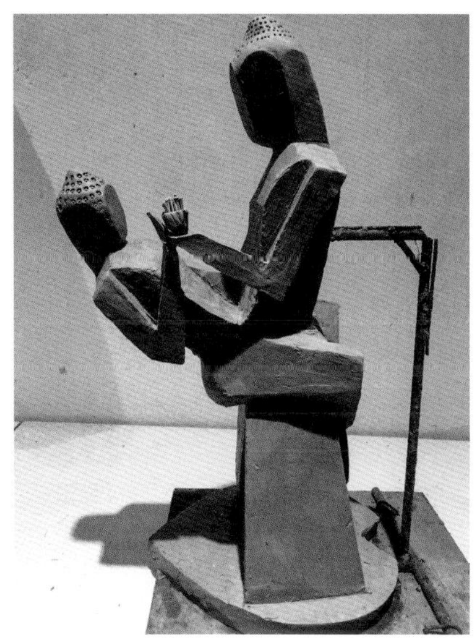
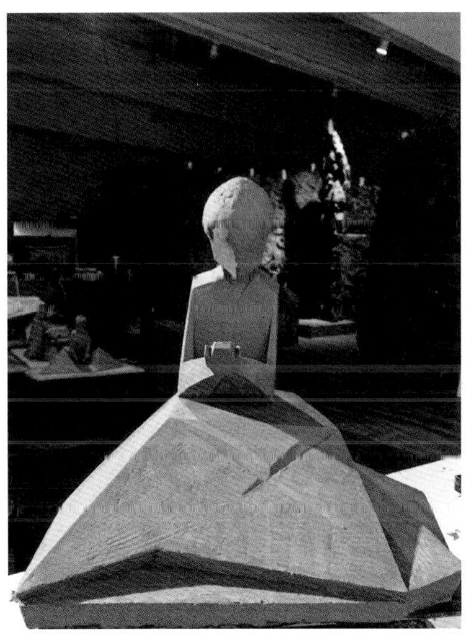
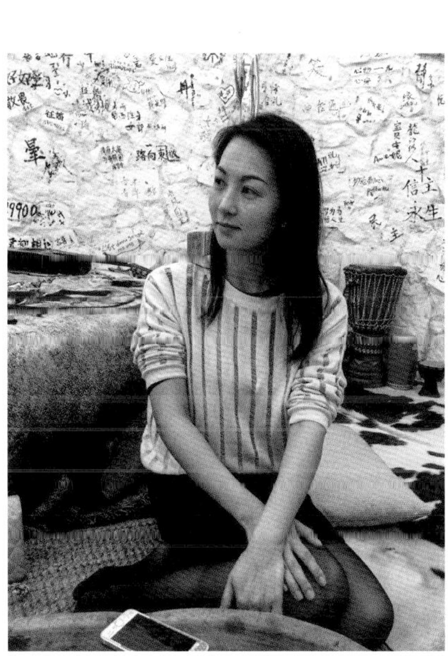
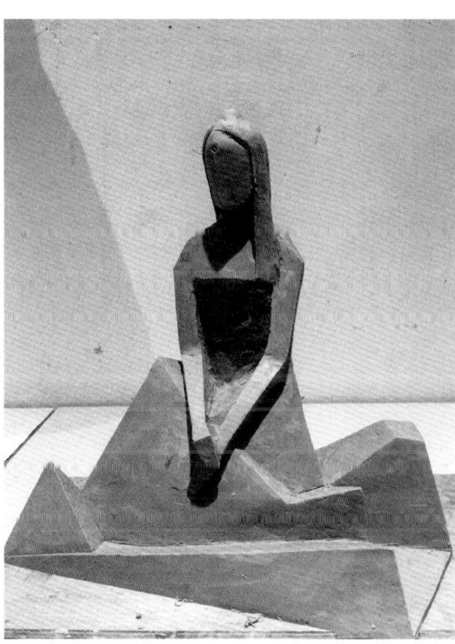

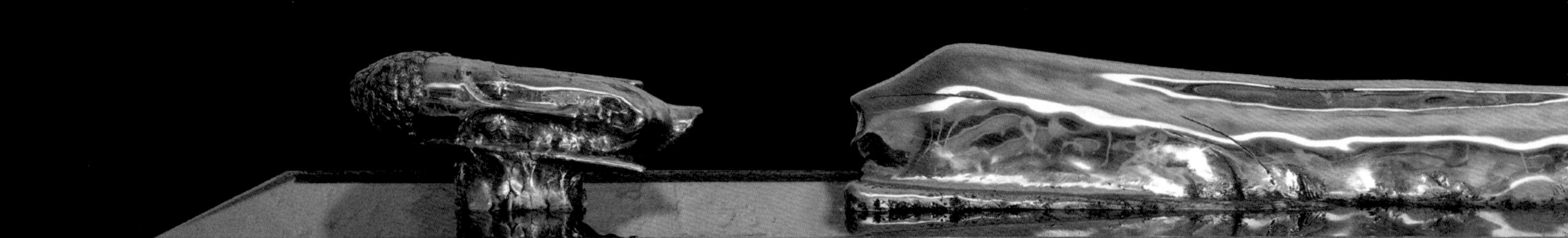

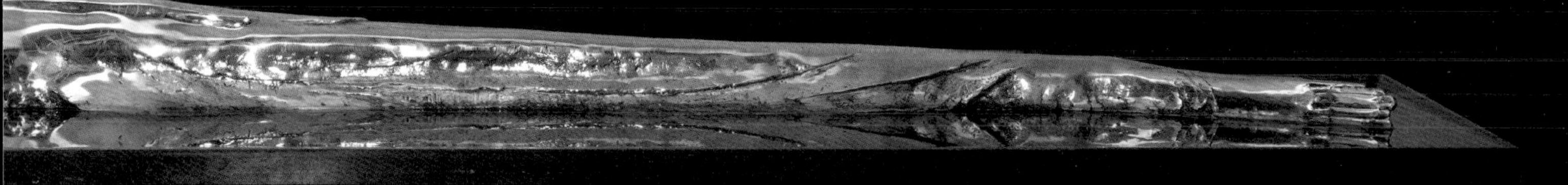

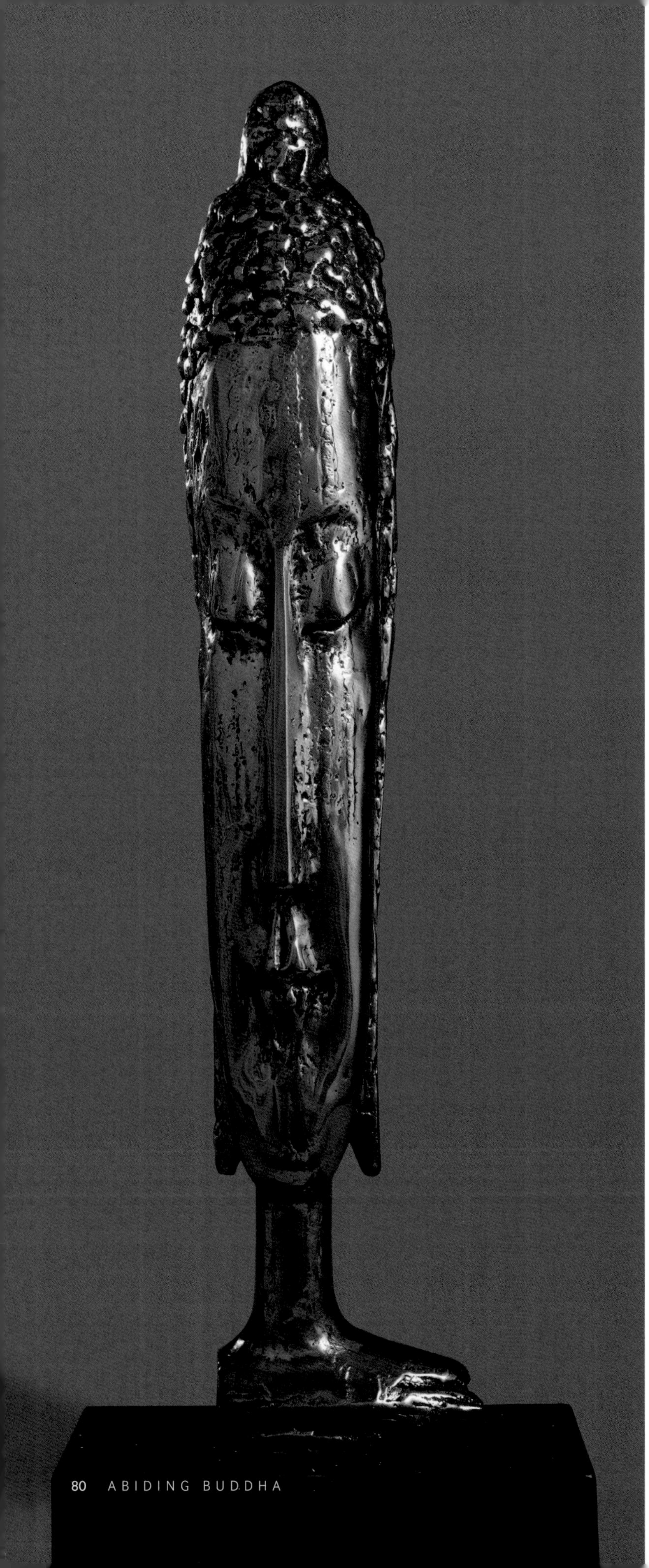

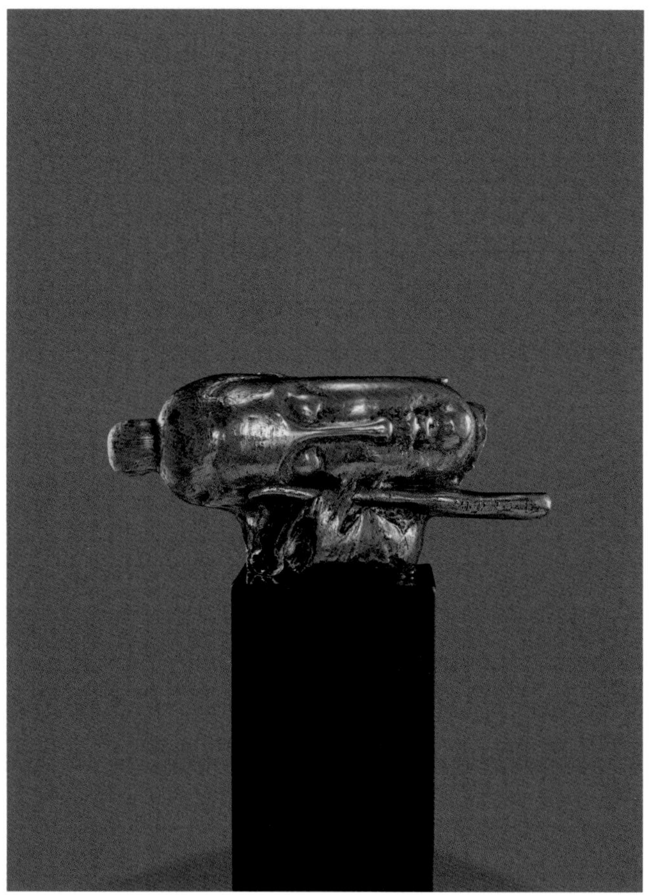

Considering the Fracture 3
Stainless steel, 12×12×27cm
2013

Considering the Fracture 2
Stainless steel, 12×12×76cm
2013

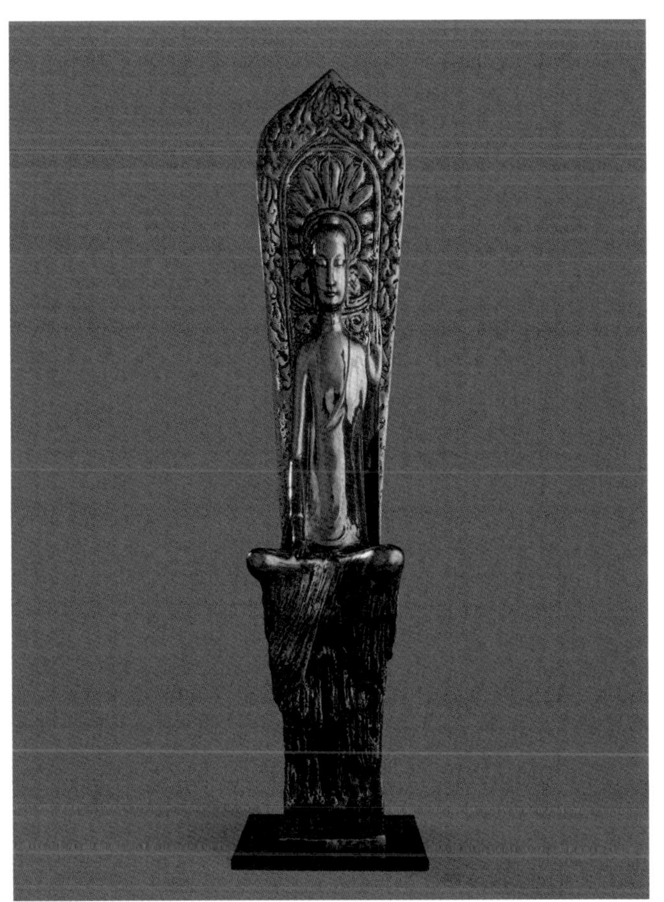 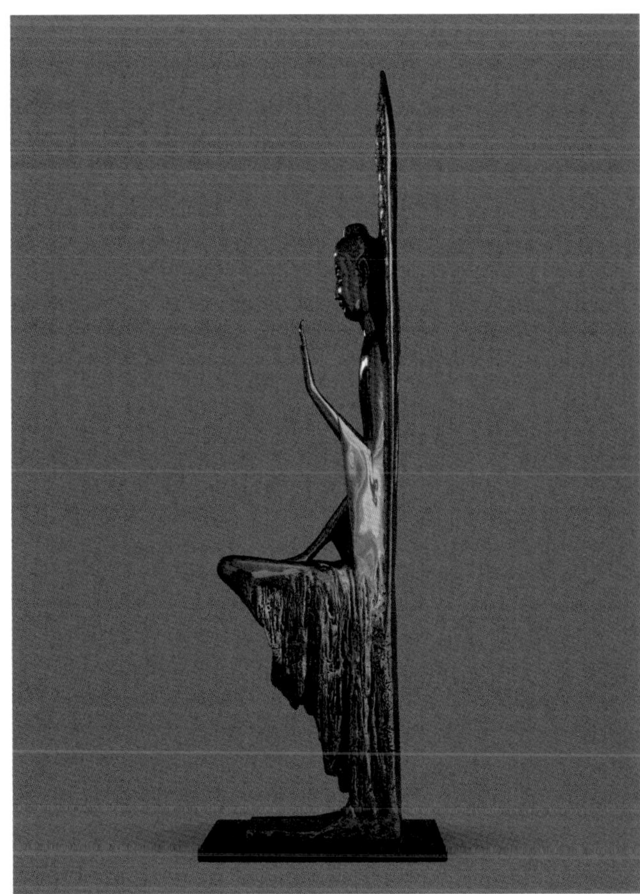

Considering the Fracture 4
Stainless steel, 25×25×108cm
2013

Considering the Fracture 5
Stainless steel, 15×15×110cm
2013

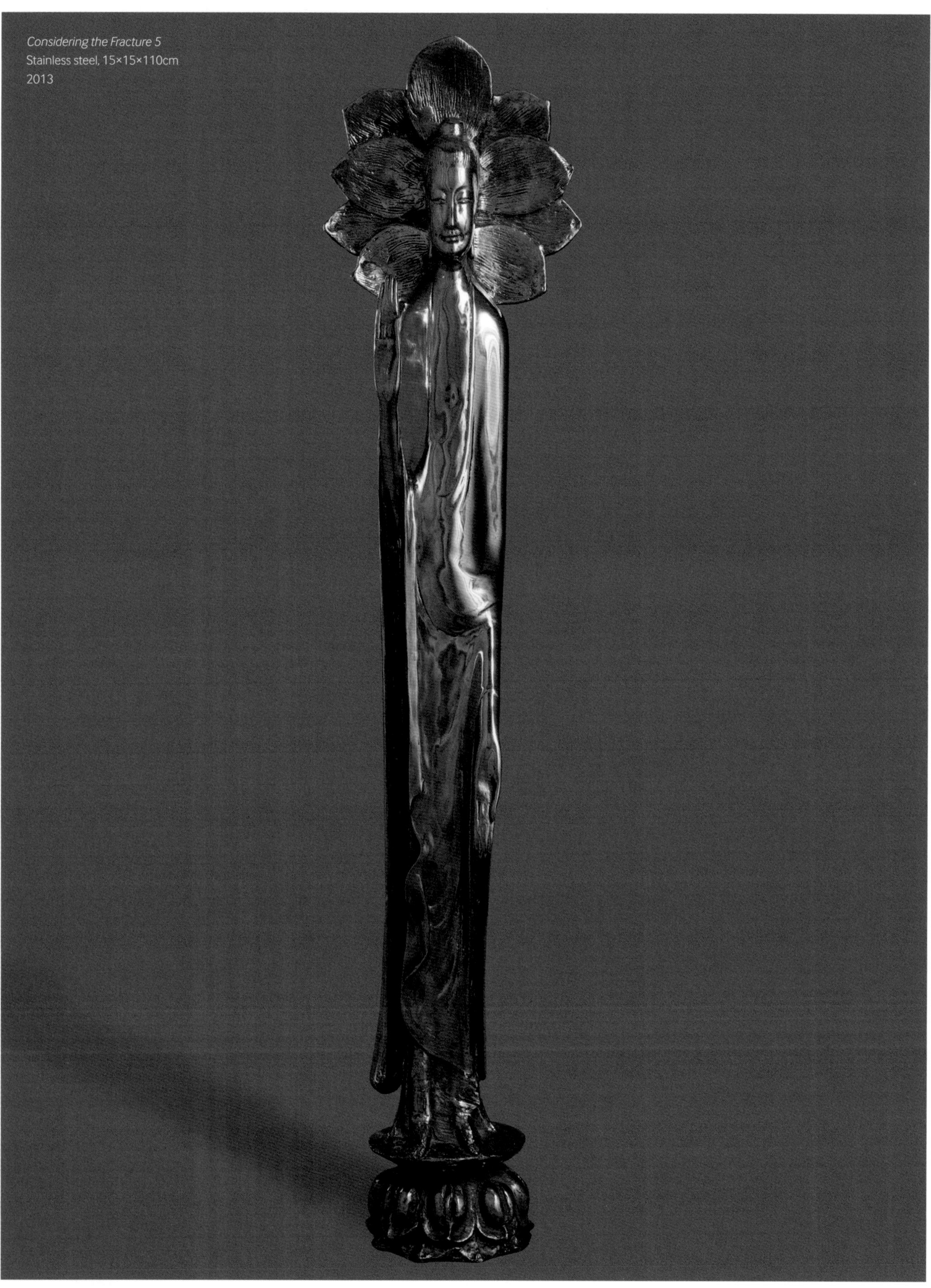

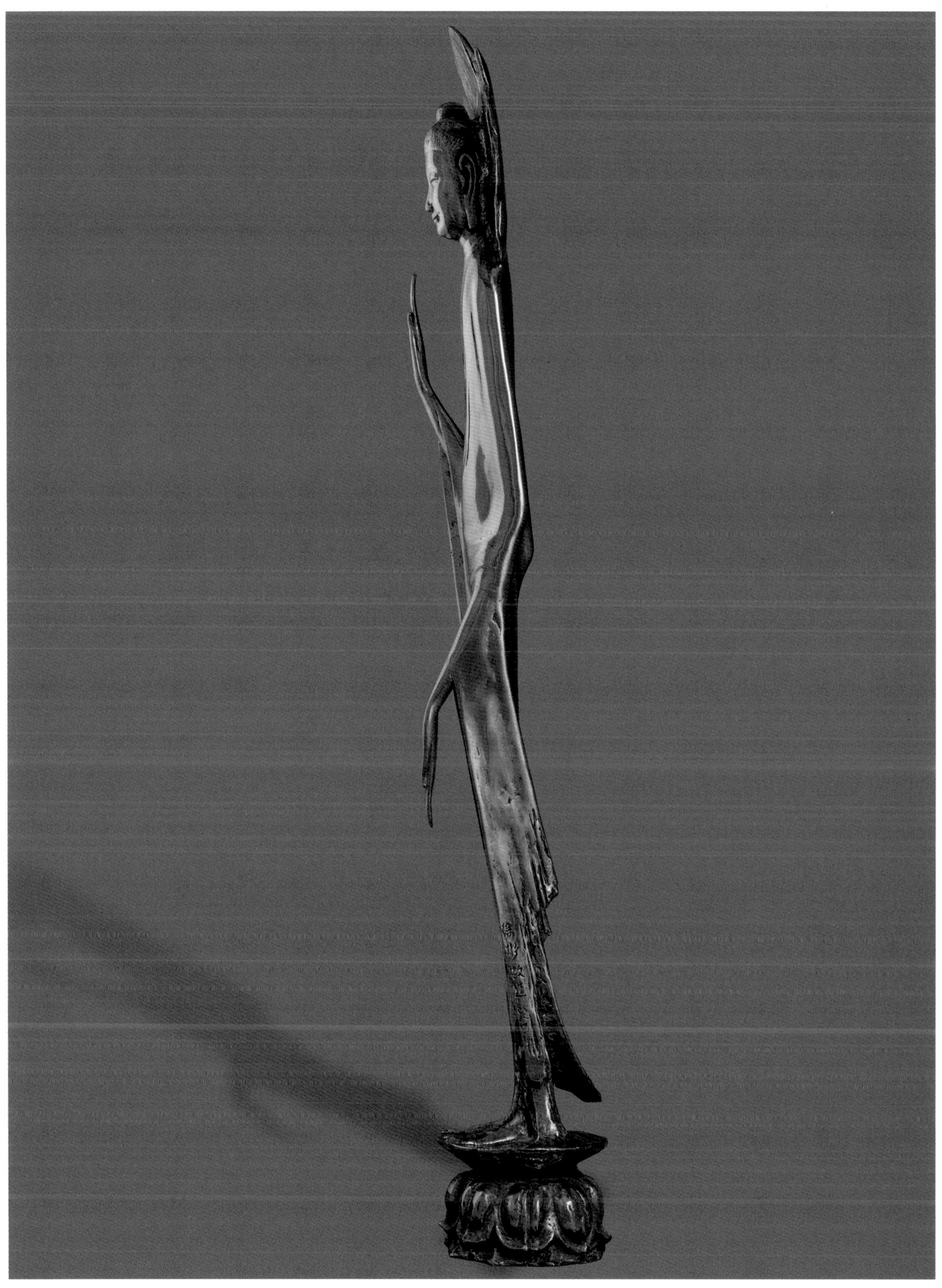

Considering the Fracture 6
Stainless steel, 26×26×90cm
2013

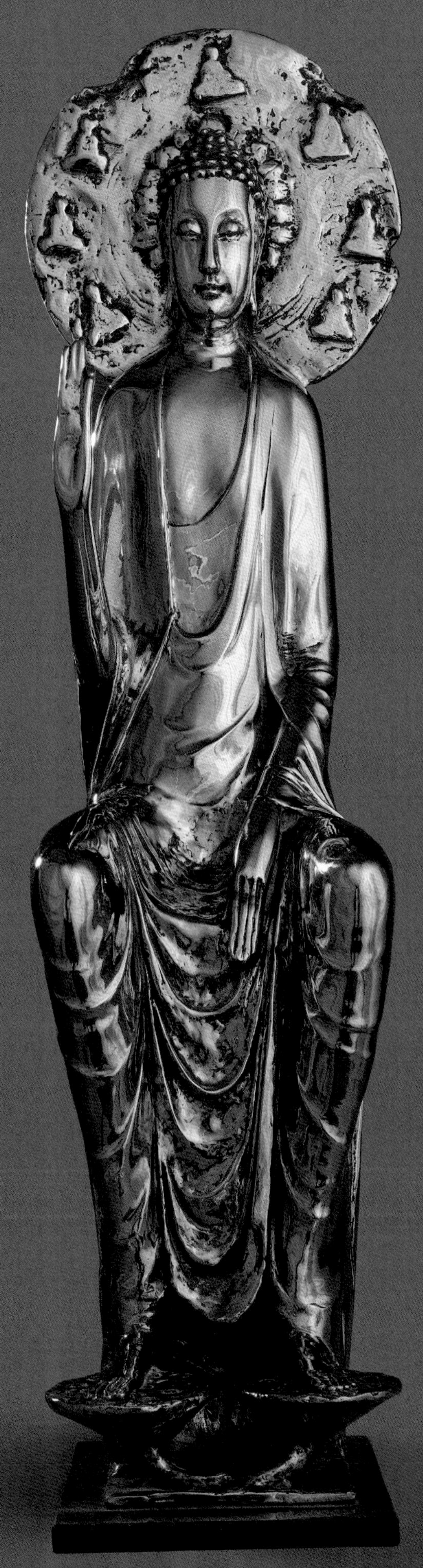

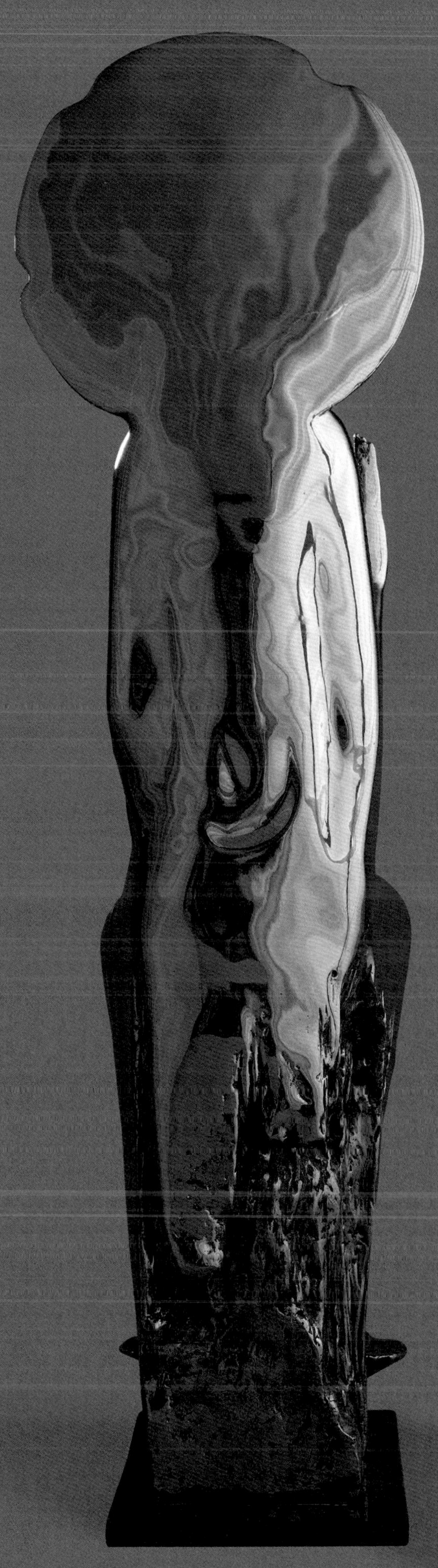

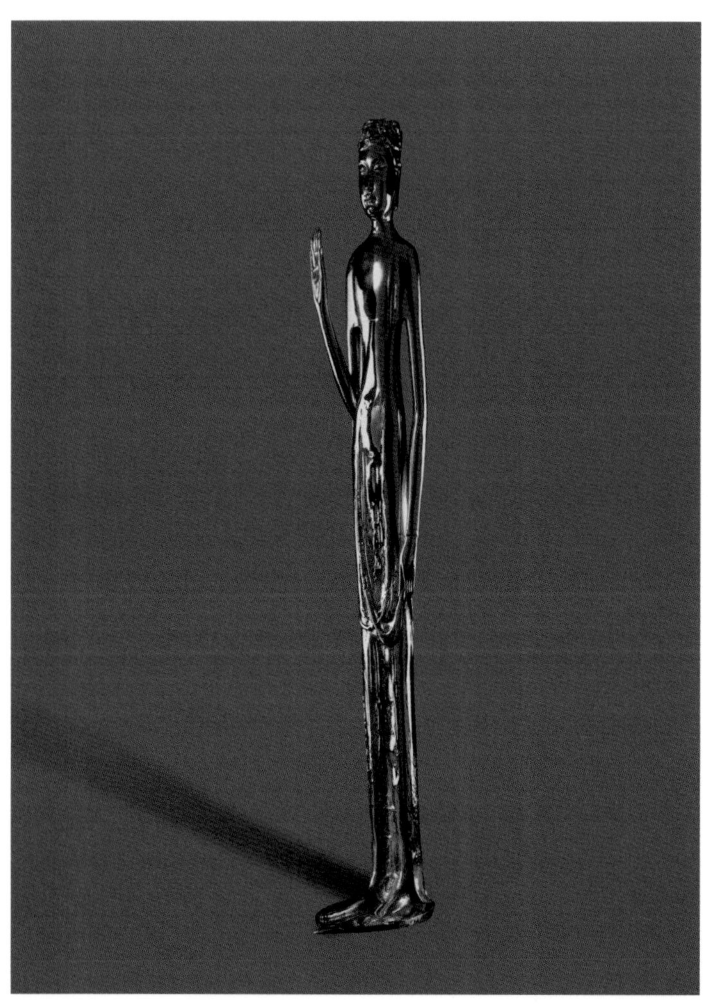
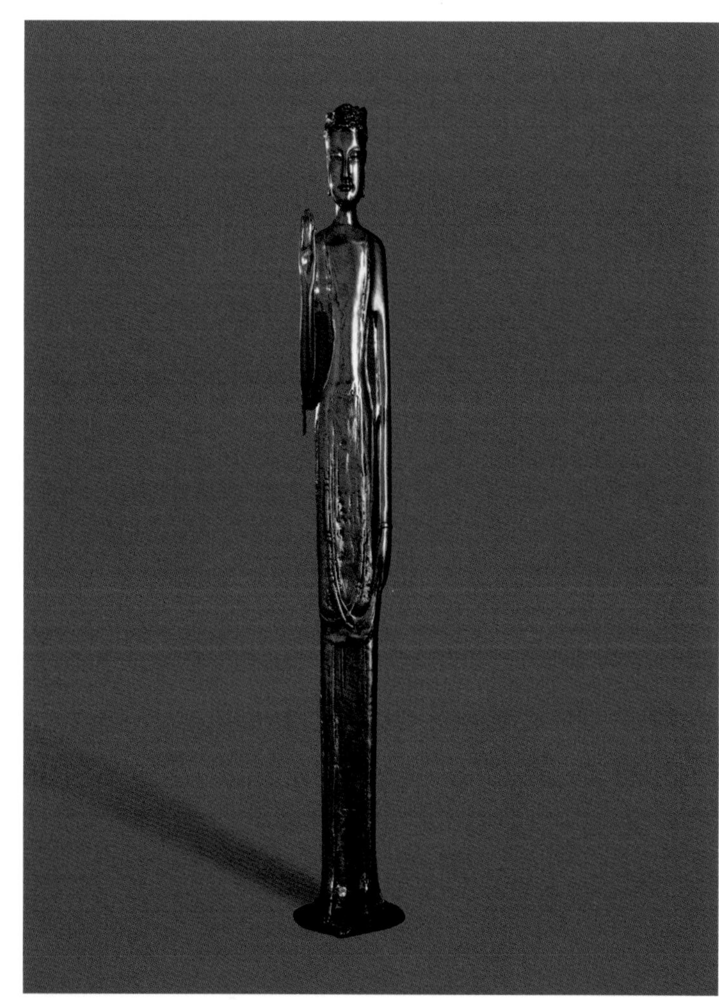

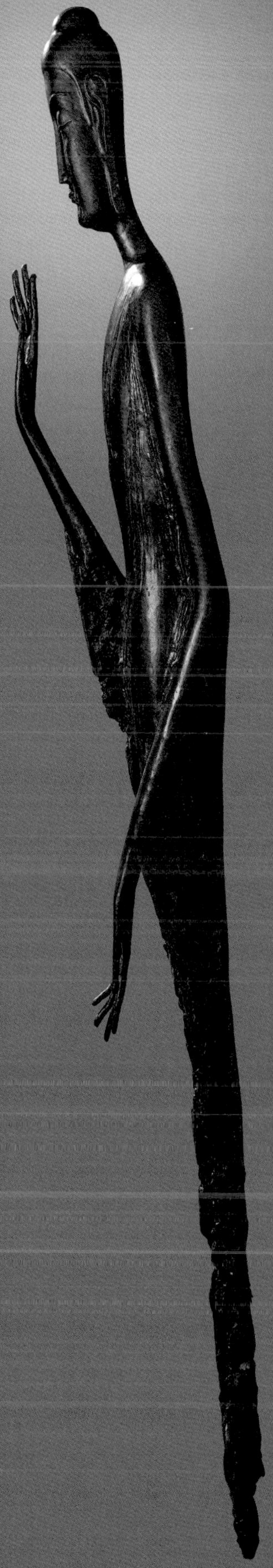

Considering the Fracture 8
Bronze, 100×48×250cm
2013

Everyone is Buddha

Spider Fort

This is a huge wall-like structure made of stones inside the shed
that is his sculpture studio ... And he made a giant steel spider out of
abandoned automobile parts, setting it in the space above the fort, so
that its legs cover the whole structure ... Another garish object is the
circular couch, so big that it is almost like a bed. Xu Bin Jueyi insists
that it is not a bed at all, that it is for people to sit on rather than for
sleeping. Guests to the fort do not agree however. They insist it is a
bed, and have inferred many bed-related associations, which they
have written on the surrounding stone walls.

- Wang Luxiang

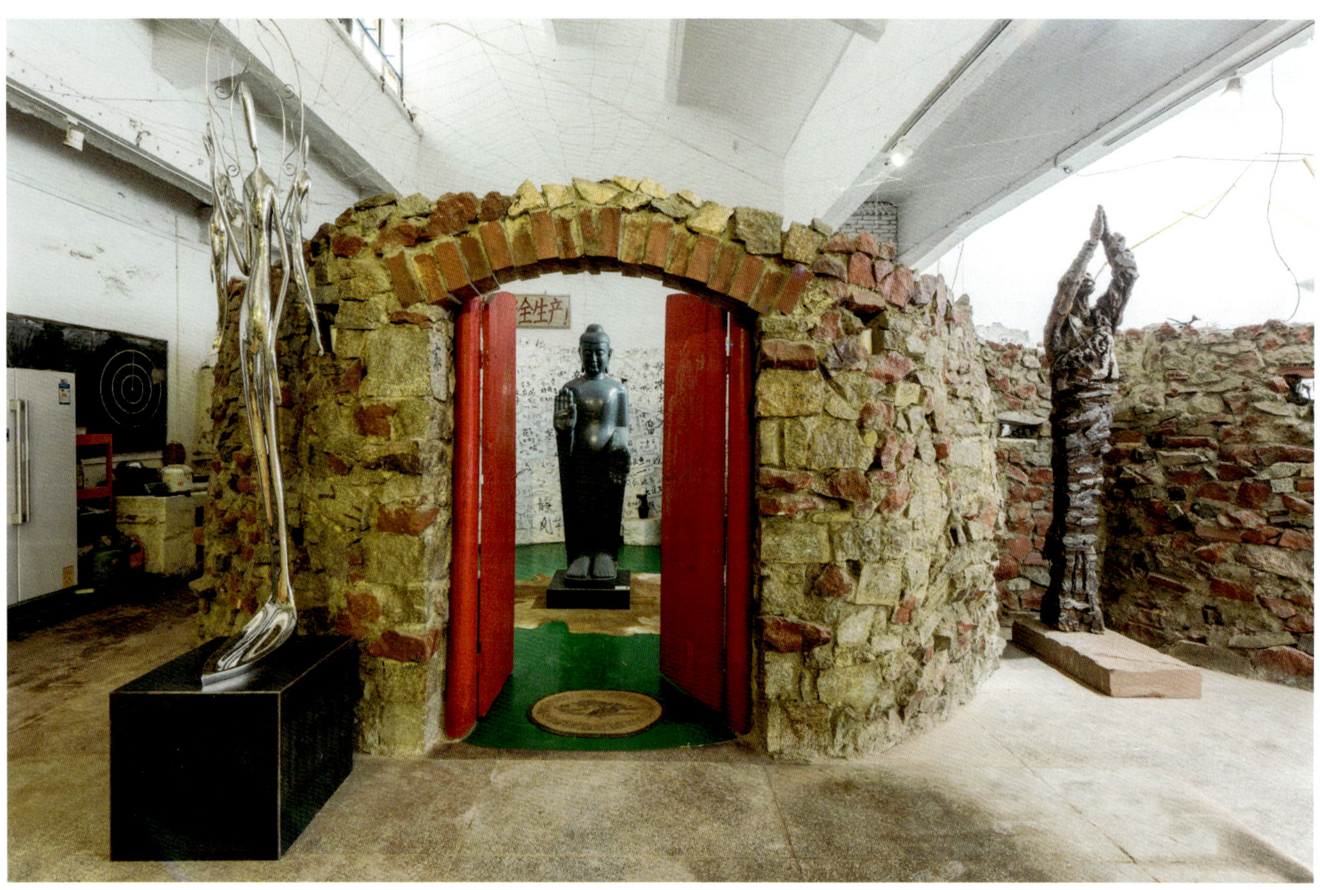

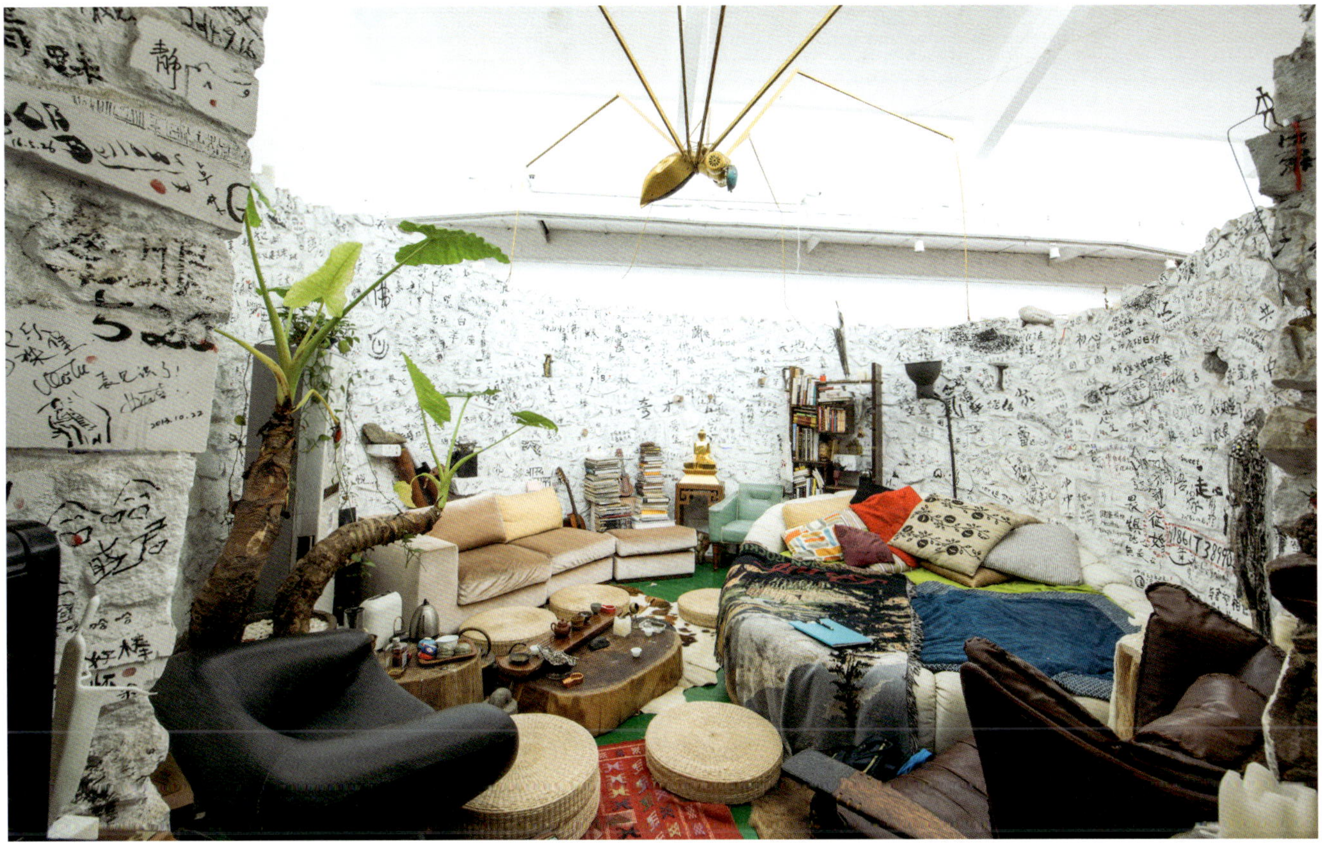

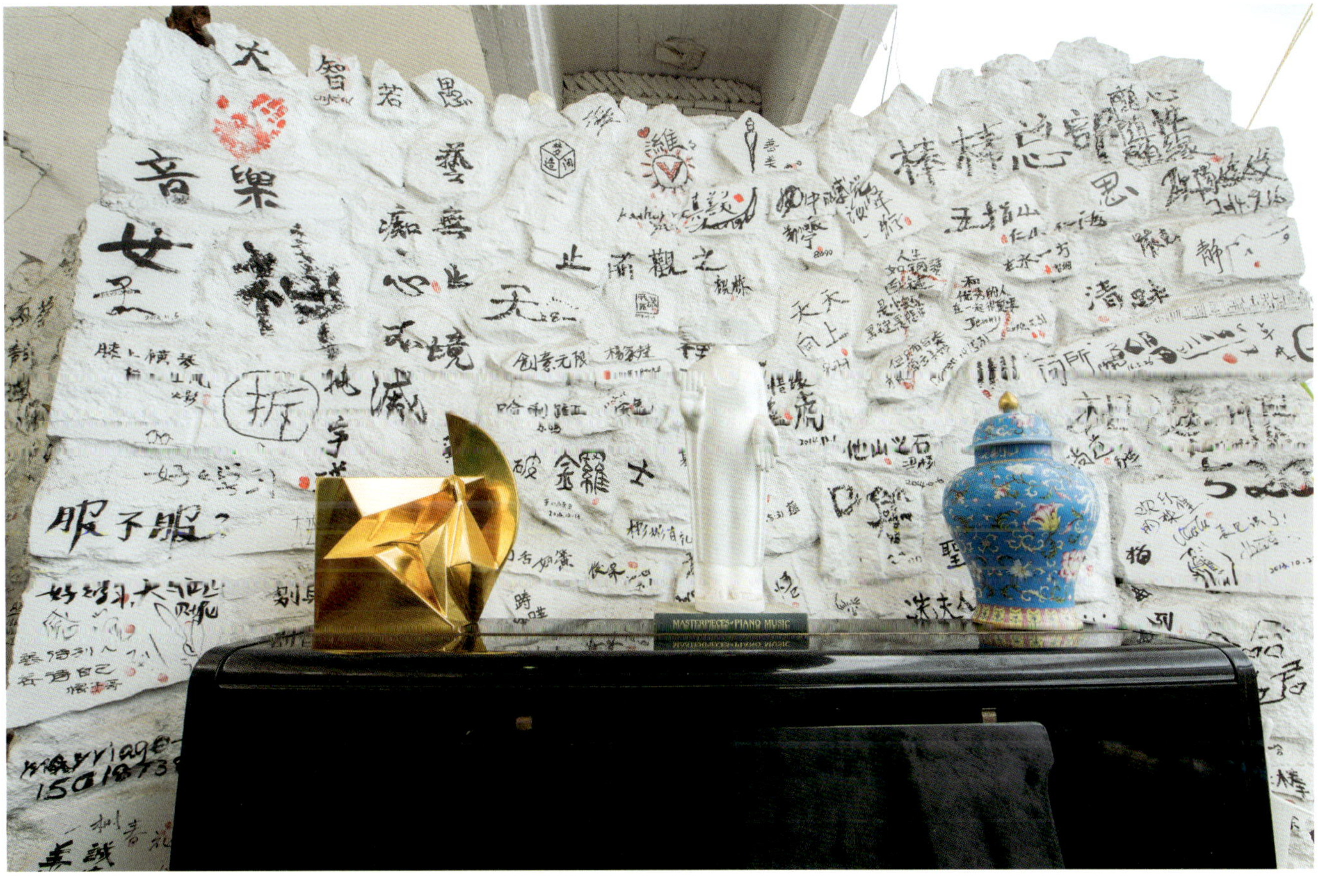
大智若愚
音樂
MASTERPIECES PIANO MUSIC

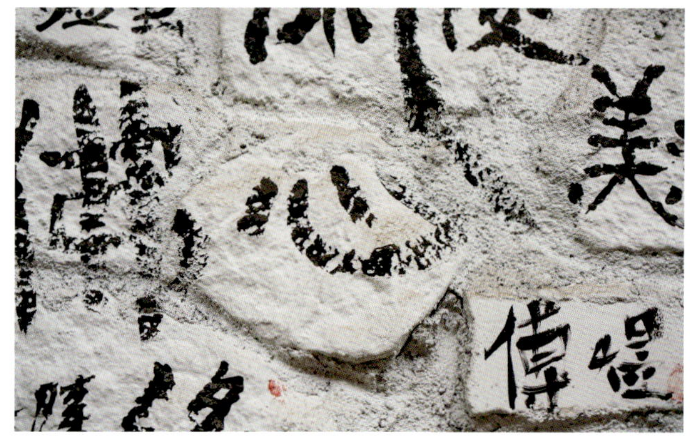
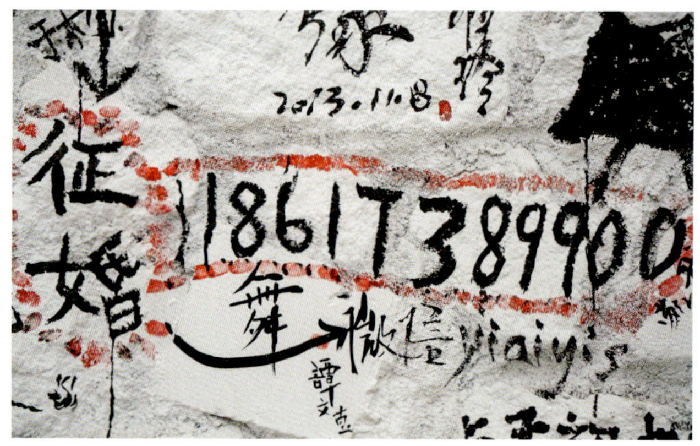
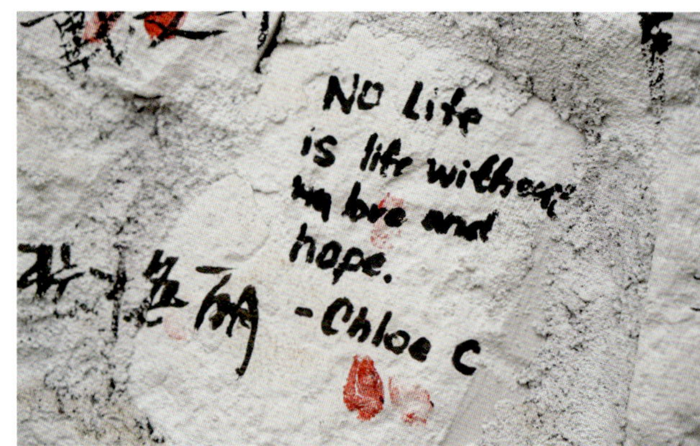

NO Life
is life without
love and
hope.
-Chloe C

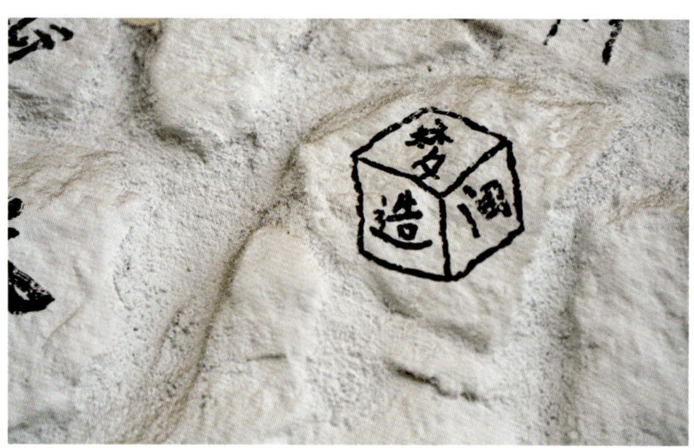
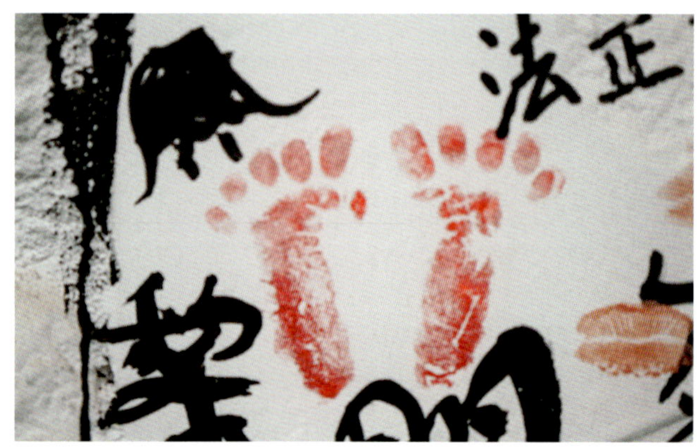

法正

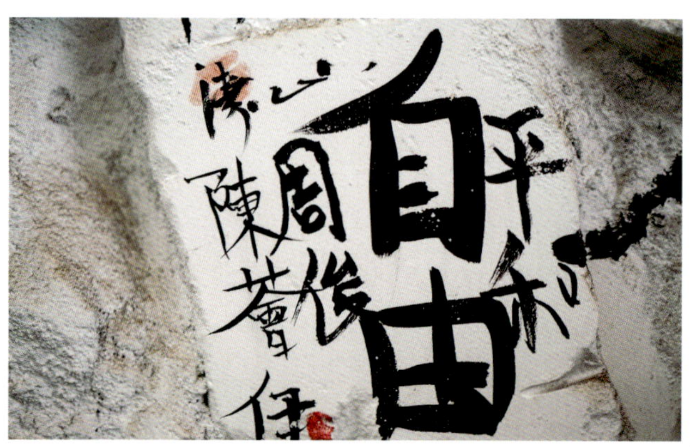
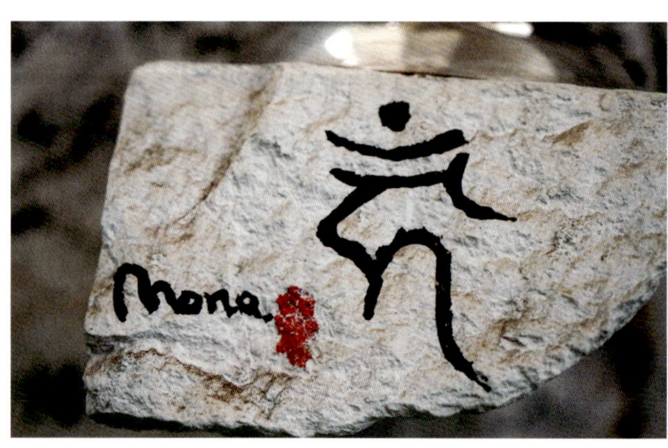

Mona

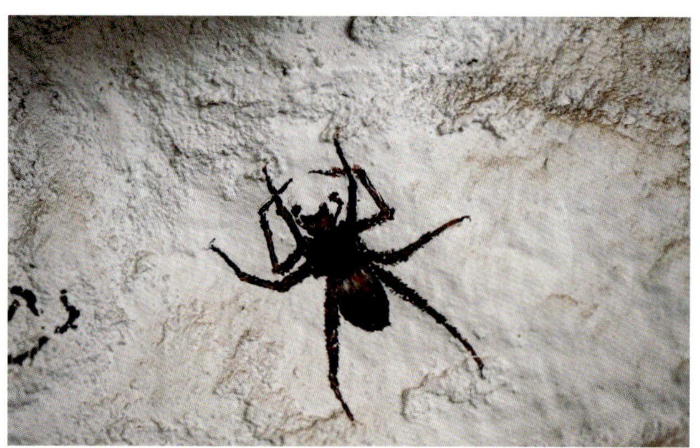

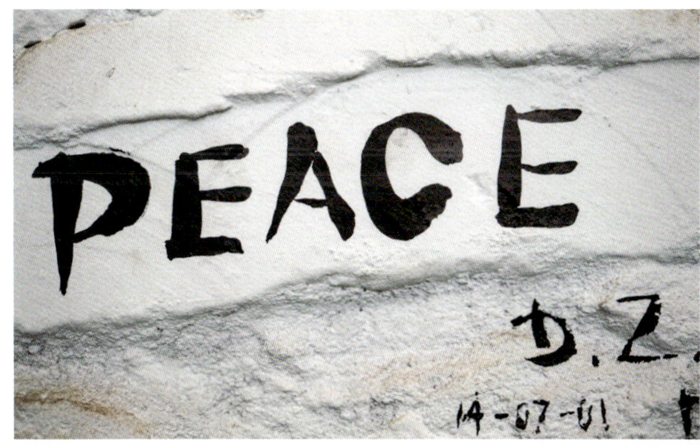
PEACE
b.z.
14-07-01

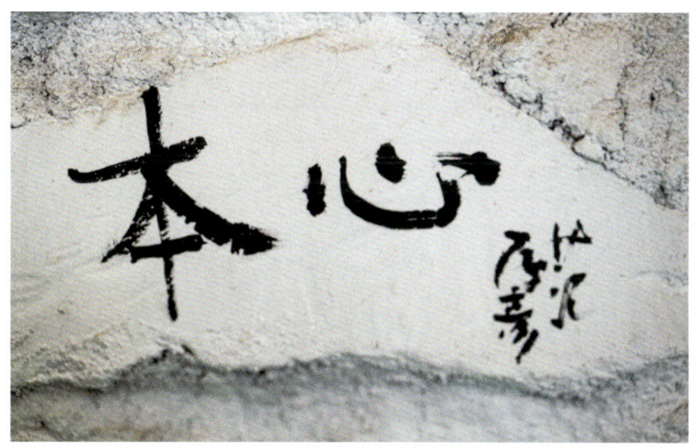
本心

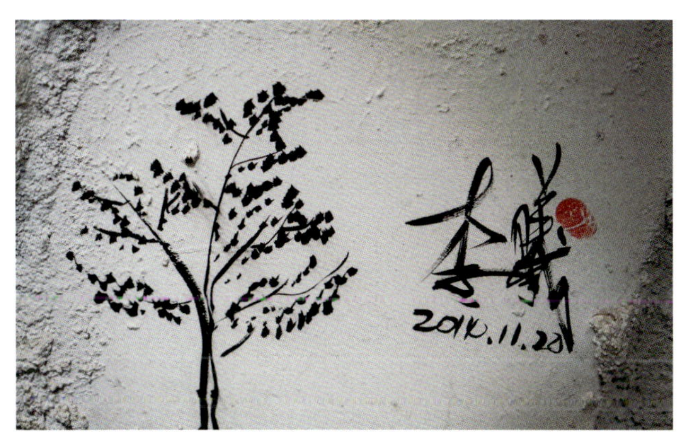
2010.11.20

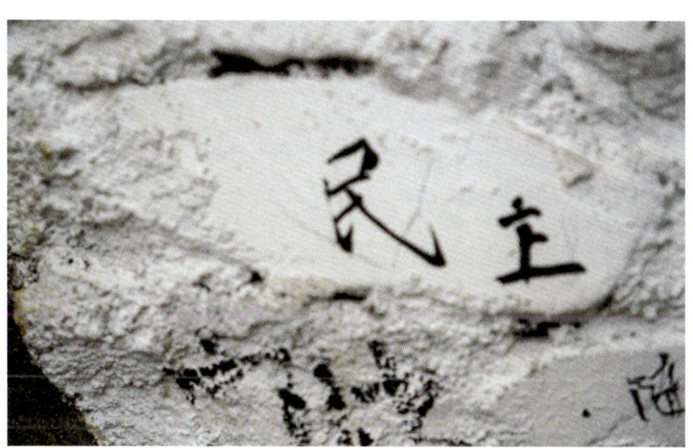
民主

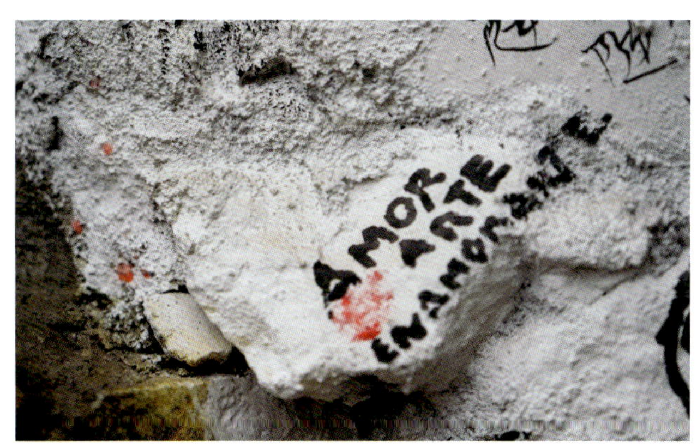
AMOR
ARTE
INAMORANTE

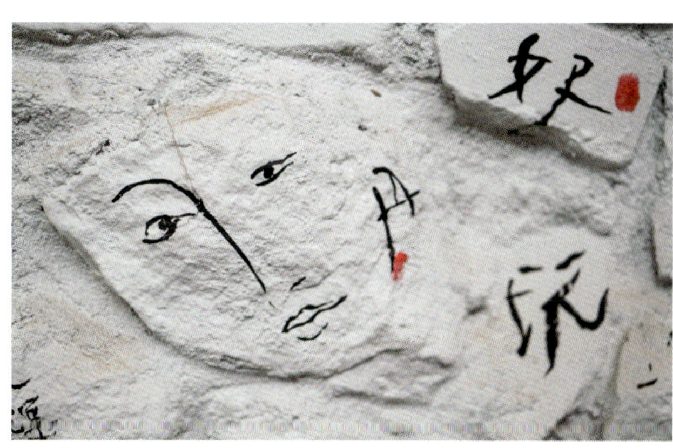

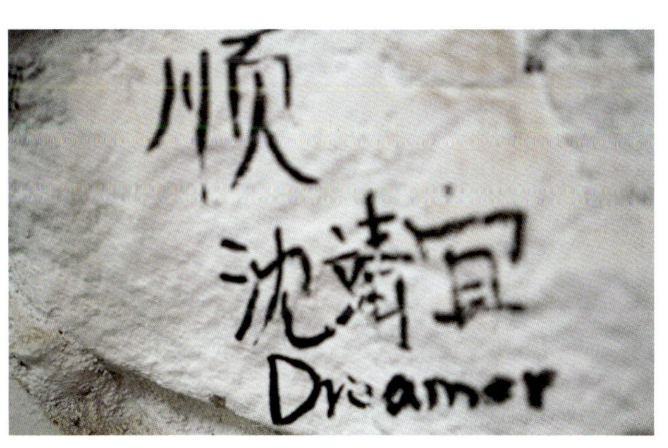
顺
沈靖宜
Dreamer

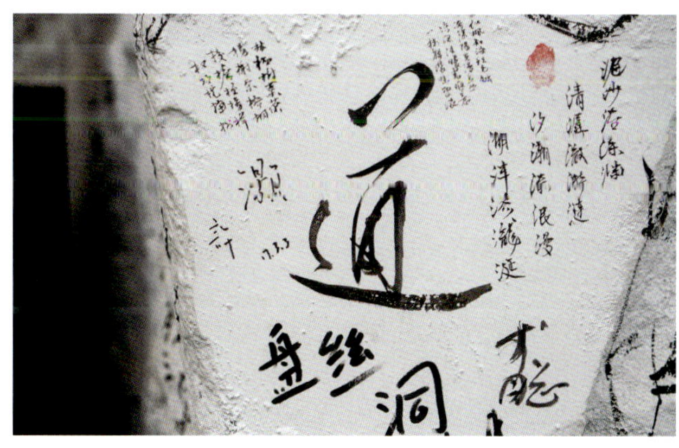
道

Encountering my Buddha-self, I see my heart and feel at ease - Comprehending Mr Xu Bin Jueyi and his Buddhist sculptural art

- Lu Guoping

One

'Floating life on a field of grass, the months and years urge us ever on.' Living in the red dust of this mortal world, how should people perceive themselves, and how cherish their souls?

. . . .

When I opened the great door made of a net of cables into the sculpture studio of Mr Xu Bin Jueyi at 'Spider Fort' in Yuancun, Guangzhou, I inexplicably immediately sensed a kind of sacred breath of spiritual mindfulness.

Here, there is no sign of rich, ornate decoration, but instead a profusion of sculptures of various types, shapes and sizes interestingly placed. There are statues embodying kindliness with mother and father as the models, a group of Tibetan-themed pilgrims figures reflecting the vicissitudes of life, and treasured images of compassion, manifesting both body and spirit, created for the Liurong Temple Flower Pagoda. Moreover, there is *State of Mind: Becoming Aware*, and several hundred pieces of non-realistic Buddha sculpture, full of feeling, and with only numbers as references.

Entering here is like coming to a kind of reality written in spider's web, confronting a variety of buddhas never seen before, as if encountering the Buddha and engaging in conversation. Unexpectedly you gain understanding of yourself, and feel as if your heart is protected!

. . . .

What Xu Bin Jueyi calls *Diamond Sutra* is a stainless-steel sculpture with a shining, tall, slender body, as if reaching for the sky, totally unlike solemn-and-quiet, realistic Buddhist statuary. Looked at from the back, it has a smoothly convex shape, like a cloak- wearing Madonna, and emanates a seemingly pure spiritual glow. The front is a recessed vertical slot, giving the illusion of strong light, large enough to accommodate someone standing; on the left side, above your shoulder, there is a small golden Buddha statue. If you stand in front, to the side, or at the back of the sculpture, taking up various positions or looking from a variety of angles, things appear different from normal. I am no longer myself: you see a myriad illusions of yourself. And if you pray or kneel before the image, or squat or stand in the recessed space, it is as if the Buddha protects you, the light of the Dharma shines, allowing introspection. At this point, you will nod and recite: 'All phenomena are dream bubbles, like dew, like lightening, and should be perceived as such' (*Diamond Sutra*). Each person finds thoughts and feelings welling up, and so it is that the Buddha and I am one!

. . . .

Thus, as I understand it, Mr Xu Bin single-mindedly uses his artistic creation to encourage people to observe their souls more consciously! His works, demonstrating superb technique and with profound nuances of meaning, go beyond the level of creating a space for manifesting form and spirit, and enter a spiritual plane of inspiration.

. . . .

I have always believed that solitary murmuring does not resonate with people, and in the end is not art. To succeed at art and to create compelling works, you must have 'three teachers and three attainments': taking the former sages as a teacher, you attain the Dharma (the Law); taking the times as a teacher, you attain heart; and taking nature as a teacher, you attain the Dao (the Way). And Mr Xu Bin's artistic creations are indeed based on a combination of the teachings of the sages, of the times and of nature. With his hands, he depicts the appearance of the soul; with sculpture, he takes on a sacred pursuit. In this way, he arrives at the integration and interpretation of myriads of mysteries, and leads people to a place of resonance and hidden teaching.

Two

Xu Bin Jueyi was born in Nantong village, Jiangsu, into an ordinary family. Chewing at grass roots, he learnt about the sweetness and bitterness of life. Smoked by cooking fires, he came to understand coldness and warmth. Home represented kindness, people were genuine. From catching shrimps as a child, he intuited, 'Poverty that is in harmony with the natural environment is a kind of wealth.'

He has never been narrow-minded: 'Ruminating on little joys and sorrows, and seeing those little sorrows as a source of grief for the whole world.' He has an innate love of natural mountains and rivers, and an appreciation of Chinese painting and photography, and brings these to his specialism in sculpture. He has wandered to the ends of the earth, retaining his sincerity of heart. He has been to France, Italy, the United States, India and Bhutan, and travelled all over China, even living in Guilin for four years, in Gulangyu for three years, in Dalian for two years, and now in Guangzhou.

His life centres on both his interests and his professional calling: he is happy to be assiduous, and stubbornly diligent.

. . . .

Known as an 'independent artist', he accepts Buddha in his heart and conveys the Buddha to others, so, both internally and externally, cultivating and sculpting the soul.

Three

The ability to interpret and express life is the fundamental strength of the artist.

Xu Bin Jueyi believes that he should explore the depths of the human spirit realm, so that his art can shape souls, with the aim of interpreting the ultimate problem of human nature and fate. He wants to be able to lead people of the world to a secluded place to find goodness, to the shadows to see the light.

To attain lasting enlightenment, you must be greatly at ease. He feels deeply that all creatures have a Buddha nature; sculpting them as buddhas is the most straightforward way to express human nature in art. In the moment a person opens their compassionate Buddha heart, their body language and facial expression are the most beautiful!

He is like a bodhisattva living in the world and embracing compassion, completely integrating his profound understanding of boundless life, and expressing his hopes for all sentient beings. He creates buddhas with flesh and bones, warmth, inner qualities and radiance, to display the compassionate Buddha Light to all, and to give the blessing of doing good and the hope of becoming Buddha.

He wants to use silent words to awaken people to see through the illusory nature of things, to subdue the impetuous heart, to gain release and to return to the stillness.

. . . .

On 10th October 2014, he began the first 'create a myriad buddhas' project, called: *'360-Degree Redemption'*.

He believes that the life state lies in complete unhindered integration, the circumference completed, no beginning or end.

He intends to describe the Buddha nature of people of every age, occupation, class and character, that is 360 degrees in the round.

He wishes to show people the completeness of Chan (Zen) Buddhism, to redeem them through art, so that sentient beings realize their true Buddha natures, and 'cross the river to the other side' (attain nirvana).

Four

All beings are equal, without distinction. Living in the world and becoming Buddha, they return to the true origin. Following their desires, integrated and unhindered.

This reflects his creative approach and sculpting process, and embodies the style of his works and main idea of his art.

. . . .

It does not matter whether it is a familiar friend, or a stranger encountered by chance. Whether a laid-back traveller at the Burning Man gathering in the depths of the Black Rock Desert in the United States; a Tibetan, encountered on his travels, who places his palms together, chants and prostrates himself, in long worship; an Indian holding a broom in front of a stupa; an old woman standing on a flight of steps with a plate of food in her thin hand; or a tired bird sitting on a street light under the crescent moon ... Xu Bin Jueyi, with his materials at hand, will do sketches there and then, and then compose one new sculpture after another.

Of the buddhas he sculpts, he has such models as the cultural scholar Wang Luxiang and the owner of Wujuezhai, Zheng Huaxing, but also his protégé Lin Yingxi, and the little girl next door and old man on the street, and even visiting strangers he has never met before.

Of course, he also intends to allow me 'to become Buddha', sculpture number 811, the first in the third year of the Myriad Buddha Programme. What a superb opportunity!

Five

Only those who 'see past and present in an instant, and take in the four seas (the world) in a moment,' (Lu Ji: *Wenfu*, AD 261-303), that is those who go out beyond their circumscribed field and experience the boundless world, can become true artists.

....

Xu Bin Jueyi believes that human beings should seek a common spiritual home, beyond the barriers of ideological and cultural tradition. Moreover, that they can stop the conflict between religions, and integrate with each other. The pursuit of the natural world in the East and the respect for God in the West can then become one.

When he saw three stakes chained together on the Grand Canal in Venice, he even thought that it would be possible to make a sculpture of Shakyamuni, Jesus and Mohammed, encircled and struggling to free themselves from the iron links. He noted: Break the chains of the boundaries between religion; peace is above religion.

He uses the artistic styles of the East and the West, of the South and the North, to create a transboundary amalgam in Buddha sculpture, inventing a new style, but without pursuing freakishness.

He does not advertise what genre the art belongs to, but instead reflects the style of the times and the integration of the world.

....

From solemn-and-quiet realistic sculpture, manifesting both form and spirit, to the creation of unrealistic and elongated Buddhas, this represents his leap in the progress of art, a major change in the history of the Buddha image!

Xu Bin Jueyi previously also created a lot of realistic sculptures. But later, he purposely ignored facial features and clothes.

He knows the dictum of the Buddhist scriptures: 'The nature of the origin is emptiness.' If you look at each predestined meeting, they can be broken down into a myriad distinctions, but are also integrated.

His '360-Degree Redemption' is intended to enable people of the world to reject the distinction-making mind, and to contemplate and become aware of the true Tathāgata.

In fact, sculpture has always been an art concerned with the concave and convex, light and ornament. Its process and essence is to subtract: starting with the rough, from the outside to towards the inside cutting out the waste, excavating step by step to reveal beauty.

The Great Way is simple. Individuals are all different, but the true Buddha nature is integrated and unhindered, diamond-like and inextinguishable.

He decided: In creating Buddhas, you can leave aside realism!

People quickly and widely understood, concurred, and welcomed this kind of non-realistic Buddha art.

Actually, the non-realistic should not be fettered by a specific name or appearance, but be more like the meaning of the Tathāgata.

Buddhism has Trikāya, or three bodies: the dharmakāya or 'truth body', sambhogakāya or 'retribution body' and nirmanakāya or 'transformation body'. The dharmakāya is all around, sambhogakāya is limitless and nirmanakāya follows predestination. What is sensed is no different to emptiness, emptiness is no different to what is sensed. Karma is like the myriads of grains of sand in the Ganges, the root of truth is the Buddha!

....

That sense of elongation is another style feature of Xu Bin Jueyi.

Once, he was in front of the Jokhang Temple at Lhasa, watching the setting sun shine on the pilgrims. As the pilgrims raised their hands, their elongated shadow passed straight through the great door of the temple ... this moment left him stunned! He realized that in this elongated form there was a sacred sense of the spirit moving upwards. Are not Tibetan flag streamers, Egyptian obelisks, elongated?

Afterwards, he created twelve *Pilgrims*, later put in the museum collection.

From this point on, he often used the elongation method for statues.

Six

Free, unrestrained and not restricted to one style; frank, but observant of propriety.

This is Xu Bin Jueyi in his life as an artist.

He likes quiet, conserving his energy, and spiritual practice; his focus is on his creativity. He is also hospitable, to develop the source of predestined meetings and inspiration.

Whether in respect of a piece of work, an emotion, or an item of property or other valuable thing in life, he will take it up with weighty seriousness, and then gently put in its place.

With simple modelling, materials and tools, he expresses ideas that are not simple, but rather reflect his grounding in self-cultivation and art.

He has a collection of hundreds of pieces of works. But for him, in respect of the artistic life he has created, the moment is also an eternity. Sometimes he will make a statue on the beach with sand; even take the trouble to collect three thousand people's handprints on mud bricks to create a Buddha, then allow the wind and rain to erode it, so that it peacefully returns to dust.

He does not expostulate on pet topics. Works are put out there, and each viewer experiences them in their own way. Appreciation of works equates to the interpretation of human nature, both concern the re-creation of art and the awakening of the Buddha nature.

He said, 'I can see joy in weather-beaten, old faces, but I cannot for the sake of the market turn an aging woman into a carefree young girl.' He has put every effort into his creation. If he gets to a difficult spot, there is unexpected help, as if God mysteriously lent a hand.

'No sudden inspiration, in fact, can replace long-term effort.' Long-term focus on creation, working day and night, no certainty as to three meals a day, sleep disturbance, tireless diligence. He was suffering from physical effects, his limbs felt numb. But these adjusted themselves, and slowly improved.

It makes him feel more that there is no trouble in life he cannot overcome.

He is convinced that Heaven has its own arrangements; everything is arranged for the best! 'I am grateful, Heaven has been so good to me!'

Seven

Speaking of sculptural art, I think of Auguste Rodin. He broke through the bounds of the official academy, with a variety of techniques, shaping powerful artistic images, with one foot in the courtyard of the classicists, and the other over the threshold of the modernists. Rodin's *The Thinker (Le Penseur)*, Balzac and many other outstanding works, representing a new kind of creativity, bestride time and space and cross borders. They exude an eternal charm and have become world classics.

It was the artistic peak of the era!

Now, it is again an era calling for art to reach a peak.

Mr Xu Bin Jueyi and other outstanding sculptors are on the road to becoming the Rodins of contemporary China!

We can expect, through the miracles produced by their many pairs of hands, batches and individual pieces of work embodying the deep flow of the spiritual world, fresh and full of genuine life, with timeless beauty and eternal feeling. Glorious works full of mighty qi (ch'i), works to be handed down, immortal works, will enter our life, and step onto the world stage of art.

Eight

It is the eternal mission of art and science to observe, understand, and
return to the true nature of the universe.

Our vast world made up of material, energy and information, is also
a 'world under the influence of consciousness'. Modern science
has shown that the universe was originally chaotic. Once human
consciousness is added, it enters a determined progressive state.

Fine art and advanced technology guide human life, improve the
world, carrying the consciousness of civilization, and possessing
lasting meaning!

. . . .

The thousands of sculptures created by Xu Bin Jueyi are today
considered fine works, and in the future will be classics, demonstrating
each passing day the increasing vitality of art's new spring.

And his *Spider Fort* has brought together countless love-destinies,
energy fields and instances of kinetic energy, and witnessed the
whole process of joint participation in incubating ideas and creating
consummate Buddha art.

All this represents a gestation of rich spirituality in art and a Madonna-
like nurturing of the meaning of life!

Spider Fort, together with Mr Xu Bin's creations there, constitutes a
complete system for the artistic life: it is indeed an extremely valuable
cultural achievement and site.

The place is worthy of care, to ensure its long inheritance!

Thus, it will not only benefit us today, but also bring value
to future generations!

Qinghai-Tibetan Plateau

The piety of the Tibetan pilgrims – the way they place their
palms together, and every third step prostrate themselves
– deeply fascinated Xu Bin Jueyi. He saw purity and serenity
in their (these women's) eyes, quite devoid of the pursuit of
material desires of contemporary urban life! His wish was to
use the ready medium of clay to create sculptures of these
very ordinary, lowly believers.

Gao Ling

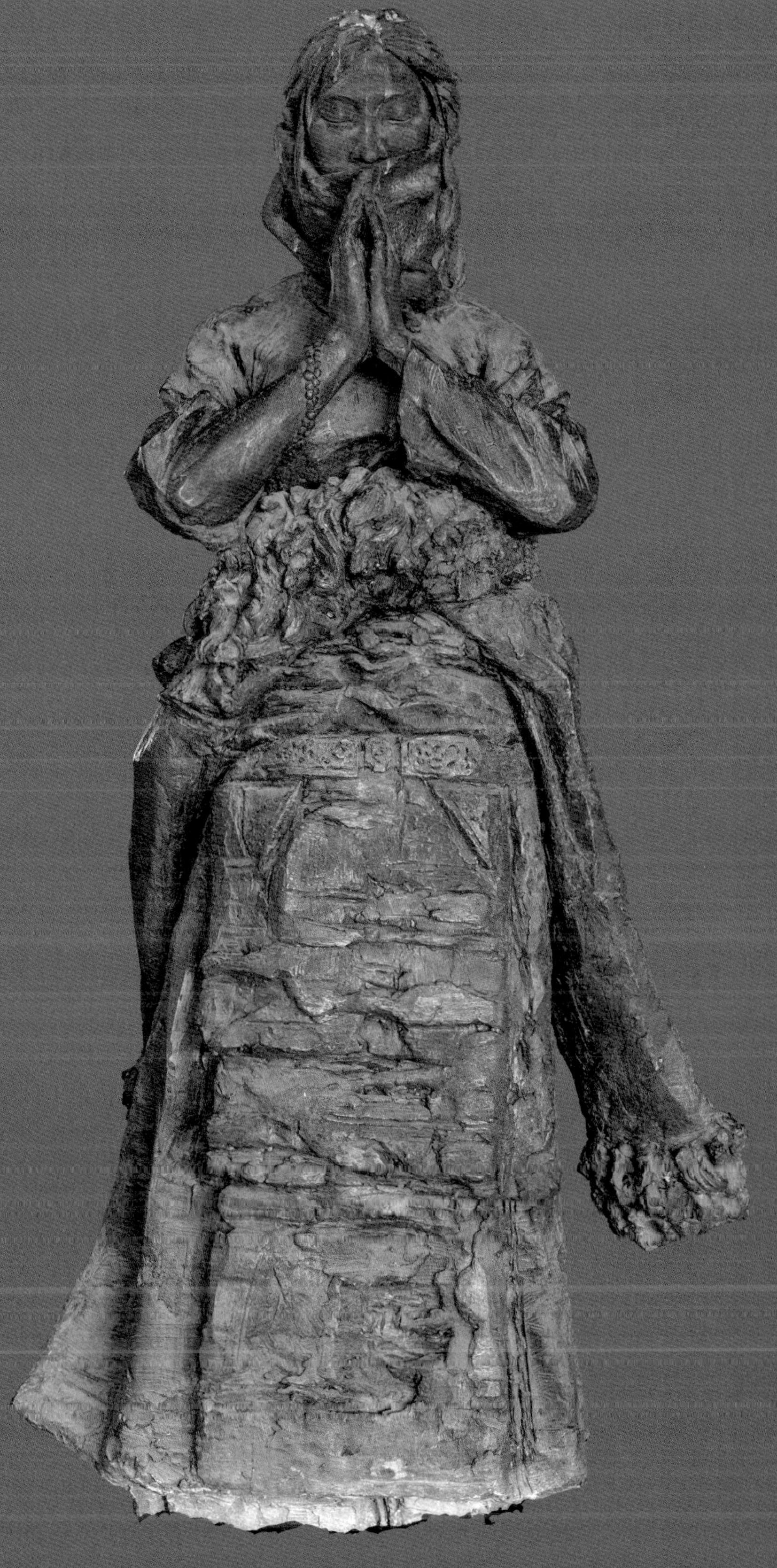

Qinghai-Tibetan Plateau
2012

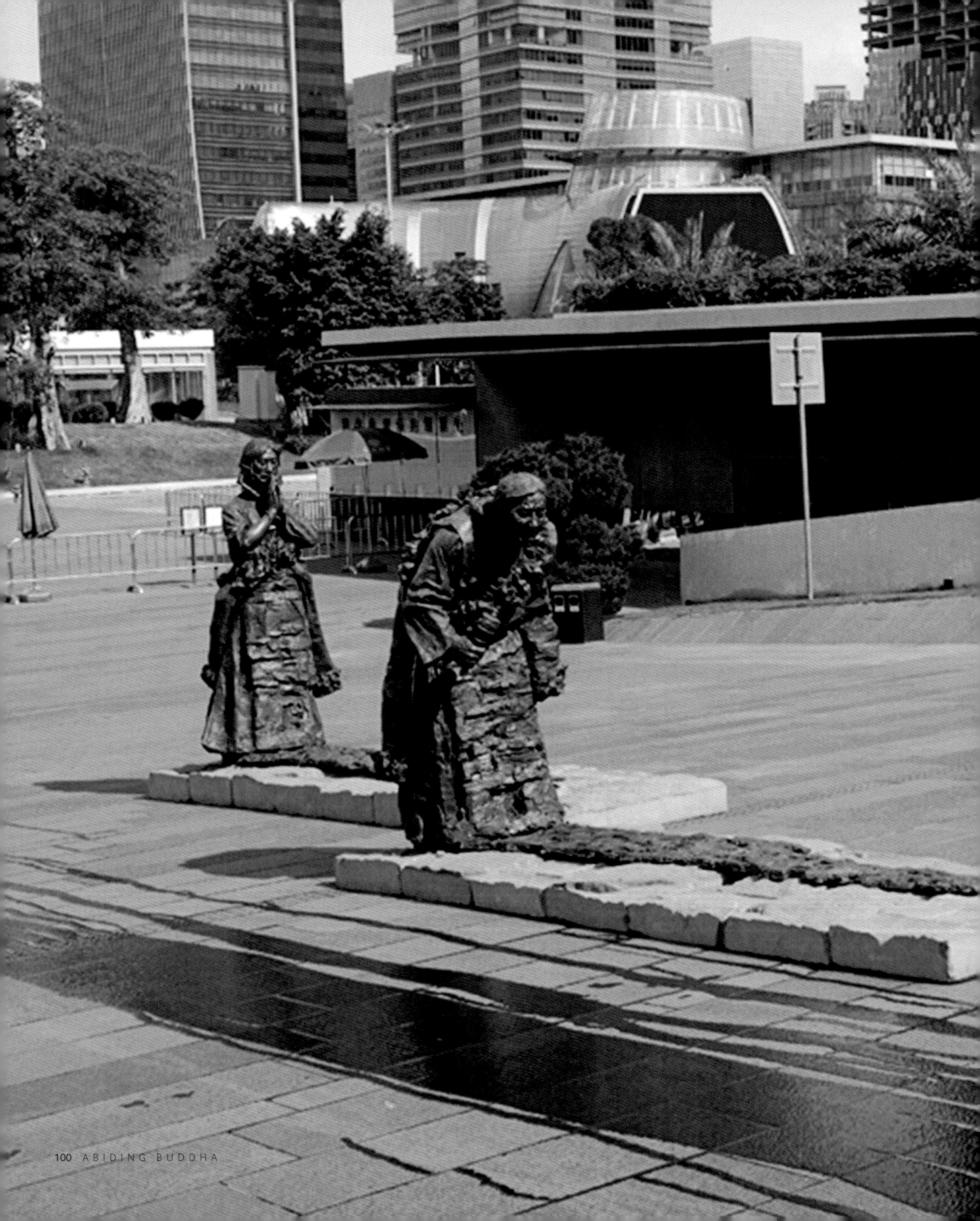

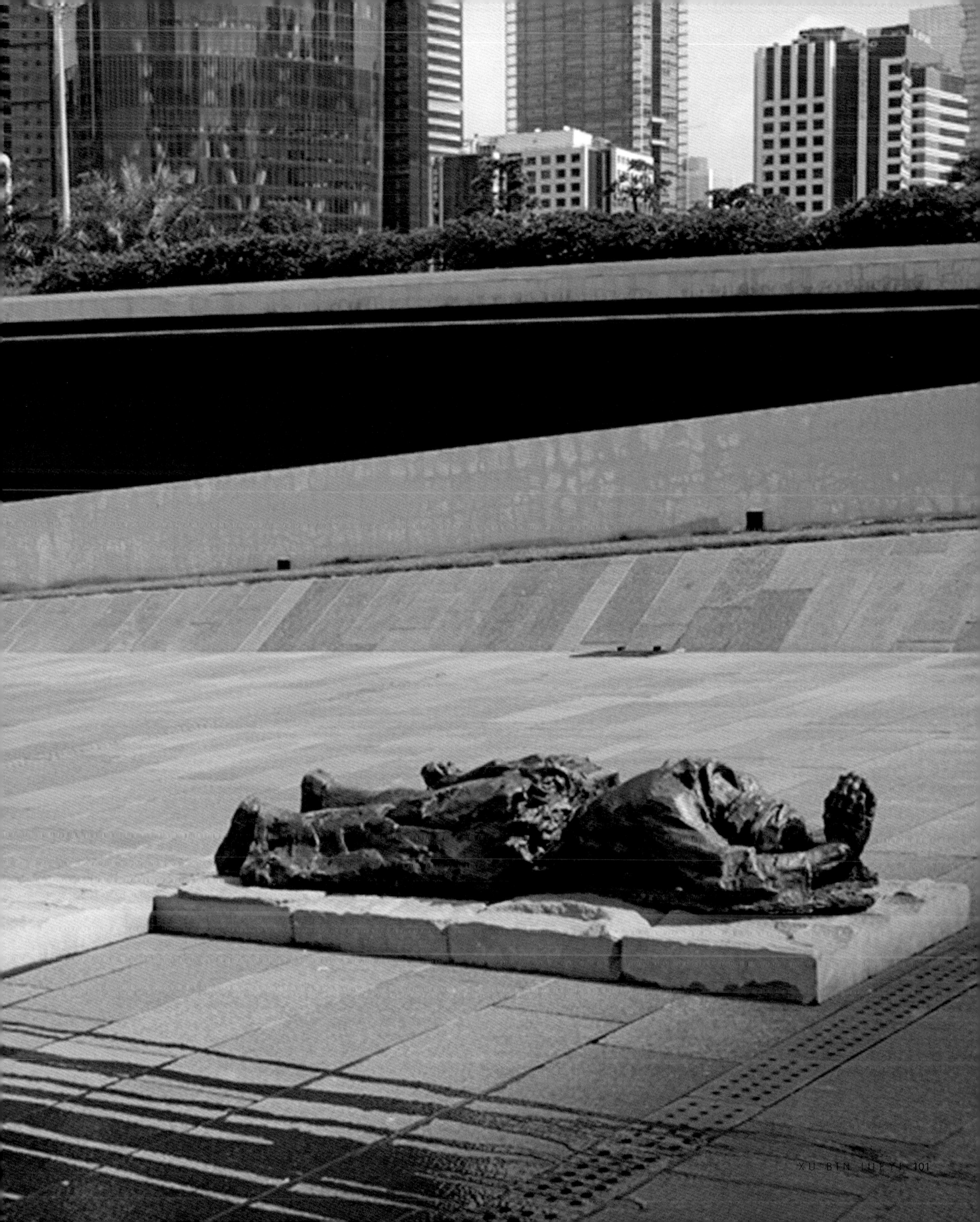

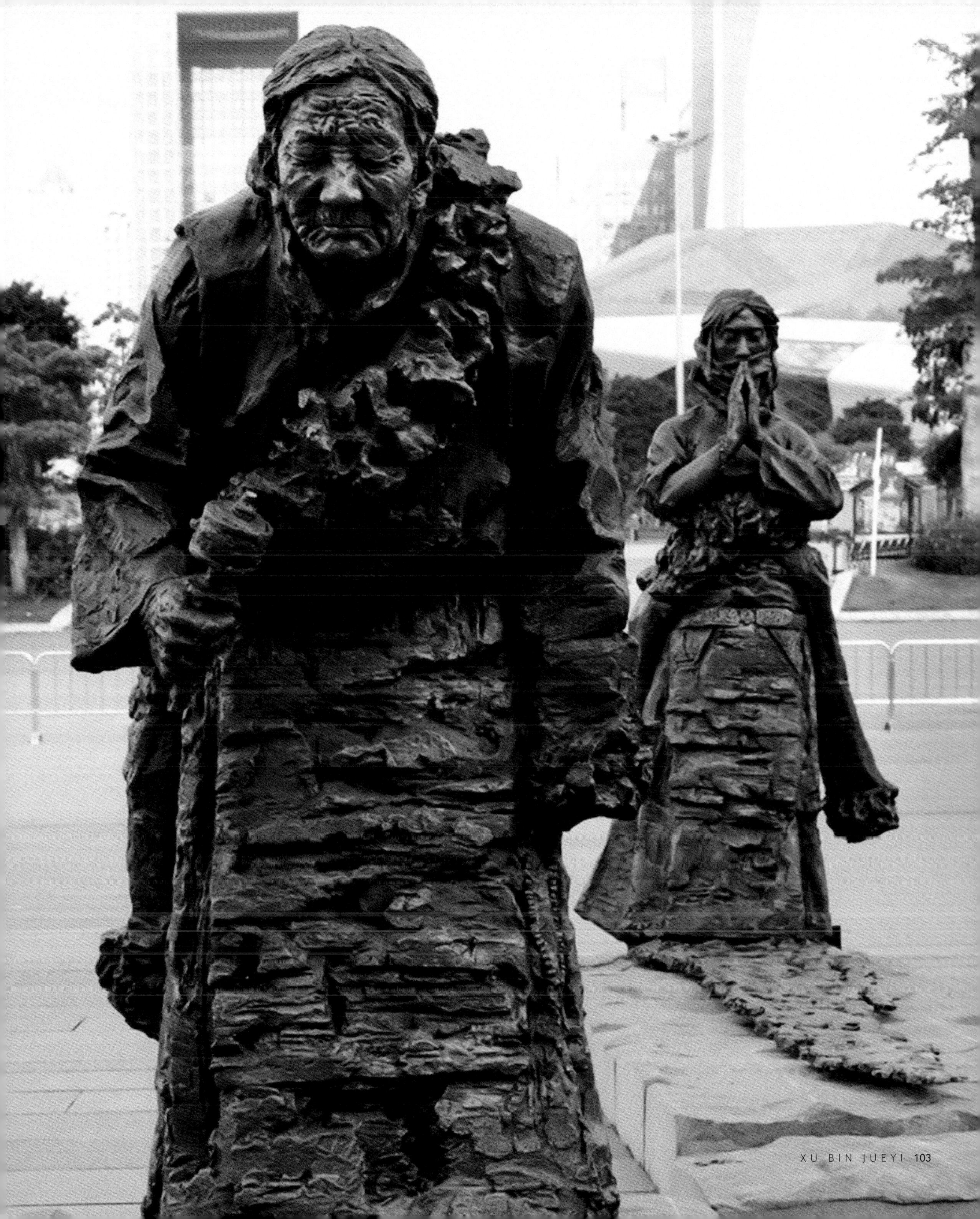

Pilgrims

Once, he was in front of the Jokhang Temple
at Lhasa, watching the setting sun shine on
the pilgrims. As the pilgrims raised their hands,
their elongated shadows passed straight
through the great door of the temple ... this
moment left him stunned! He realized that in
this elongated form there was a sacred sense
of the spirit moving upwards. Are not Tibetan
flag streamers, Egyptian obelisks, elongated?
Afterwards, he created twelve Pilgrims, later
put in the museum collection.

Lu Guoping

Pilgrims
150×300cm
2012

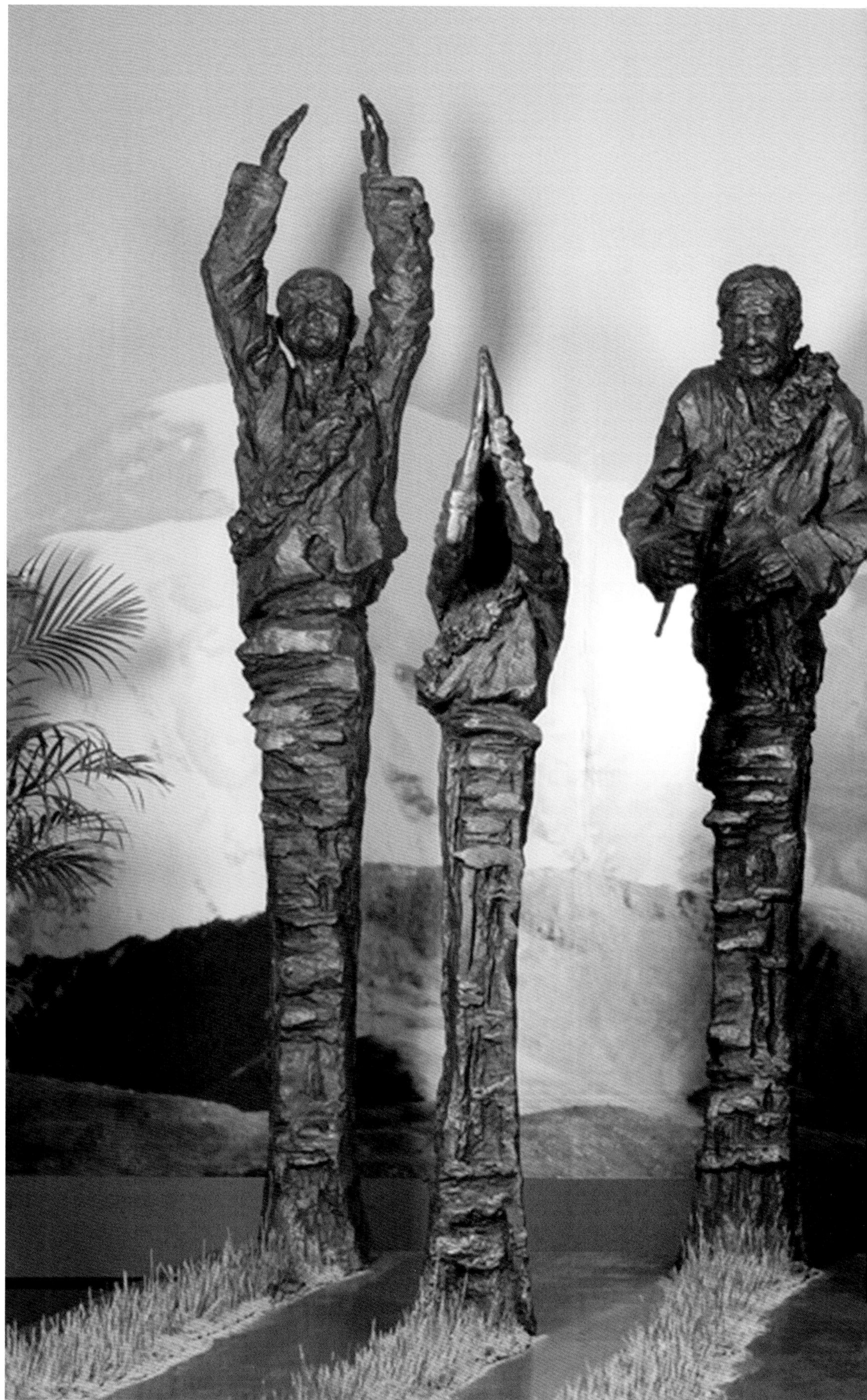

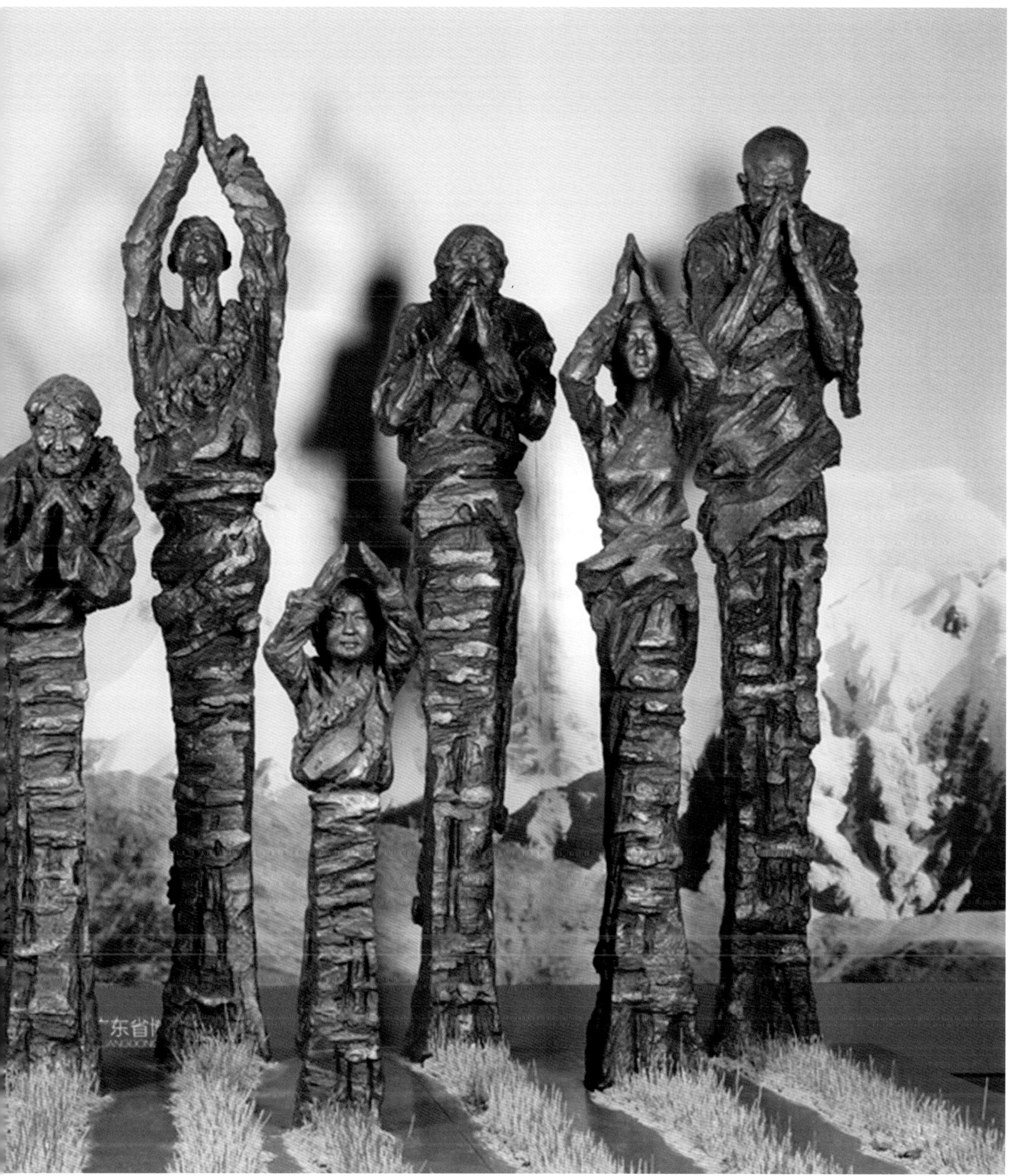

360-Degree Redemption
- Impressions of
Xu Bin Jueyi
- Wang Luxiang

Making a sculpture of Lady Xian

It was in the Lady Xian Memorial Park in Dianbai District, Guangdong, that I first met Xu Bin Jueyi. The huge bronze sculpture of Lady Xian (AD 512-604) in the park is one of his works.

Mr Zheng Huaxing told me that in order to find a suitable artist to create the Lady Xian sculpture, he sought out many accomplished sculptors in mainland China, Hong Kong and Taiwan, but all to no avail. When he first met Xu Bin Jueyi, the artist gave him an impression of purity and clarity, with a strong ability in both realistic and abstract sculpture.

Xu Bin Jueyi created Lady Xian in a seated pose, rather than as the kind of tall standing statue more usually associated with revered personalities. This brings Lady Xian closer to us, so that we can see her facial expression clearly. Moreover, the composition, with Lady Xian sitting with both hands on her knees, draws our attention to her full womanly figure -- this is Xu Bin Jueyi's real artistic focus. The reason is that Lady Xian's greatest contribution in history was her 'Acting only from good intentions', that is her generosity of heart, in uniting different regions of Lingnan, protecting the unity of the nation, and benefitting the people of the South China Sea. This maternal generosity makes her a great woman, and is the root of her valiant achievements, and the core reason why through the ages generation after generation have admired her deeply.

A woman, but one in military uniform, moreover in a seated pose often taken by ancient military generals within their tent headquarters. This signifies Lady Xian's historical identity: She truly was a female hero who led the troops into battle, and her posture expresses her resolute character. Her face, however, is unmistakably that of a middle-aged peace-loving mother, with only her eyes gazing into the distance indicating her identity as a visionary politician. Xu Bin Jueyi had no images to draw on, so he looked for inspiration among the ordinary women of Dianbai District. Surprisingly he found inspiration in Mr. Zheng Huaxing's mother. It was only later we discovered that his mother possibly shared some ancestry with Lady

Xian's father's side — it was quite extraordinary. Xu also studied some Song-period (AD 960-1279) Guanyin (Avalokiteshvara) sculptures, in an effort to bring the image of Guanyin as understood by the common people and the real face of a Lingnan woman into one, so that Lady Xian looks both ordinary and other-worldly at the same time. So, this sculpture of Lady Xian sits as still as a mountain, with a heart wide as the sea, a posture of steel and a gentle face: she is somehow real and yet not quite mortal, not exactly deified but attaining reverence.

First learning of the '360-Degree Redemption' programme

The second time I met Xu Bin Jueyi was during the official book launch for *Shallow Relief* at Artron Art Centre in Shenzhen. He told me about a project he had made up his mind to work on: one Buddha sculpture per day for a total of three thousand sculptures. These Buddha sculptures represent living and breathing real-life men and women, of different professions, ages and personalities. I asked about the process and he replied: 'I observe the subject when they are fully submerged in the self and capture the moment when their essential character is revealed.' 'How do you know when the subject is fully submerged in the self?' I asked. 'The moment when the character is revealed is different for each person,' he said. 'For some it happens when they are brewing tea, for some when meditating, for some when dancing, and for others in conversation. And for you,' he pointed at me, 'it may happen when you are reading.' As predicted, when I was perusing some catalogues of foreign ceramics, Xu Bin Jueyi took a photo of me flipping through one of the two oversized books on my crossed legs. He captured the moment when the hard cover of the book formed a distinctive angle with my body. 'From your reading position,' he noted, 'your essential character is revealed to me. At that moment, the Buddha lives within you, and the Buddha nature is your essential character. I simply see you as Buddha.' After I returned to Beijing, a WeChat photo message arrived. I saw that I had become Buddha.

It was a fascinating experience. I had planned, at some point in my life, to invite a sculptor friend to create a bust of me, to put on my bookshelf for me to appreciate myself, and in a hundred years for my descendants to admire. I did not expect a Buddha sculpture of me to be created before a human one. I know that Sun Wukong (Awareness-of-the-Void), the Monkey King, after he had travelled to the West to bring back the sutras, was transformed into the Victorious Fighting Buddha. So what kind of buddha will I become in middle age? A Reading Buddha. Book pages are stacked high to form a pyramid, at the top of which the Reading Buddha emerges. He holds open a large, thick book, immersing himself in the ocean of knowledge. If I think about it carefully, this attitude probably does reflect the moment when my essential character is revealed most fully. It is the one I adopt most commonly in life, in which I forget myself most completely, become most intoxicated and am most relaxed. I am also at my most arrogant, or feel most inferior. It is true – it scares me a little when I think about it – this pose is indeed the one in which my essential character is most apparent. Of course, I am not always quite so elegant.

Xu Bin Jueyi plans to cast it again in a gilded version. This golden Buddha he will put in his collection of three thousand Buddha sculptures, creating a realm of contemporary myriad-Buddha niches. This is a splendid vision. The greatest contribution to Indian religion and world religion Shakyamuni made was his elimination of external forces in redemption of the self. All beings have a Buddha nature, and only self-awareness brings release, not reliance on external forces. Huineng (AD 638-713), the sixth patriarch of Chan (Zen) Buddhism, who was born in Guangdong, implements this point of faith of Shakyamuni's most thoroughly. How do we stay firm in the belief that the essential character of each of us has a Buddha nature, it is only through awareness that we can awaken the Buddha nature of the mind, and there is no other way to achieve release? Xu Bin Jueyi perhaps thinks, by means of his grand art project, in the course of several years, to sincerely meet with three thousand sentient beings, to discover everyone's essential character, and to awaken everyone's Buddha nature. I am not certain that his own psychic power, or the psychic power of three thousand people, can really achieve what he wants: all of us finding our own lost heart-likenesses of the self, observing ourselves, finding the beauty of compassion and spreading the greater love, with psychic power penetrating the universe. Rather, I prefer to understand more in more concrete terms the artistic difficulties of this activity of his.

Three thousand sentient beings, three thousand Buddha natures
Three thousand sentient beings do not only share a common Buddha nature, but also have three thousand different karmas, created in the course of aeons (kalpas), and have become three thousand individual selves. For me, it is how Xu Bin Jueyi uses simple forms to express the conflict and struggle between the karma and the inextinguishable Buddha nature that is the most exciting. Moreover, it is how he creates three thousand geometric abstract sculptures without categorizing them into supposed types, while omitting details like facial features and clothing, that is the test. He has made about eight

or nine hundred sculptures and I have seen several hundred: none of them are the same. But how will that work for one thousand, two thousand and three thousand? I expect in a few years we will have an unimaginable scene in front of us, and that at first glance I will be able to pick out the lost heart-likeness of myself among the three thousand Buddhas.

The third time I met Xu Bin Jueyi was at the Liurong Temple in Guangzhou. In the Abbot's room, we drank tea and listened to the monk Faliang expounding. The pagoda in the temple needed eighty-eight Buddha sculptures and invited Xu Bin Jueyi to create them. In contrast with his three-thousand-sculpture Beauty of Compassion programme, the emphasis for these sculptures was on historical tradition. So, he did a lot of documentary research, travelled to many Buddhist caves, and visited many traditional sculptures in old temples and museums both in China and abroad. He also analysed techniques in bronze and gold sculpture-making for the Ming (1368-1644) and Qing (1644-1911) palaces, and brought back many books from Japan on Buddha sculpture. After repeated comparative study, he determined that these eighty-eight sculptures needed both to fully reflect the excellent tradition in Chinese sculpture making, and to combine this basis of the historic sculpture-making with contemporary culture and modern aesthetics. Xu Bin Jueyi's concept is, 'If you do not follow the ancients, then there are no rules; but if you follow the ancients too slavishly, there is no place for oneself.' These sculptures are intended to reflect the stately flow of the metaphorical river of the history of Buddhism in China, from the Northern and Southern Dynasties (AD 420–589); through Sui and Tang (581–907); to Liao, Jin and Song (907–1279); and on to Yuan, Ming and Qing (1271–1911). They will fuse the aesthetics of Buddha sculptures of the various dynasties with modern aesthetics and hence represent it. Xu Bin Jueyi is now directing his assistants in the studio and making clay models; I have seen some of those that have been finalized, which do indeed achieve a Buddha solemnity, something close to divinity, and supreme respectfulness. When these eighty-eight sculptures are complete, cast in bronze, gilded and installed in the pagoda, the Liurong Temple with its long history of more than sixteen hundred years, will surely revive its glory. Such a remarkable achievement by Xu Bin Jueyi is of great merit.

An amazing installation – 'Spider Fort'
The fourth time I met Xu Bin Jueyi was at his studio, or to be exact, 'Spider Fort'. This is a huge wall-like structure made of stones inside the shed that is his sculpture studio. The floor plan looks like the

Arabic numeral 8 or the symbol for infinity ∞. [The number eight is considered lucky, so,] whichever it means, the Cantonese like it anyway. The stones are left over from a previous project; since it seemed a pity to get rid of them, Xu Bin Jueyi brought them back to build the stone fort. And he made a giant steel spider out of abandoned automobile parts, setting it in the space above the fort, so that its legs cover the whole structure. Thus, *Spider Fort* came about.

Of course, you can read the fort from another cultural perspective -- the Gossamer Cave in the Ming-period novel Journey to the West is where the spider becomes a demon and wants to have sex with the Tang monk (Xuanzang) to destroy his diamond-like inviolate body. The interior of the fort is full of double meanings: The main entrance is in China red lacquer, and door gods taken from Han-period portraits, Shentu and Yulei, stand watch. When you open the door, you encounter an abstract standing Buddha made of stainless steel, reflecting light like a mirror. So, as people enter, they see both the Buddha and their own reflection in the Buddha at the same time. Except that both the Buddha and the reflection are a little warped, like looking in a distorting mirror at a fair. An important feature of the fort is the foreign piano. Host and guests all play on it, or, if they cannot play, just strum away. Another garish object is the circular couch, so big that it is almost like a bed. Xu Bin Jueyi insists that it is not a bed at all, that it is for people to sit on rather than for sleeping. Guests to the castle do not agree however. They insist it is a bed, and have inferred many bed-related associations, which they have written on the surrounding stone walls. This scrawl covers the surfaces of Spider Fort. Such writing on walls is in fact a major part of the Chinese cultural landscape. The Tang-period poet Li Bai (AD 701-762) wrote compositions on Yellow Crane Tower when he was drunk; the Song-period rebel leader Song Jiang wrote poems of resistance on Xunyang Tower. In new China, placards and slogans have covered areas of the countryside, and Chinese tourists write, 'I was here,' at tourist sites abroad. Xu invites every guest to write on the walls of the fort. This is actually a psychological test. Guests get a whiff of the doubleness and confusion of the place, and inevitably some idea will surface. Some write boldly, others obscurely - some nakedly, others coyly. Some people see pornography, others Chan (Zen) delight. It is like the Qing-period novel *Dream of Red Chamber*, which some see as stirring up lust and violence, others as full of thoughts on revolution. My interpretation is that Xu Bin Jueyi creates an field of energy (Qi or Ch'i) with this spider fort, and the cultural references within the field are confused and ambiguous. Like our thinking and culture in contemporary China, there is a little bit of everything, but no

dominant influence: a little of the West, China, religion, lust, tradition, fashion, seriousness, humour, propriety, and playfulness. In a word, it reflects a game mentality, and provides a relaxing environment. So guests feel free to lie, sit, recline or stand, to adopt the lotus position on the Chan (Zen) chairs, or stretch out on animal skins on the floor. It does not matter, there are no requirements on how to position yourself. Thus, in this environment, Xu Bin Jueyi can observe what situations people create, how their emotions change when conditions change, and capture the moment of revelation. These all become the blueprints for the three thousand sculptures.

I told Xu Bin Jueyi, 'Whatever your intention, you've made a great installation. Every day performance art takes place, and the building, sculpture, furniture, music, calligraphy and images come to life. Everyone participates and everyone observes. This is like a Buddhist rite. If possible, you should really take it to the Venice Biennale.'

Xu Bin Jueyi is a fun person, immensely energetic and full of life, with boundless creativity and enthusiasm. Sculpture takes a combination of physical labour and mental work, with the main emphasis on physical labour, and he really excels at it. He is also a loving person who cares about society: It is moving to see the huge energy he puts into the creation of several public sculptures commemorating Anti-Japanese War veterans. He is an endlessly creative artist. Whenever you see his eyes sparkling, you know that his brain has been running at full speed. During his trip to Europe, he found artistic inspiration everywhere. The landmark architecture of Western civilization he combined with Eastern Buddhist sculpture to make a whole, a perfect fusion without obstruction.

This quality of 'perfect fusion' runs through the whole of Xu Bin Jueyi's life. To him, art and life, religion and secularism, the East and West, are all perfectly fused without obstruction. Therefore, when I was asked to write this essay 'Impressions of Xu Bin Jueyi', I decide to entitle it with the name of his art project, with its allusion to a soul crossing a river to reach Nirvana: '360-Degree Redemption'.

- Wang Luxiang
Beijing
3rd September 2016

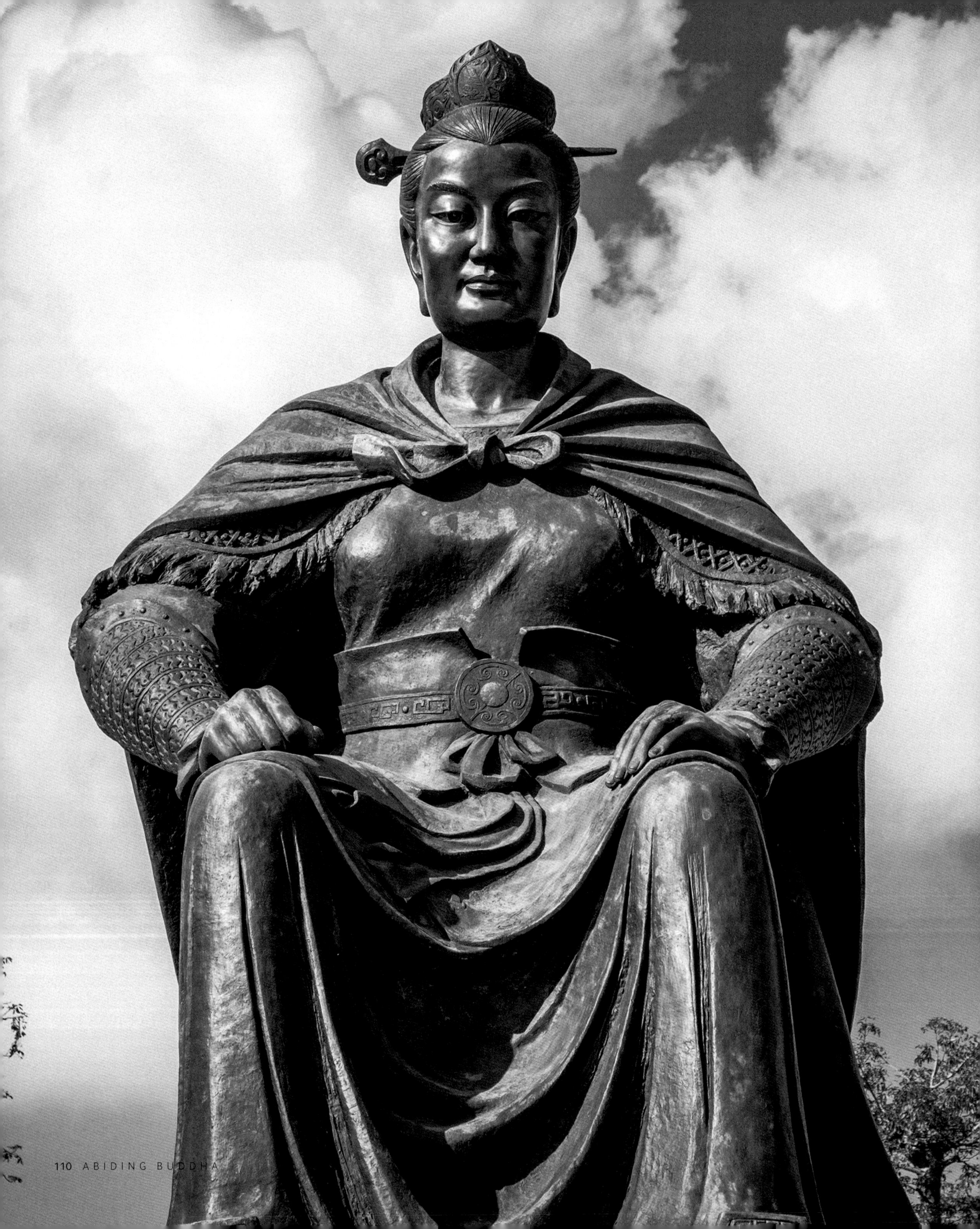

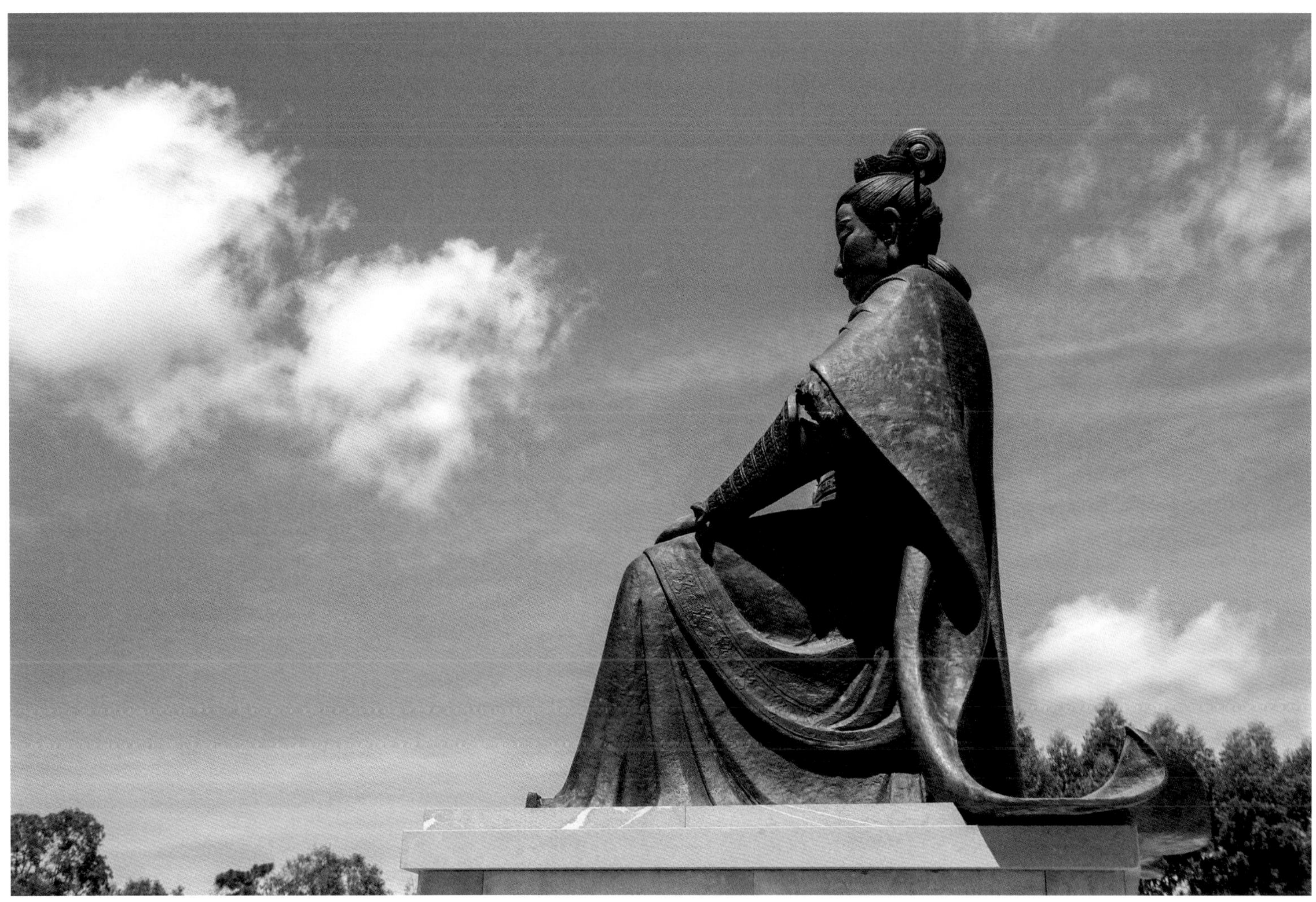

Lady Xian

A woman, but one in military uniform, moreover in a seated
pose often taken by ancient military generals within their tent
headquarters. This signifies Lady Xian's historical identity: She truly
was a female hero who led the troops into battle, and her posture
expresses her resolute character. Her face, however, is unmistakably
that of a middle-aged peace-loving mother, with only her eyes gazing
into the distance indicating her identity as a visionary politician.

Wang Luxiang

Lady Xian
Height: 900cm
2014

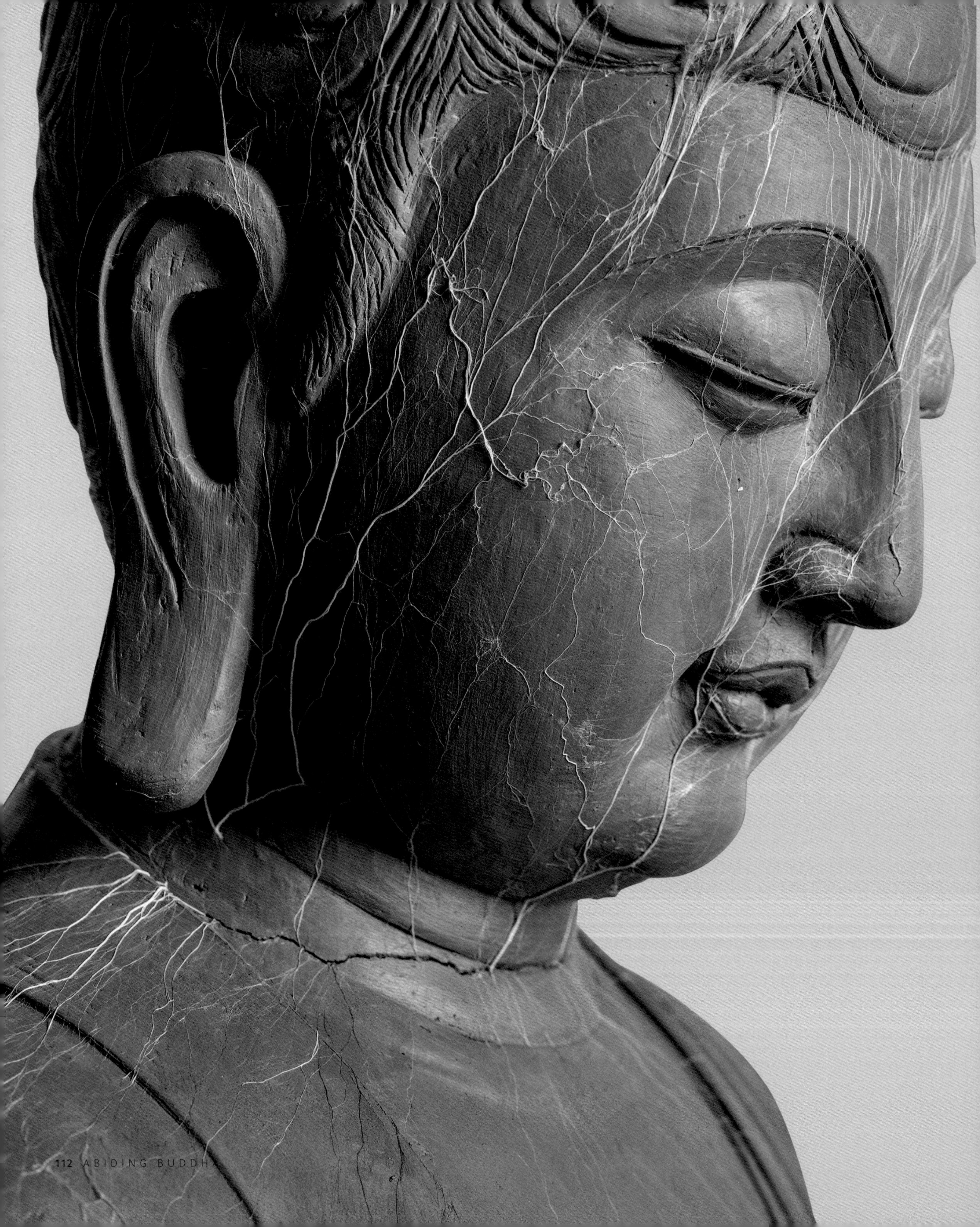

Liurong Temple Buddhas

After repeated comparative study, he determined that these eighty-
eight sculptures needed both to fully reflect the excellent tradition in
Chinese sculpture making, and to combine this basis of the historic
sculpture making with contemporary culture and modern aesthetics.
Xu Bin Jueyi's concept is, 'If you do not follow the ancients, then there
are no rules; but if you follow the ancients too slavishly, there is no
place for oneself.'

Wang Luxiang

Liurong Temple Buddha series 1
Clay, 57×42×88cm
2016

Buddha Shakyamuni
Bronze, 49×39×68cm
2016

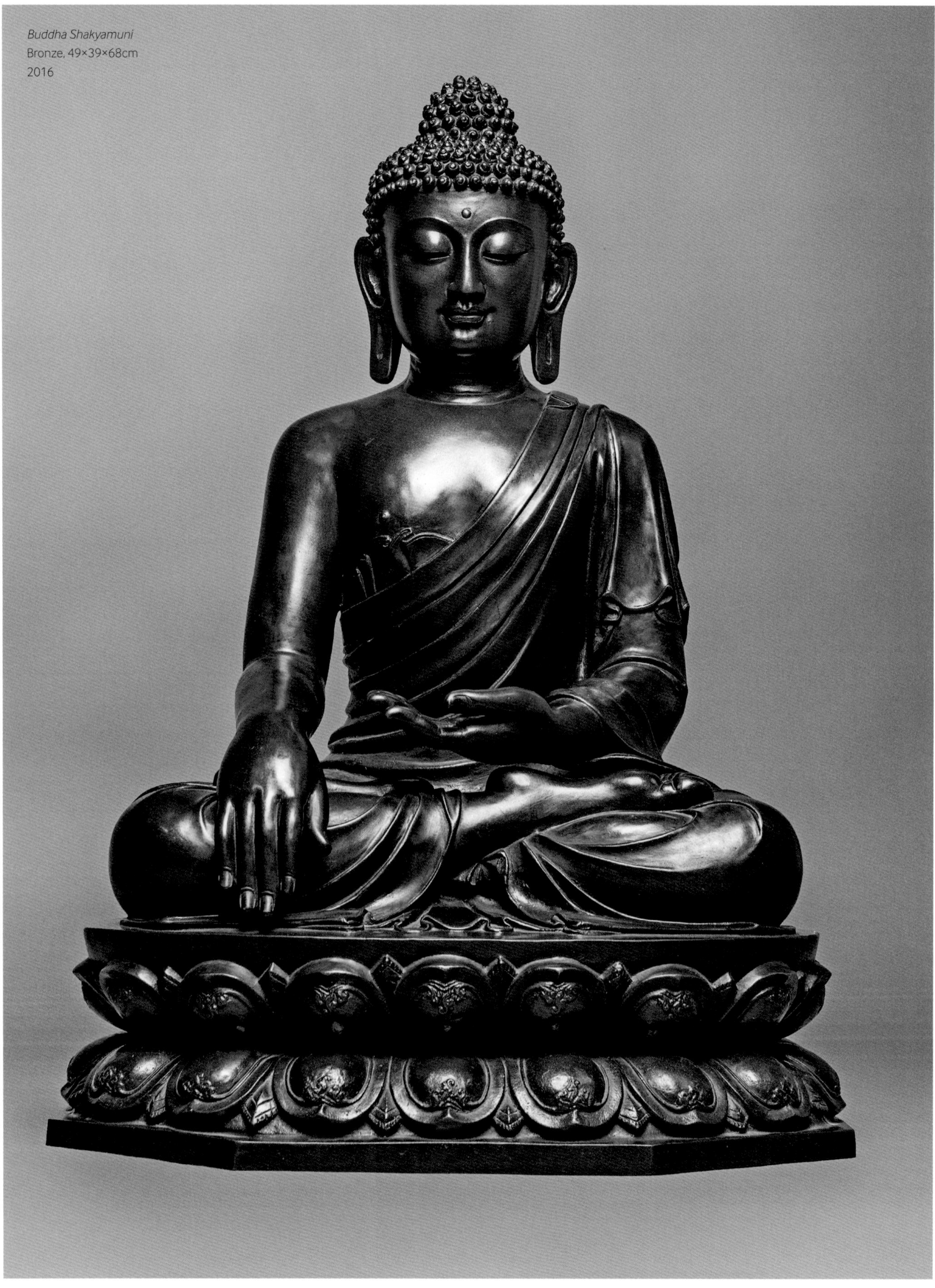

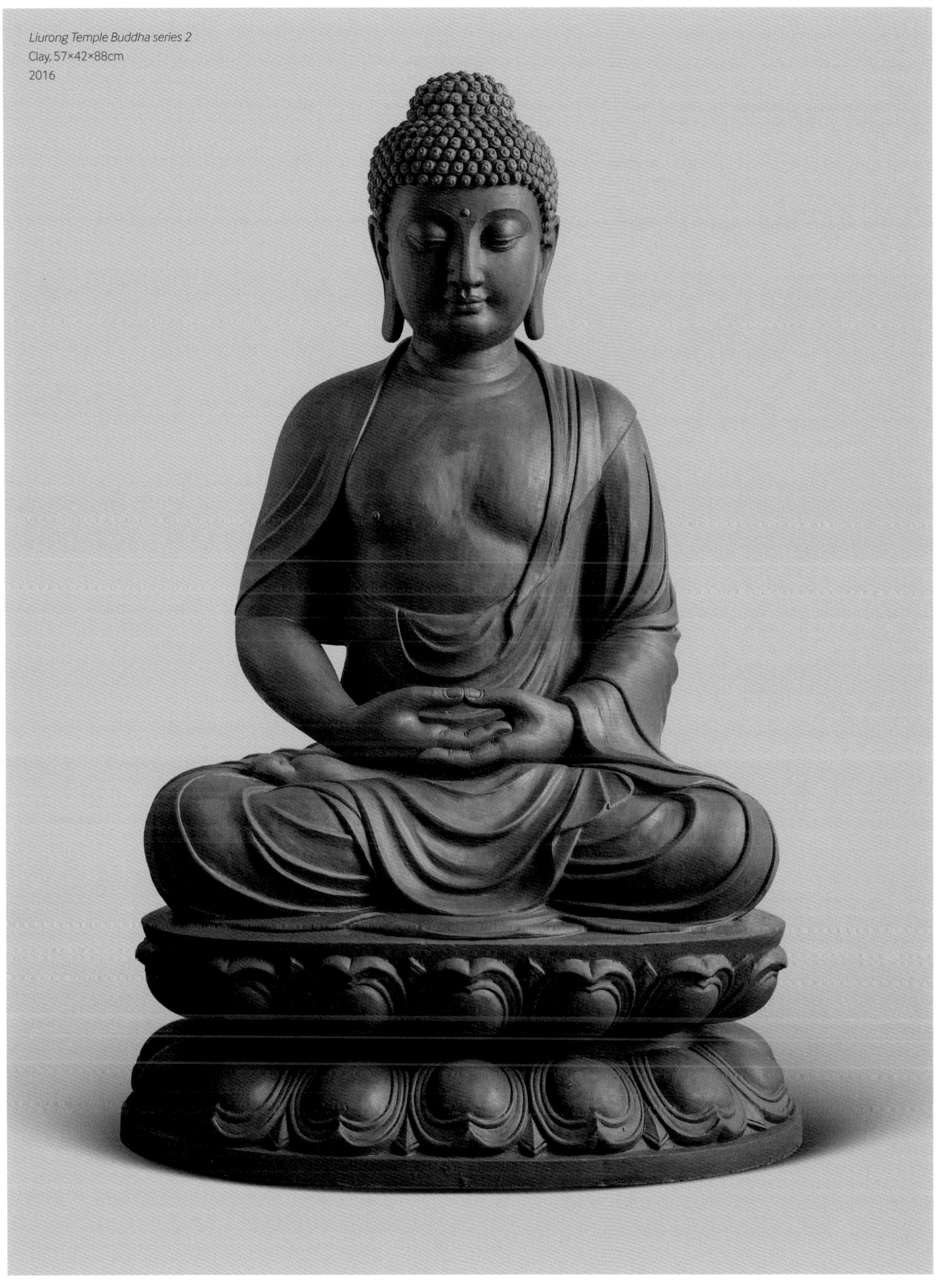

Liurong Temple Buddha series 2
Clay, 57×42×88cm
2016

Liurong Temple Buddha series 5
Clay, 49×38×68cm
2016

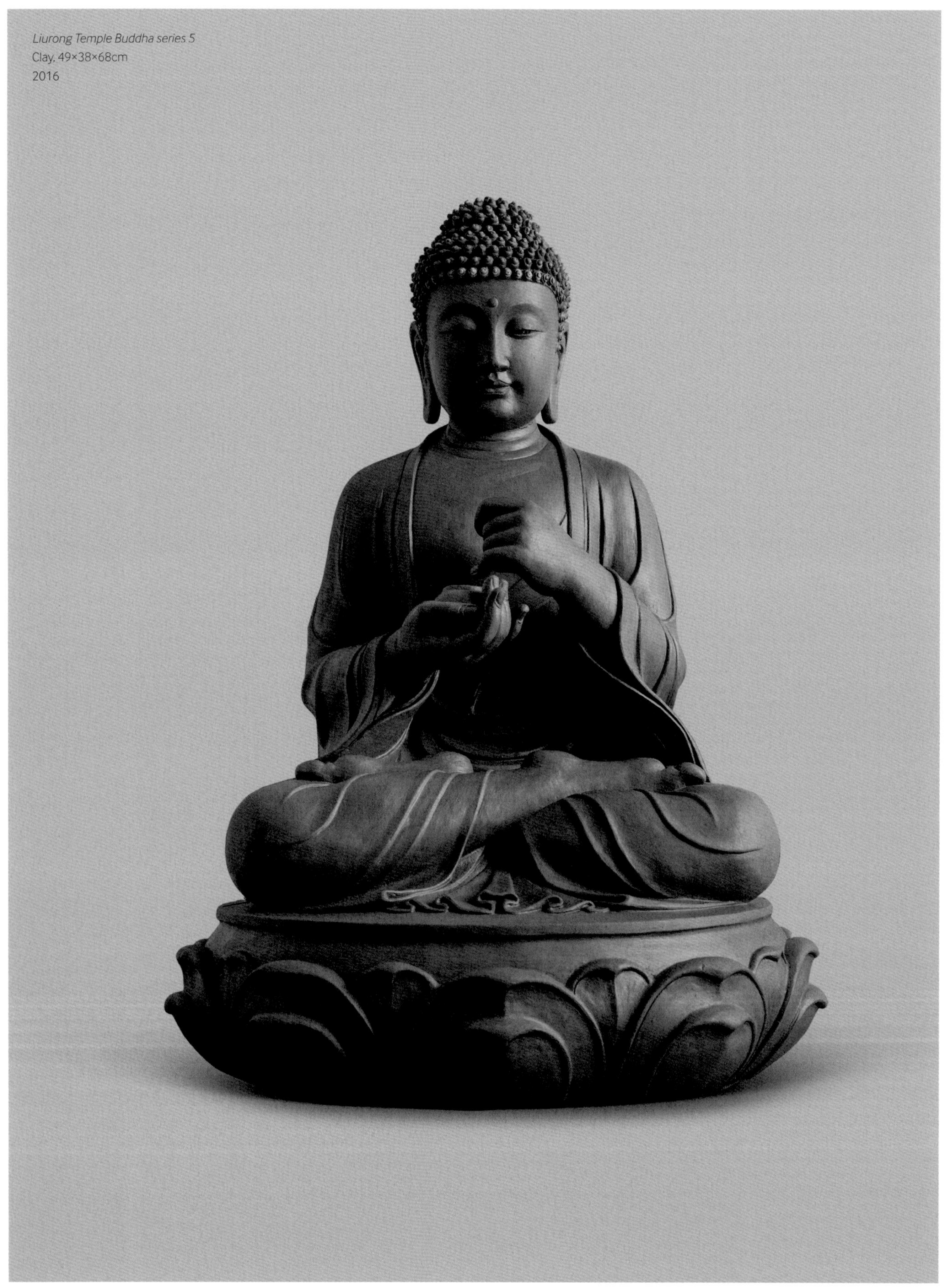

Liurong Temple Buddha series 7
Clay, 49×38×68cm
2016

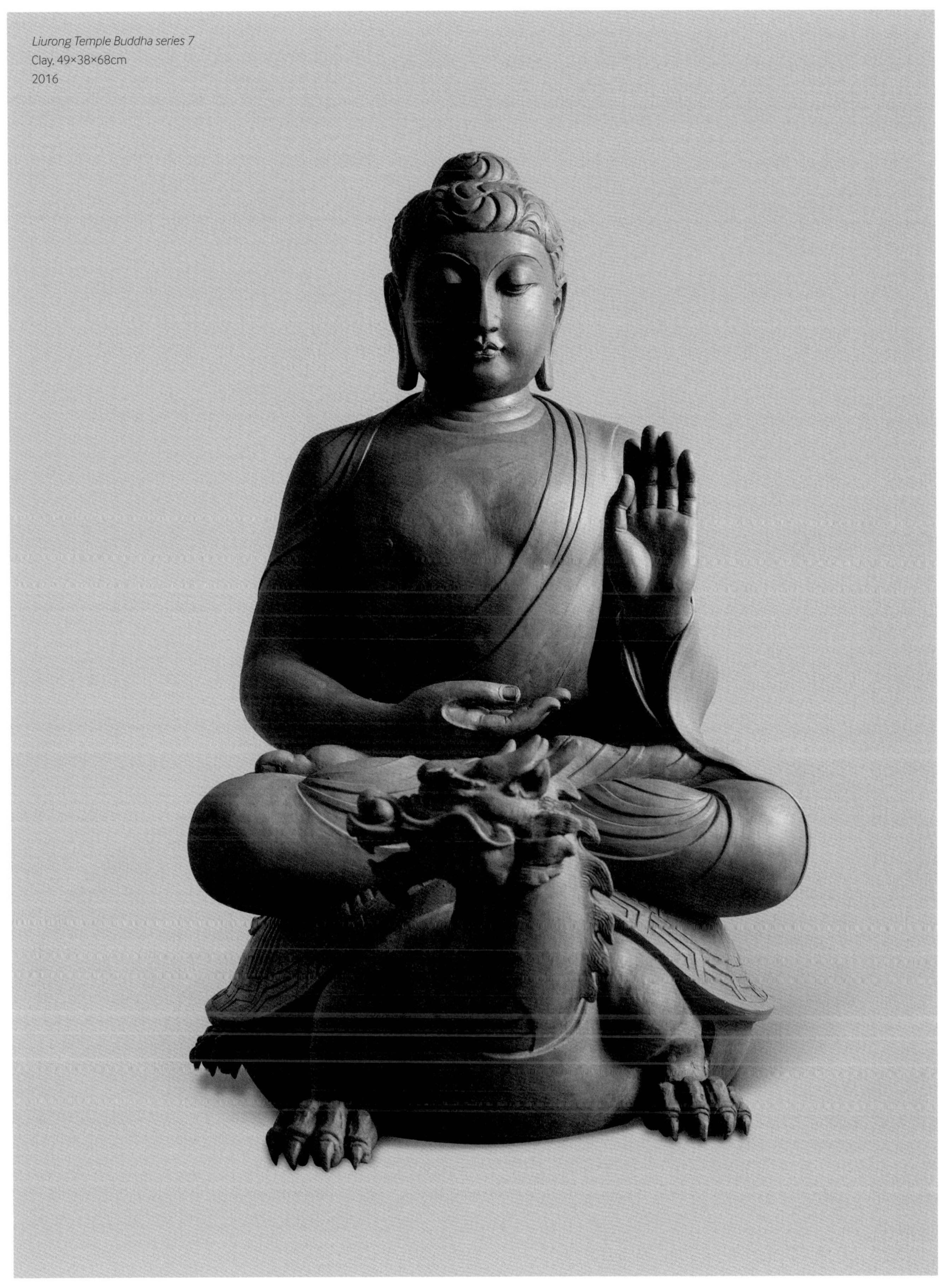

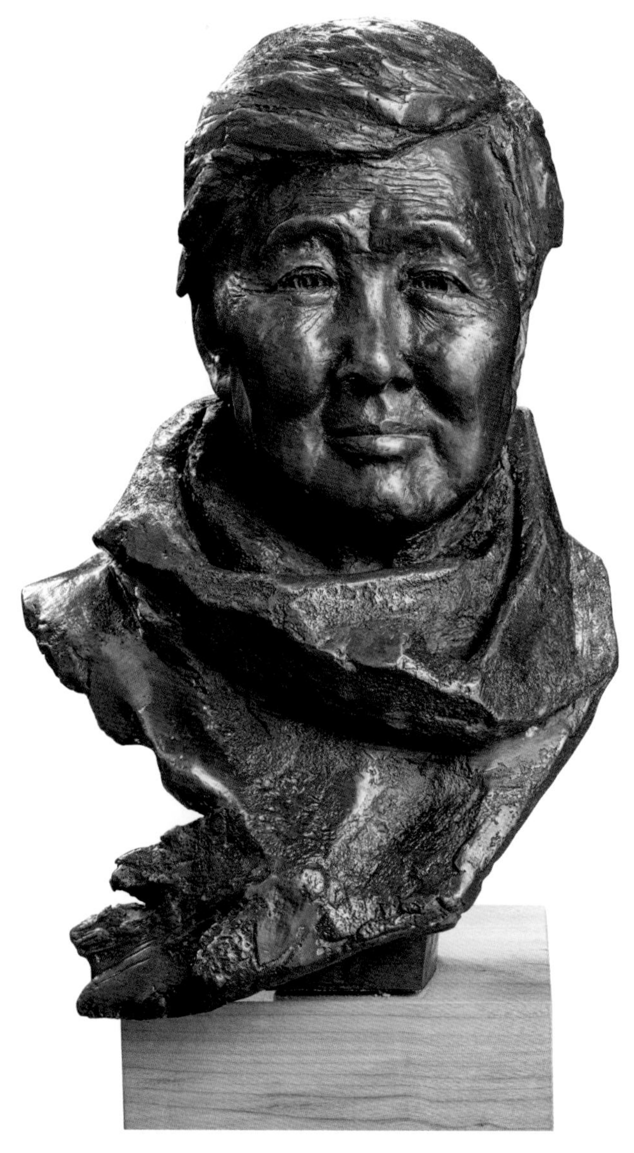

Mother
Bronze, 36×34×71cm
2016

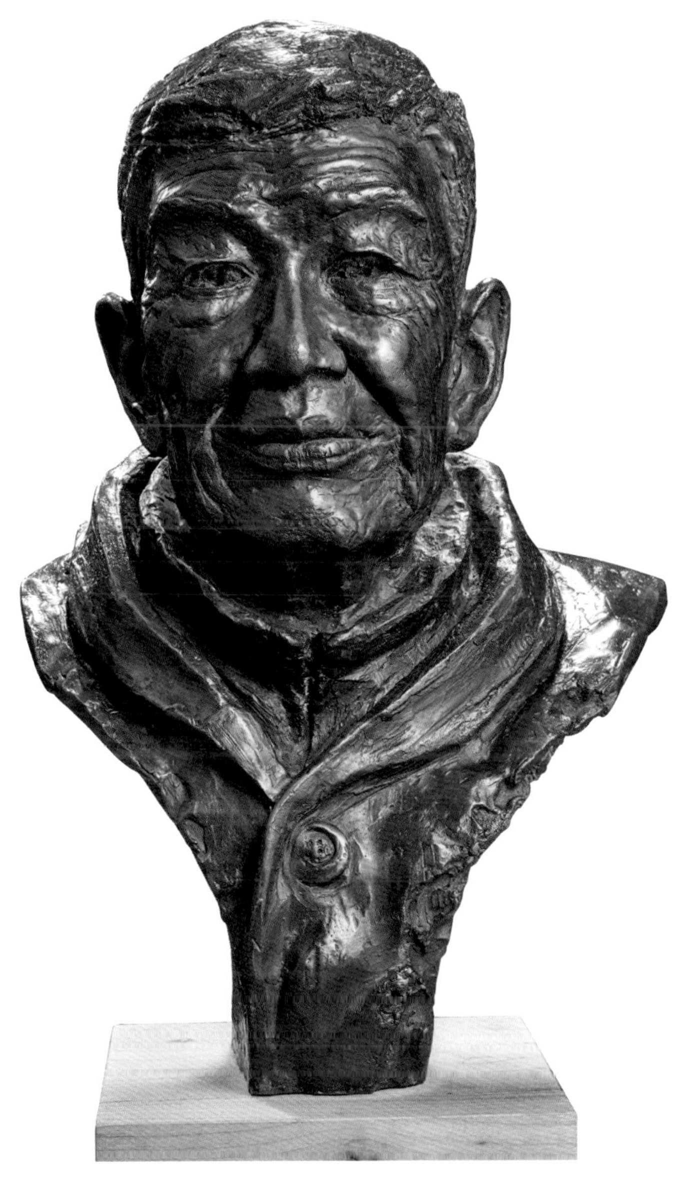

Father
Bronze, 36×25×72cm
2016

Wind
Bronze, 24×22×48cm
2008

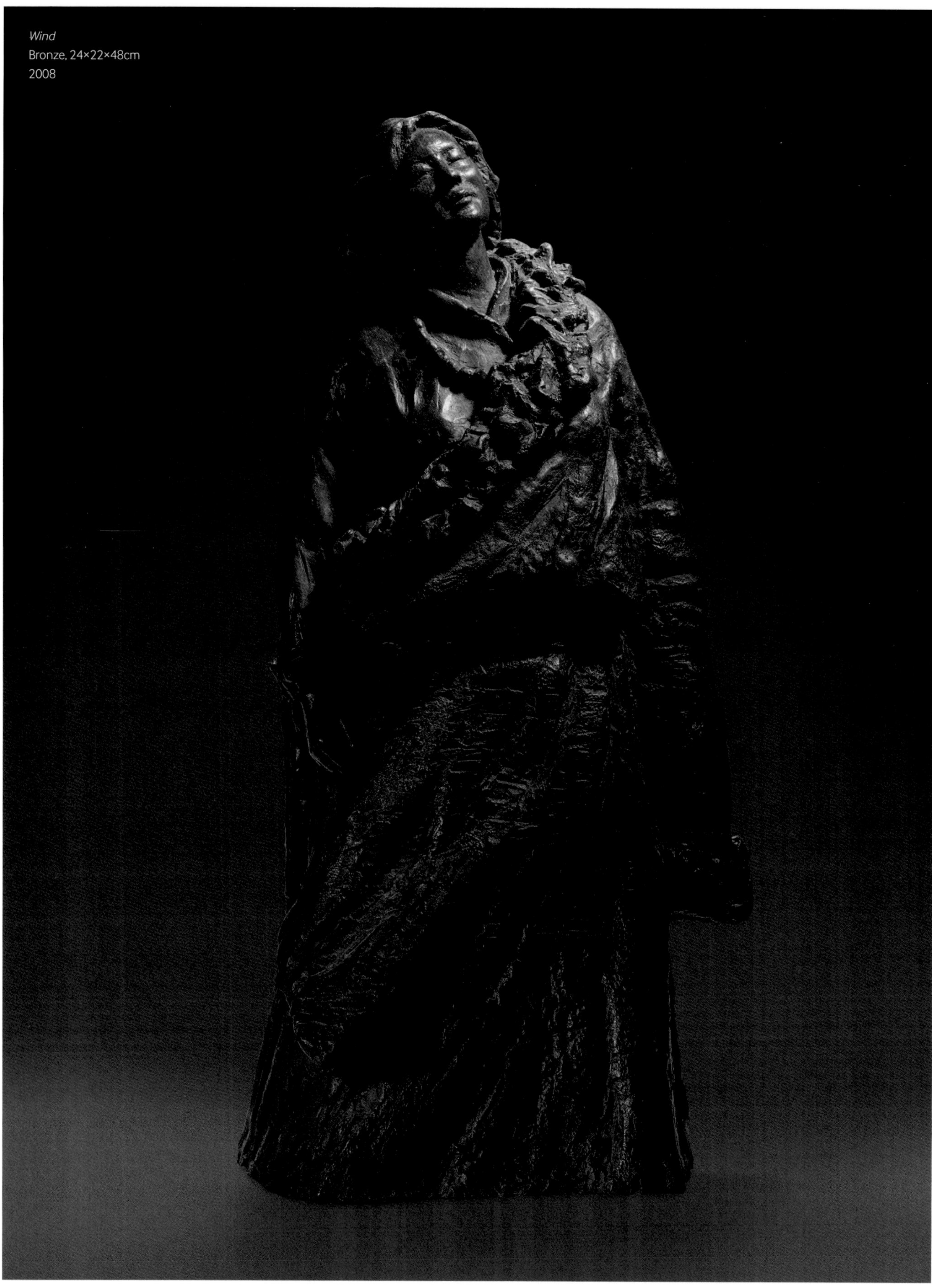

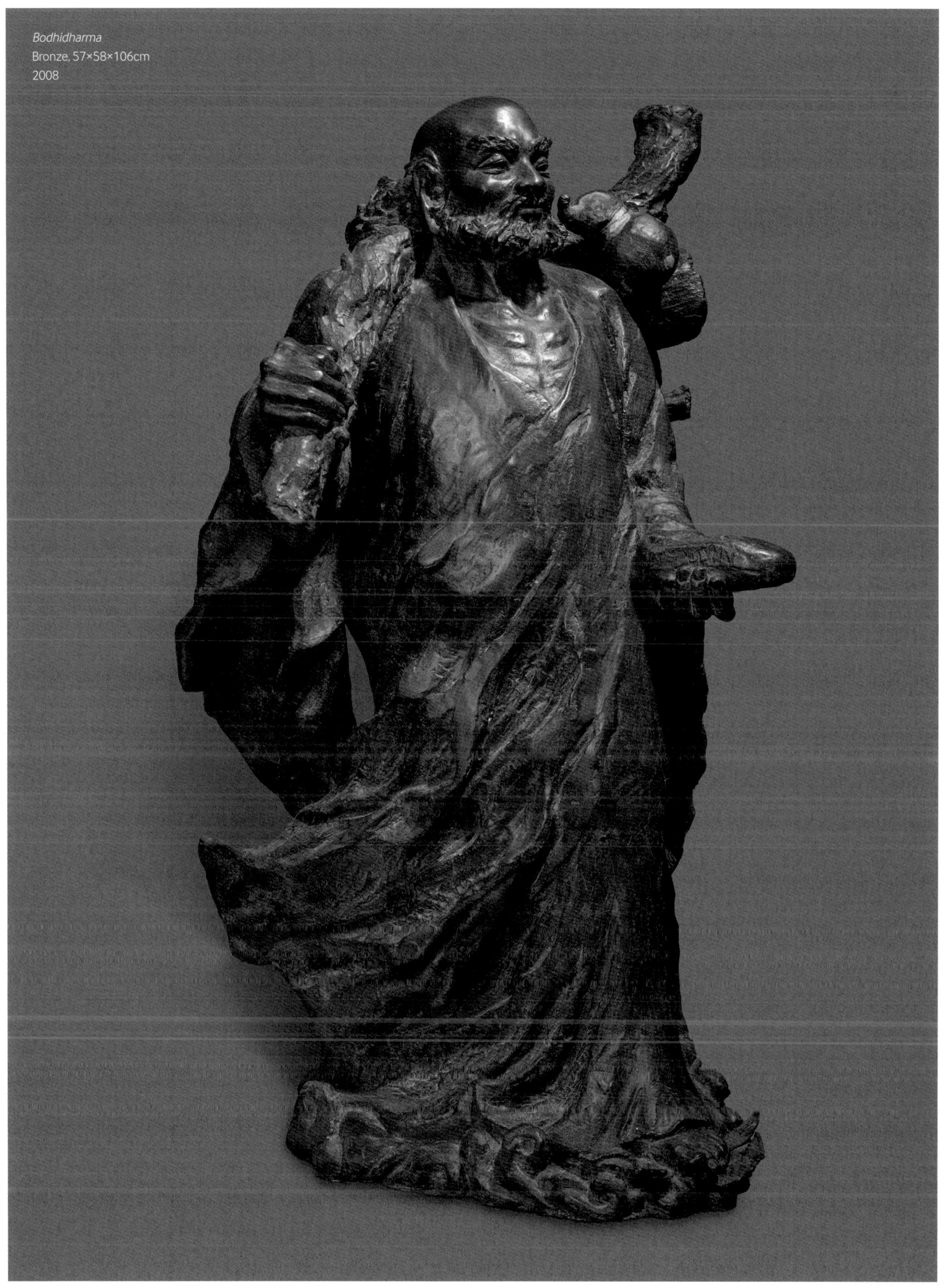

Bodhidharma
Bronze, 57×58×106cm
2008

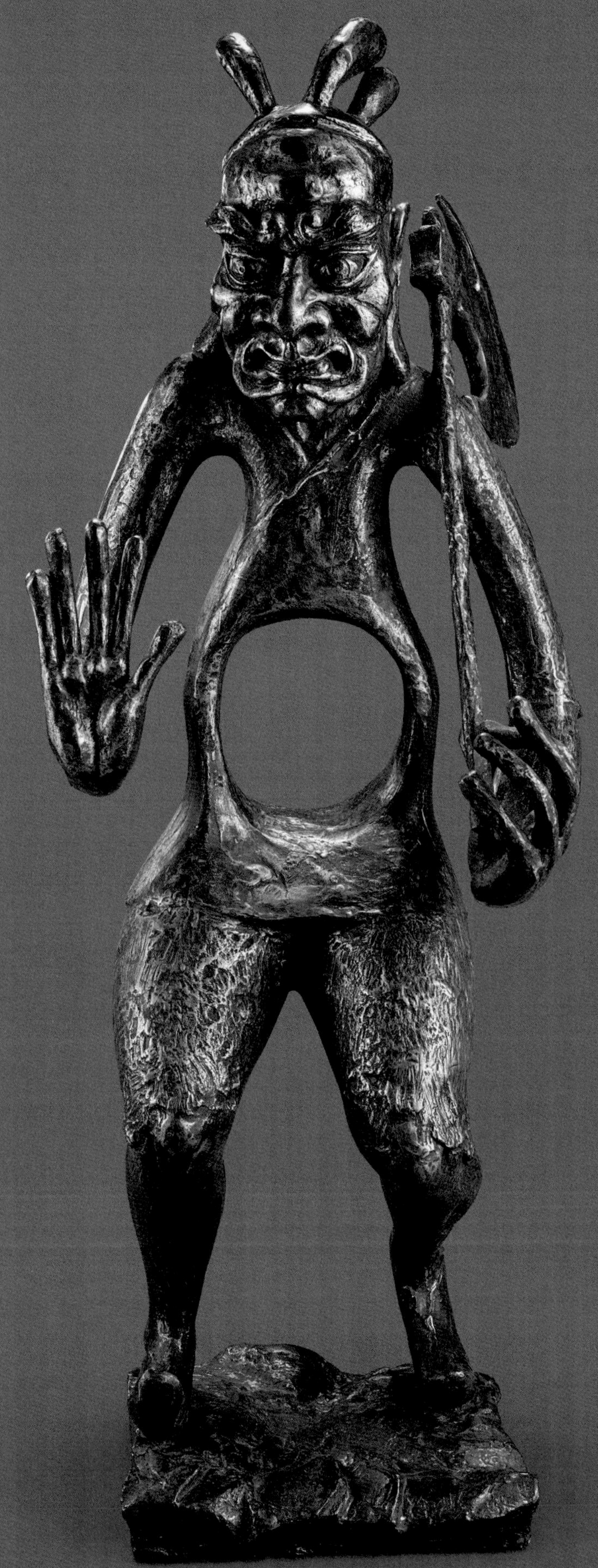

Door Gods 1
Iron, 40×44×113cm
2014

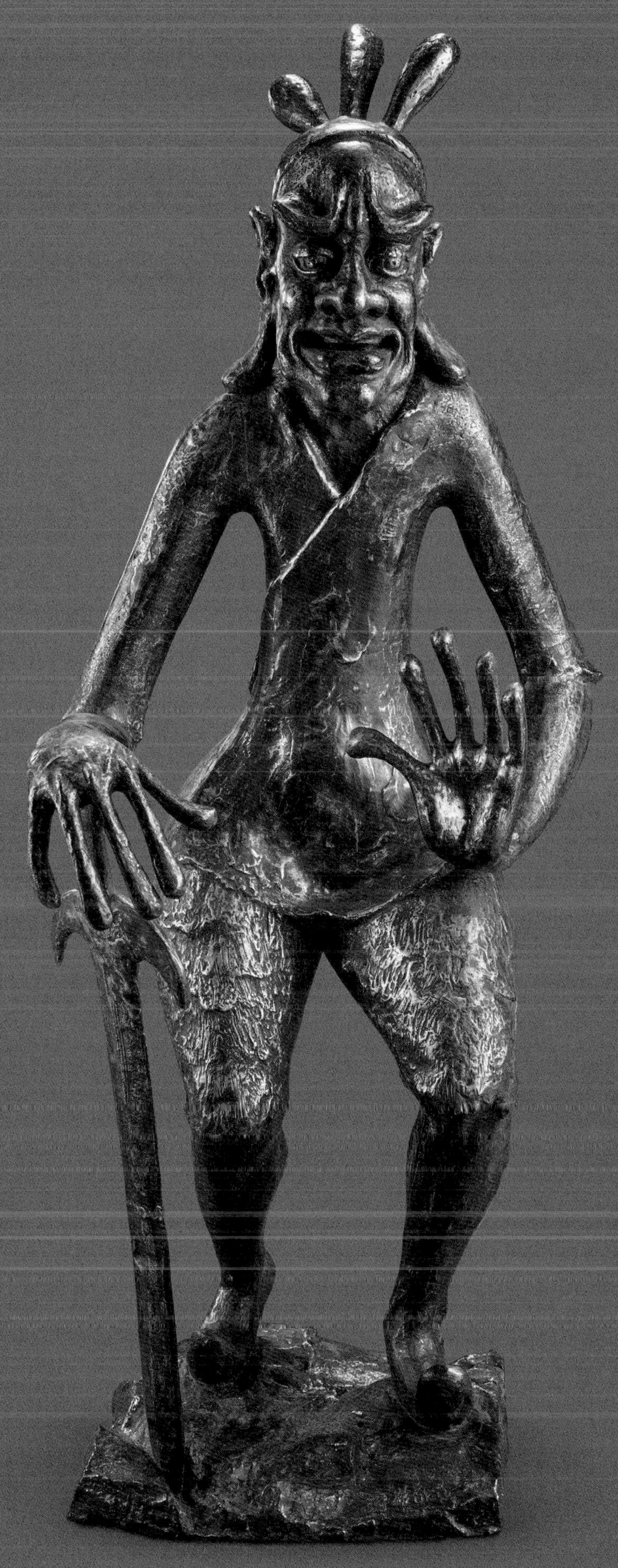

Door Gods 2
Iron, 45×40×112cm
2014

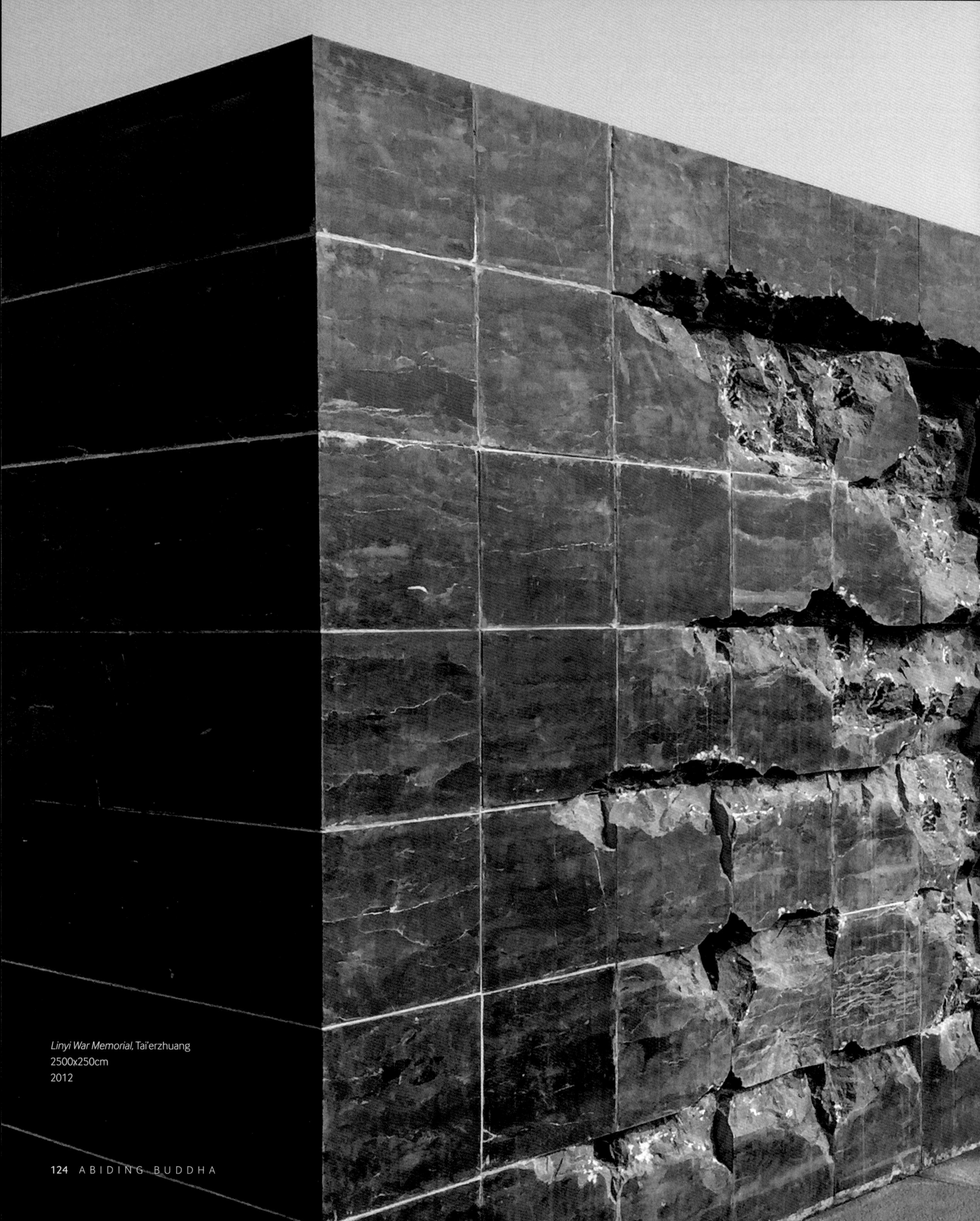

Linyi War Memorial, Tai'erzhuang
2500x250cm
2012

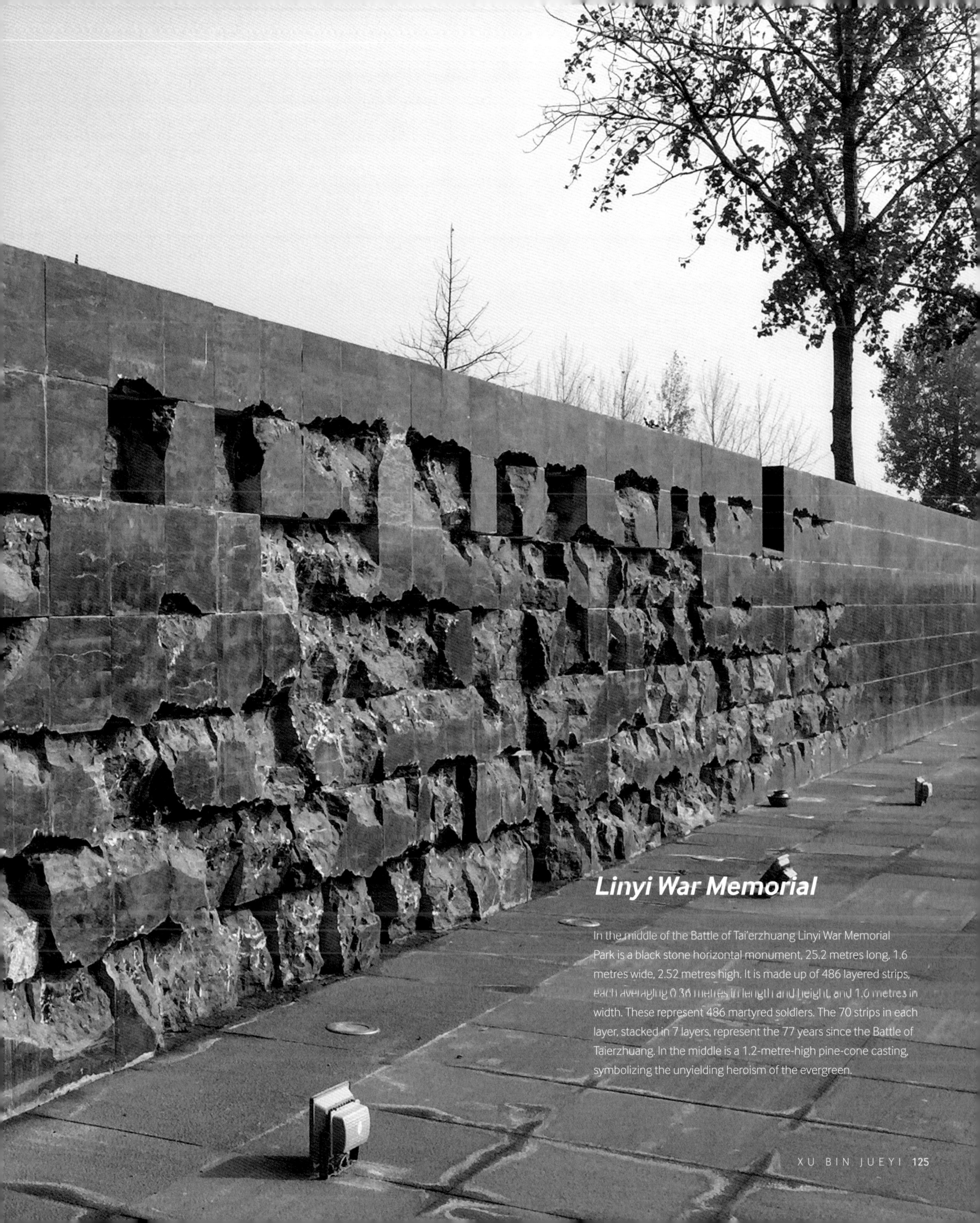

Linyi War Memorial

In the middle of the Battle of Tai'erzhuang Linyi War Memorial
Park is a black stone horizontal monument, 25.2 metres long, 1.6
metres wide, 2.52 metres high. It is made up of 486 layered strips,
each averaging 0.36 metres in length and height, and 1.6 metres in
width. These represent 486 martyred soldiers. The 70 strips in each
layer, stacked in 7 layers, represent the 77 years since the Battle of
Taierzhuang. In the middle is a 1.2-metre-high pine-cone casting,
symbolizing the unyielding heroism of the evergreen.

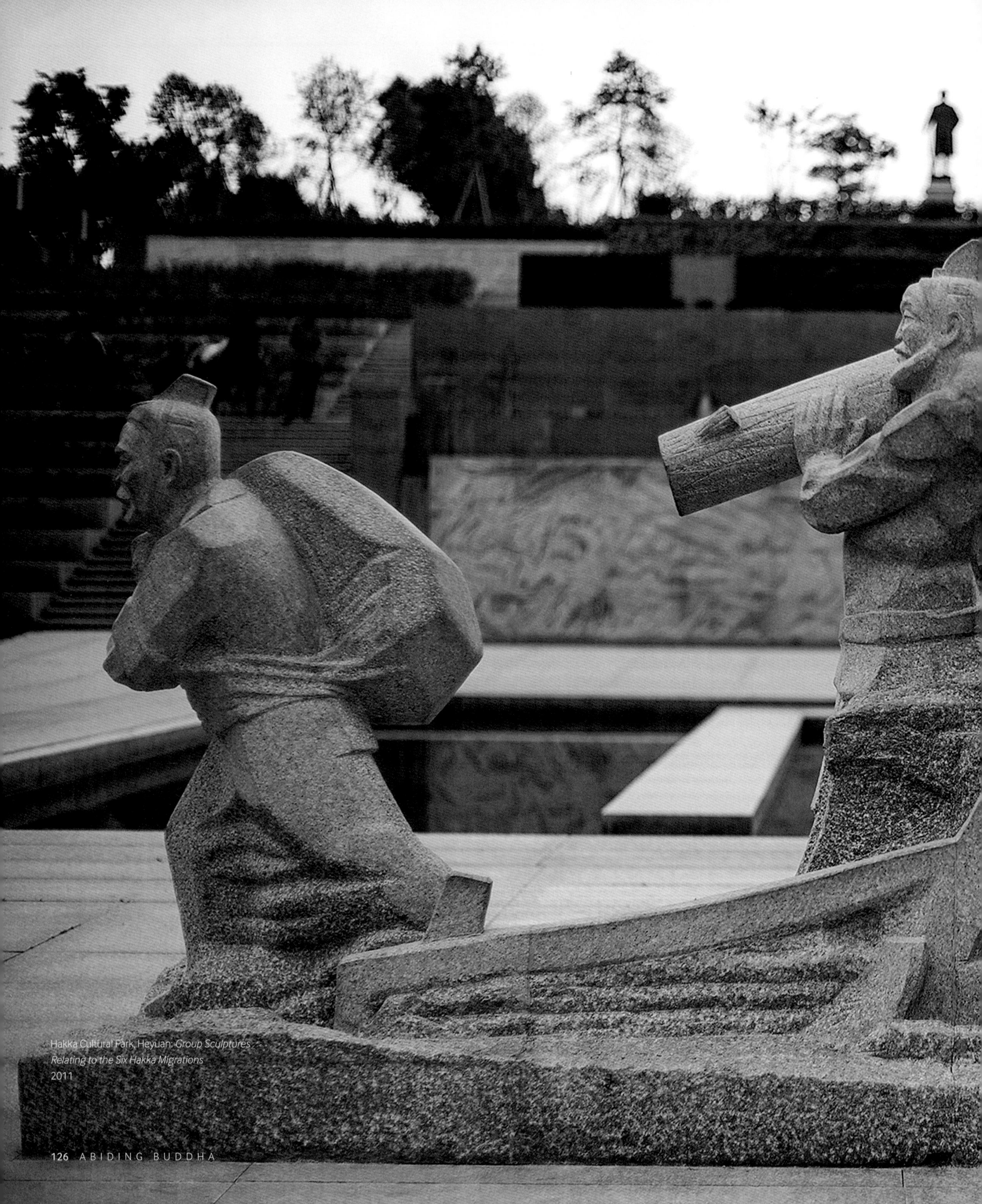

Hakka Cultural Park, Heyuan: Group Sculptures
Relating to the Six Hakka Migrations
2011

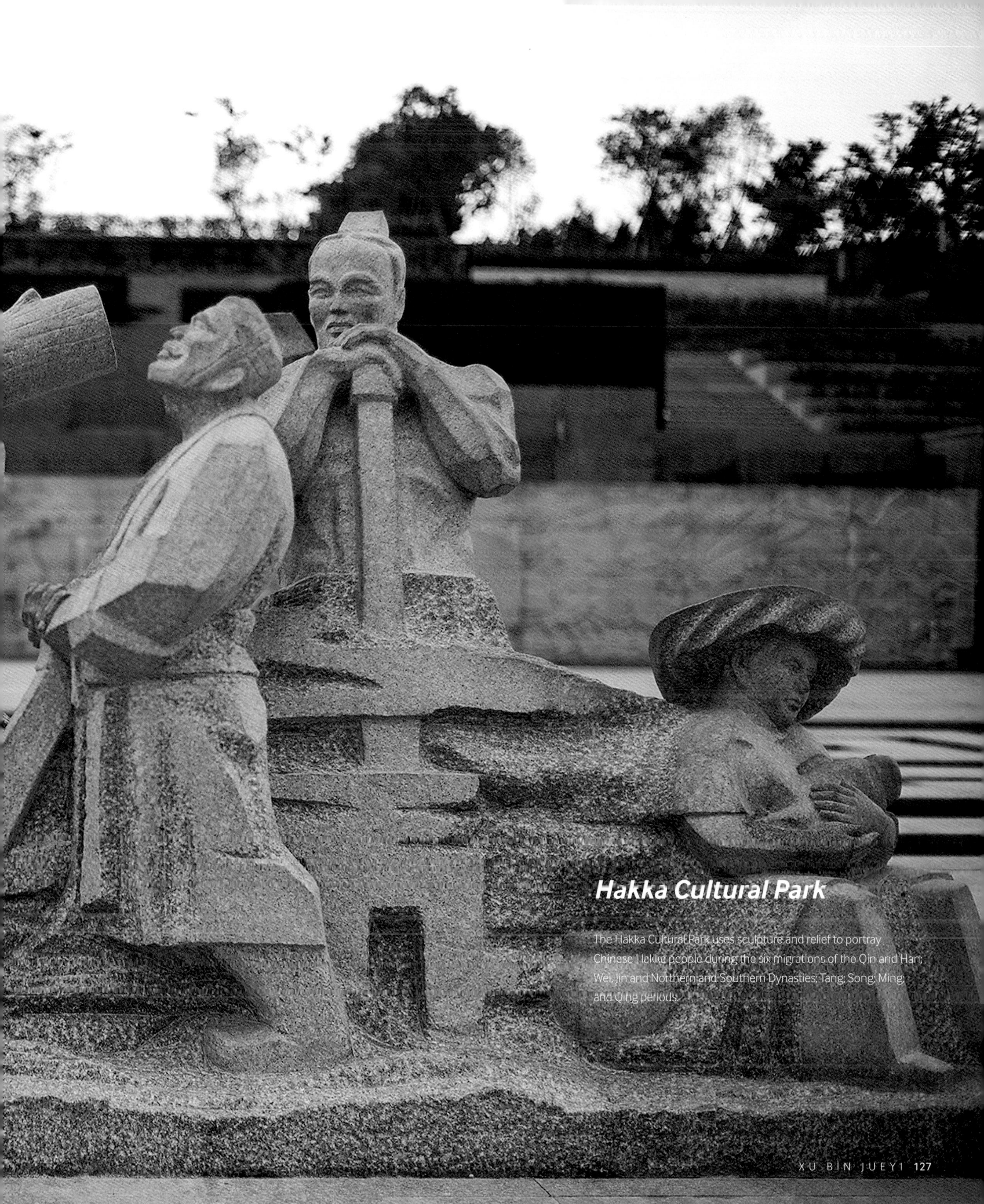

Hakka Cultural Park

The Hakka Cultural Park uses sculpture and relief to portray
Chinese Hakka people during the six migrations of the Qin and Han;
Wei, Jin and Northern and Southern Dynasties; Tang; Song; Ming;
and Qing periods.

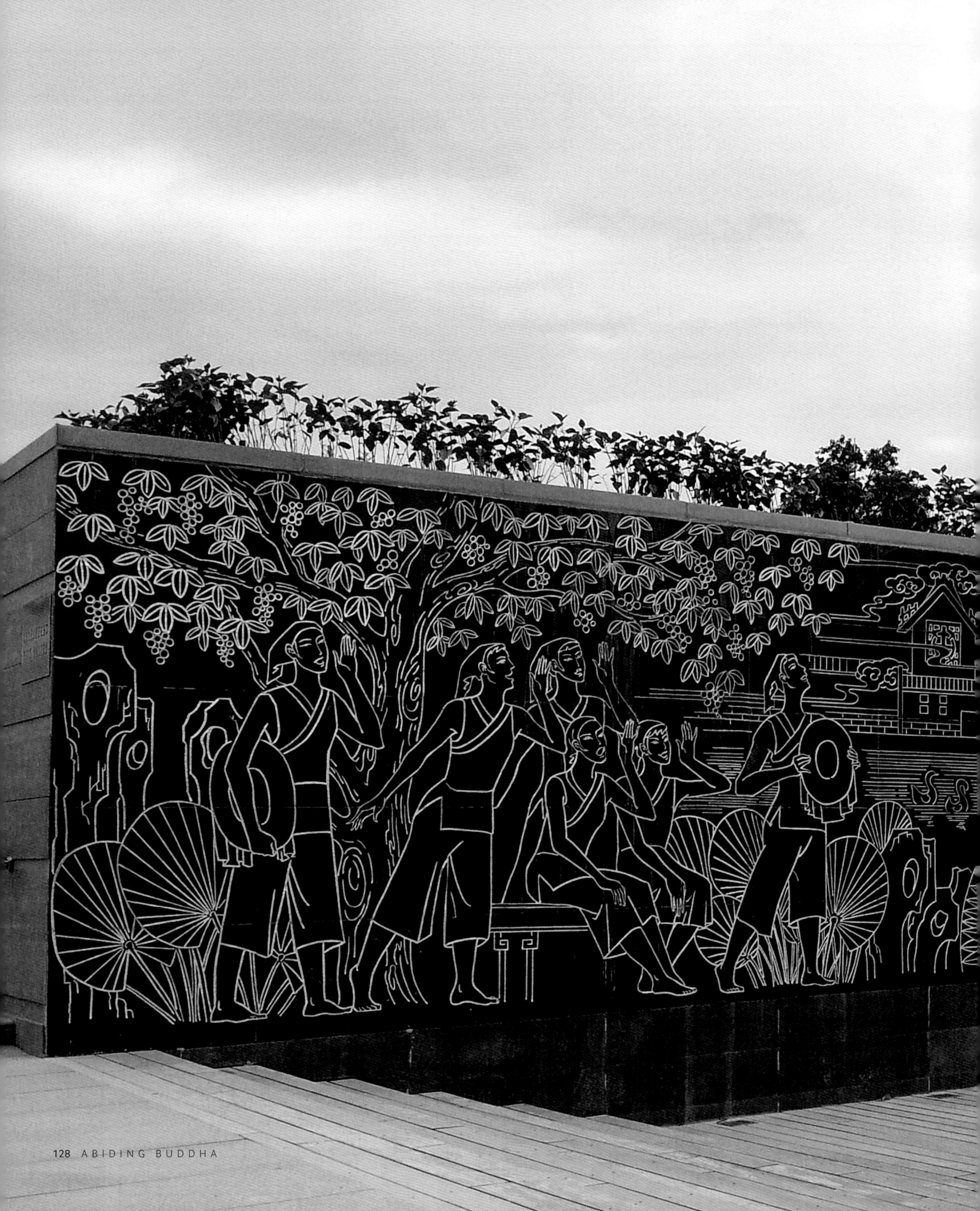

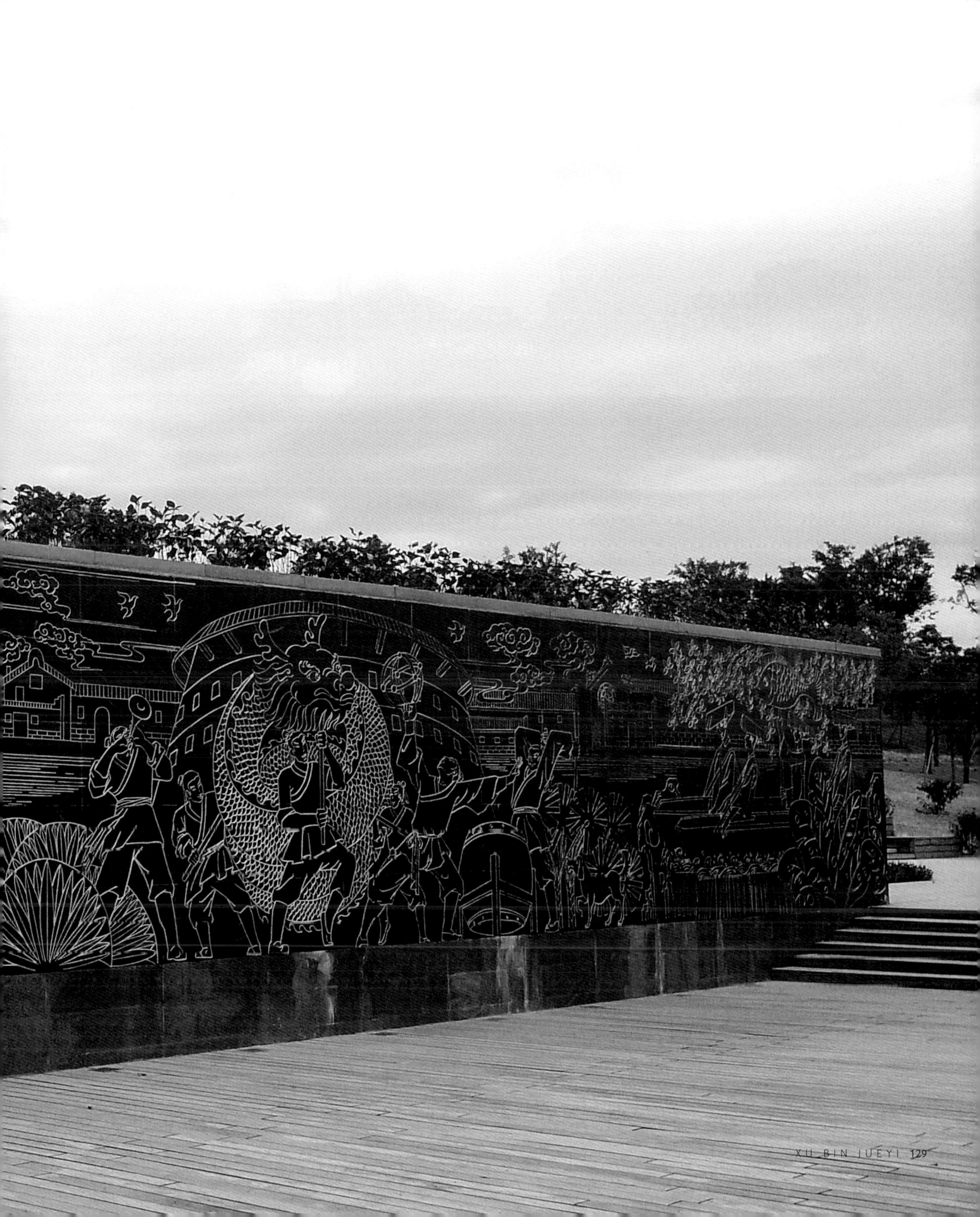

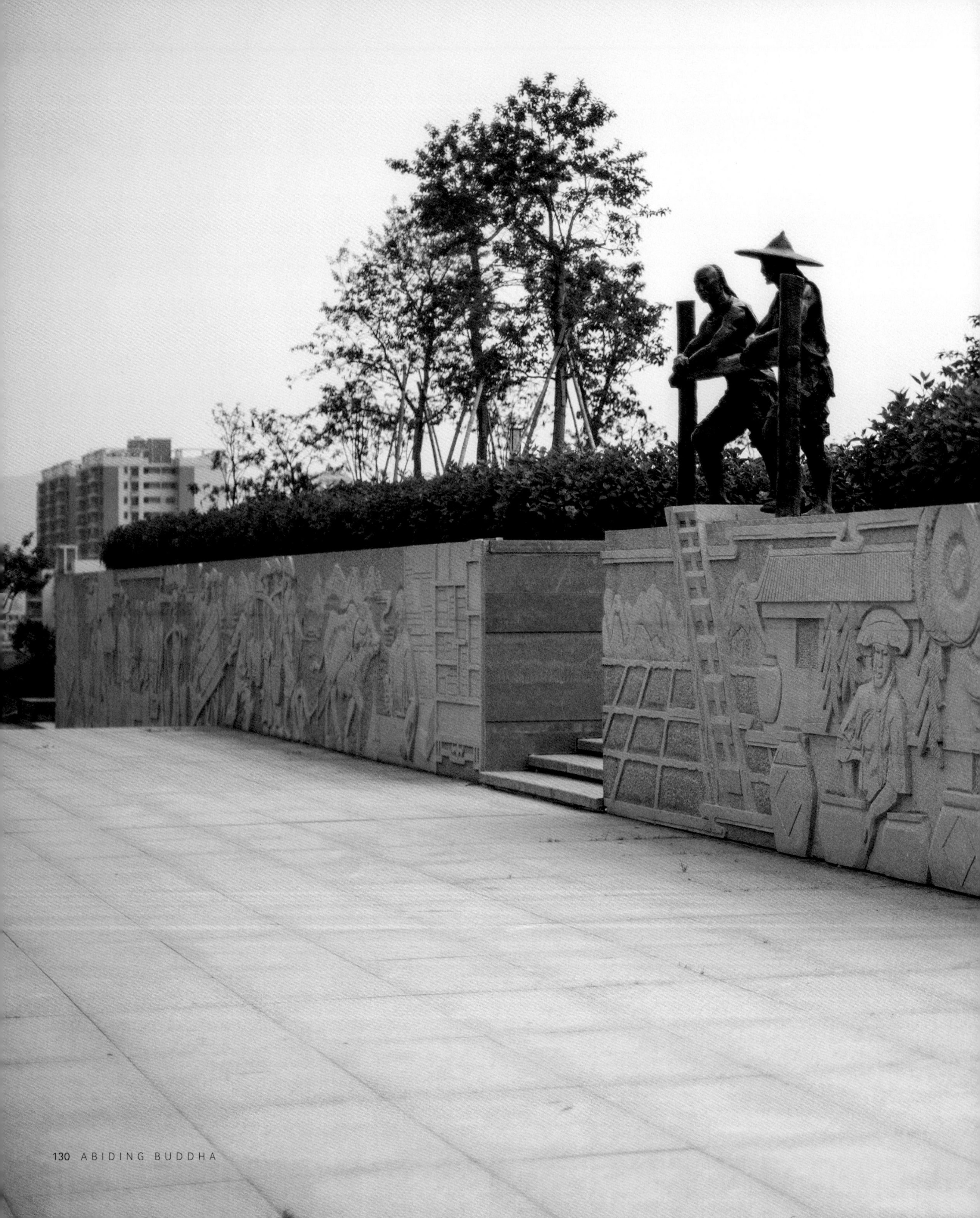

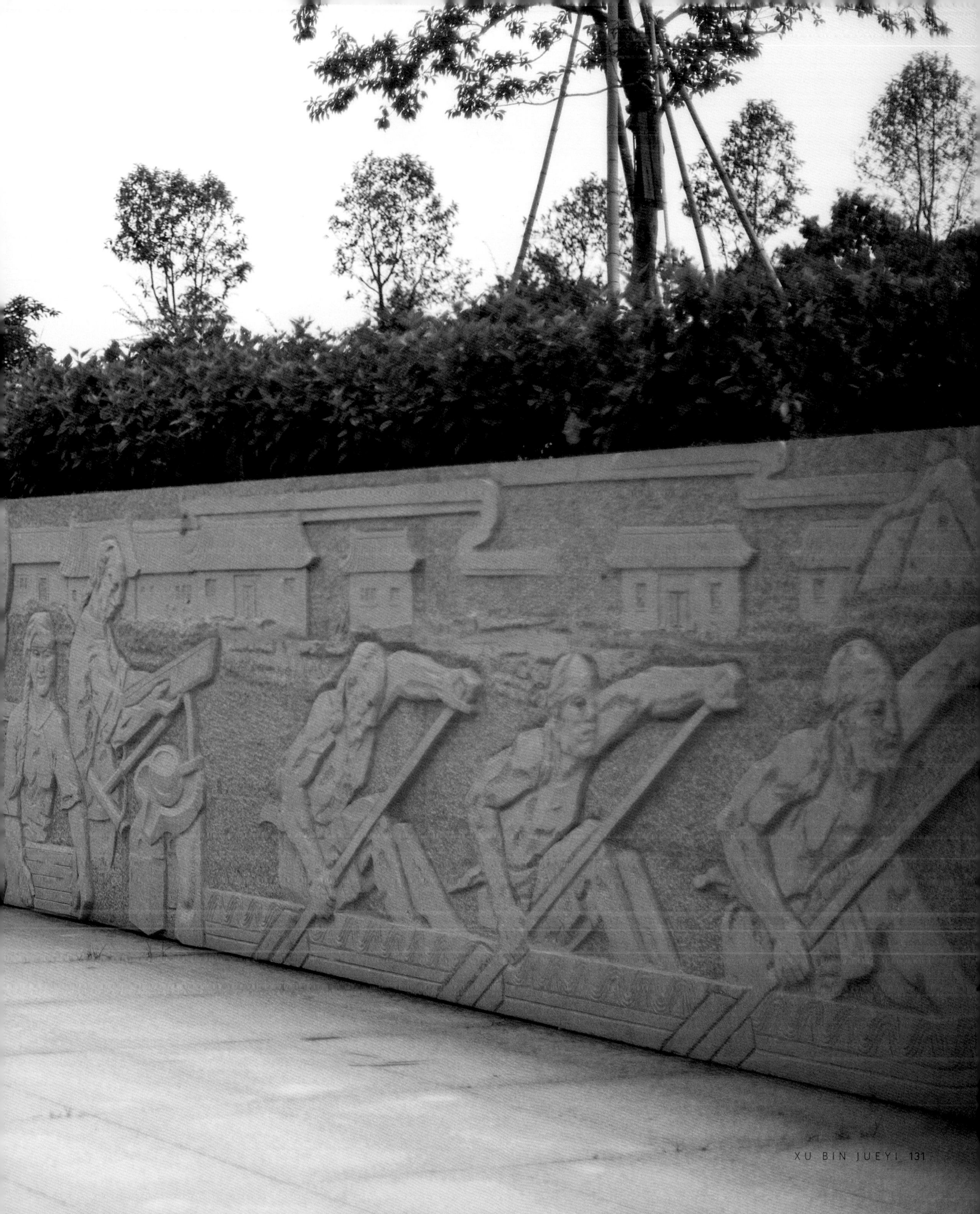

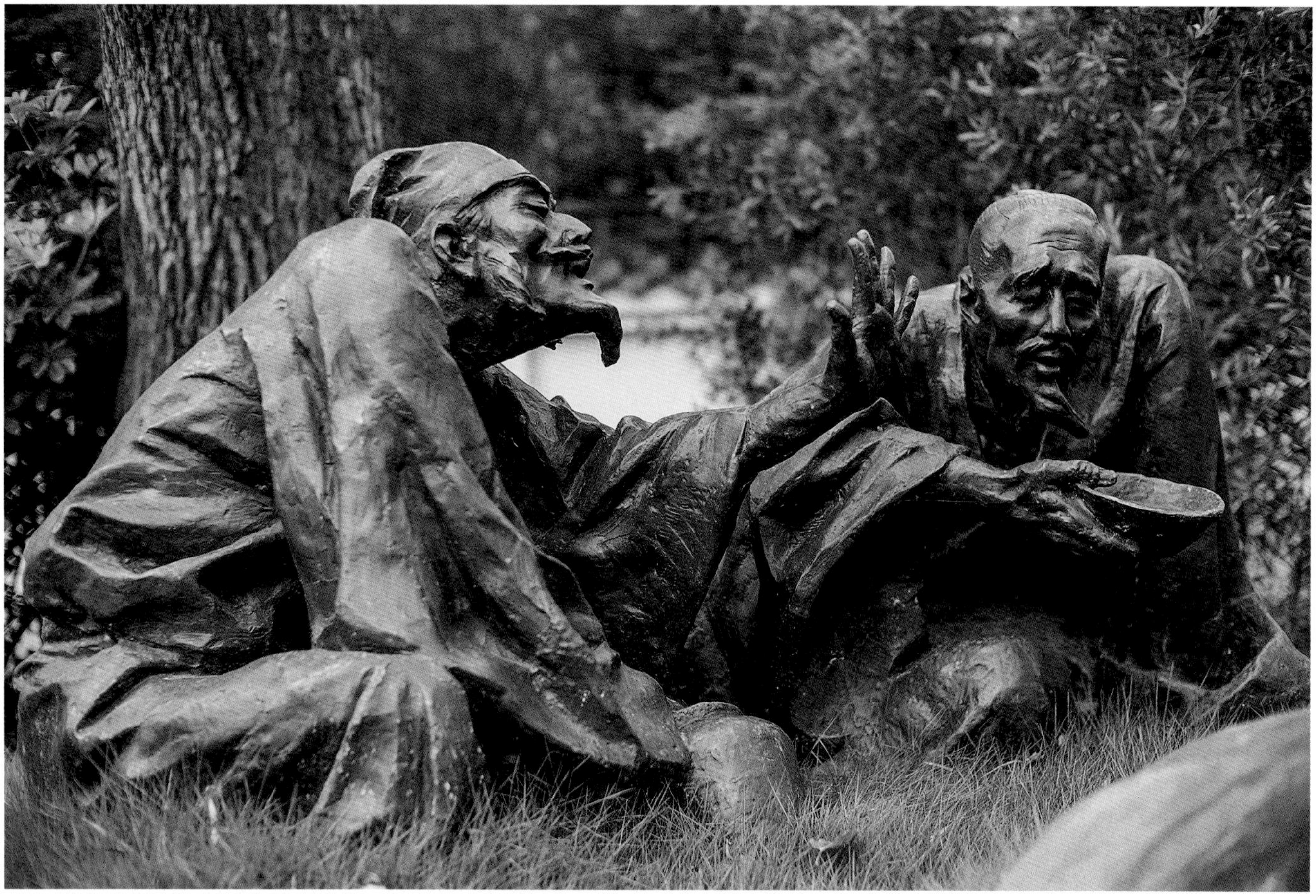

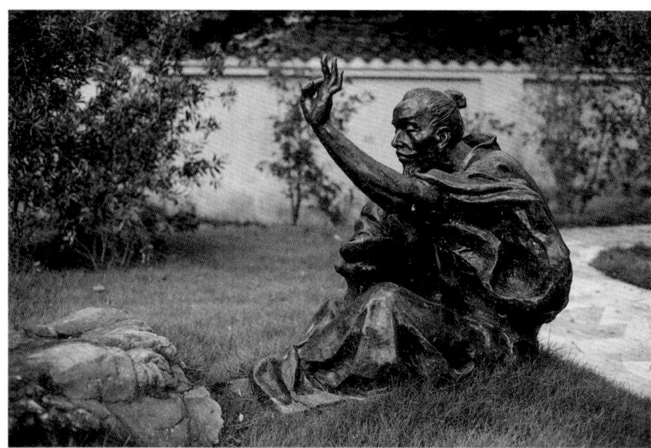

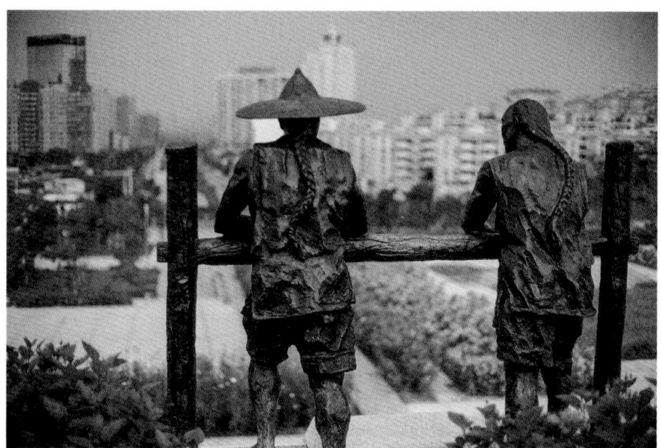

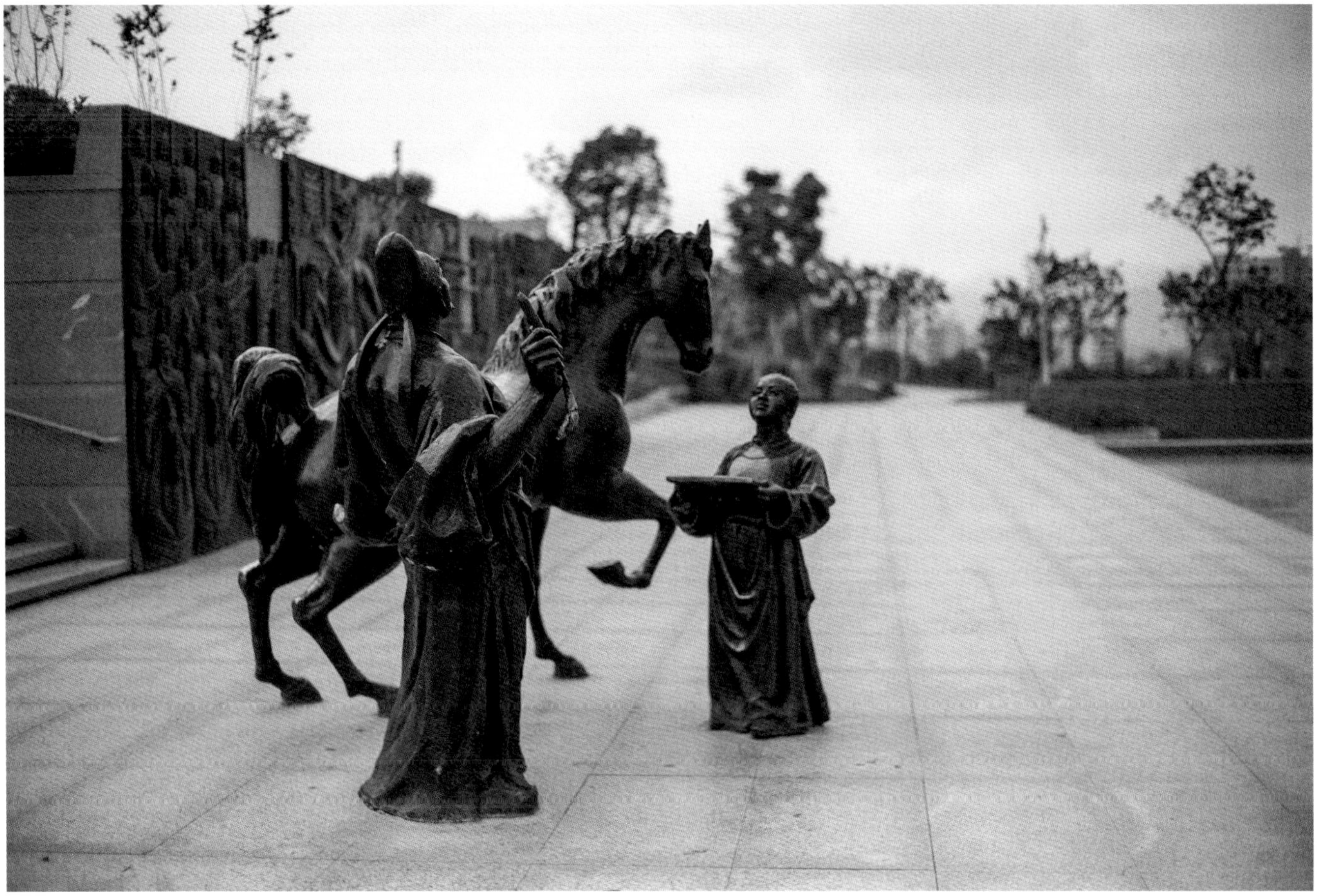

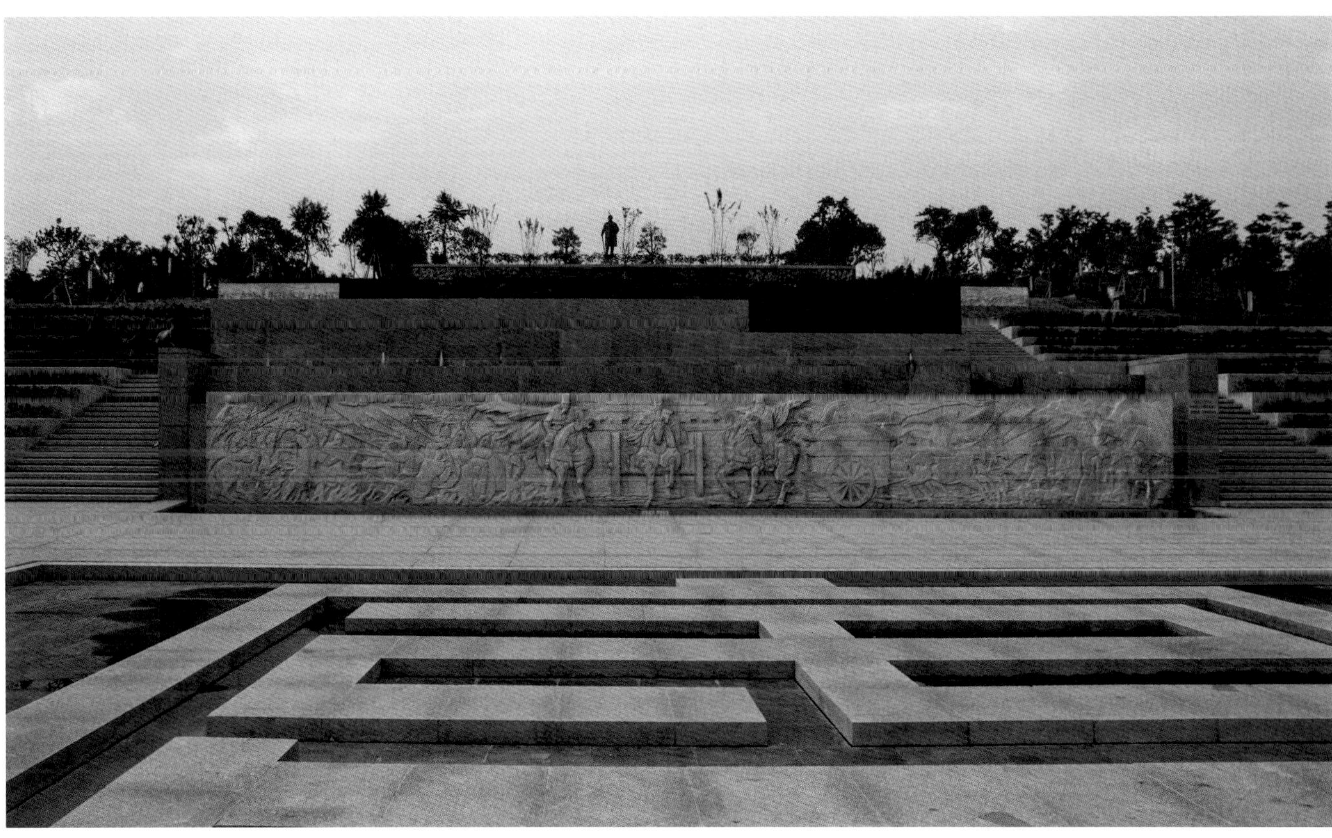

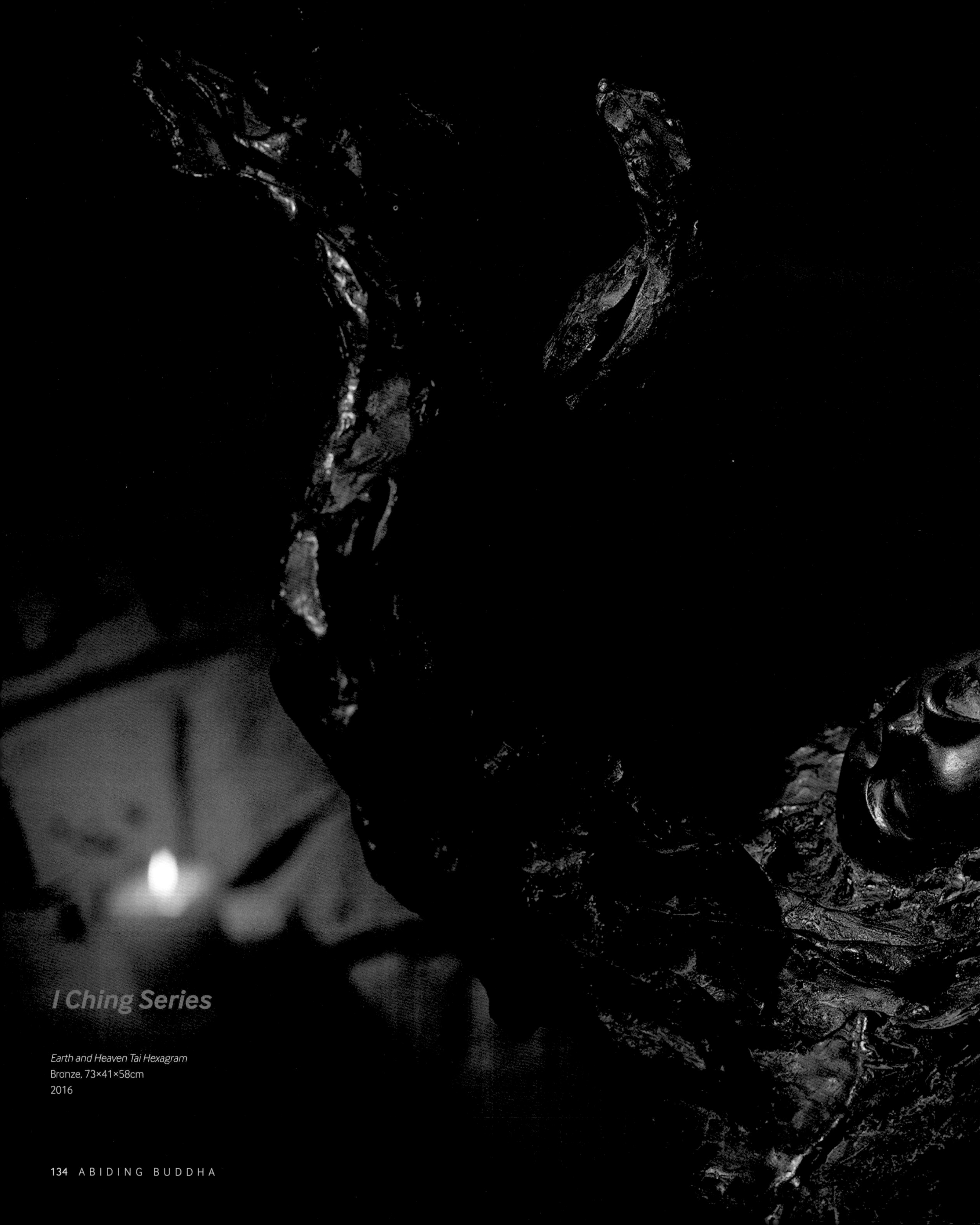

Earth and Heaven Tai Hexagram
Bronze, 73×41×58cm
2016

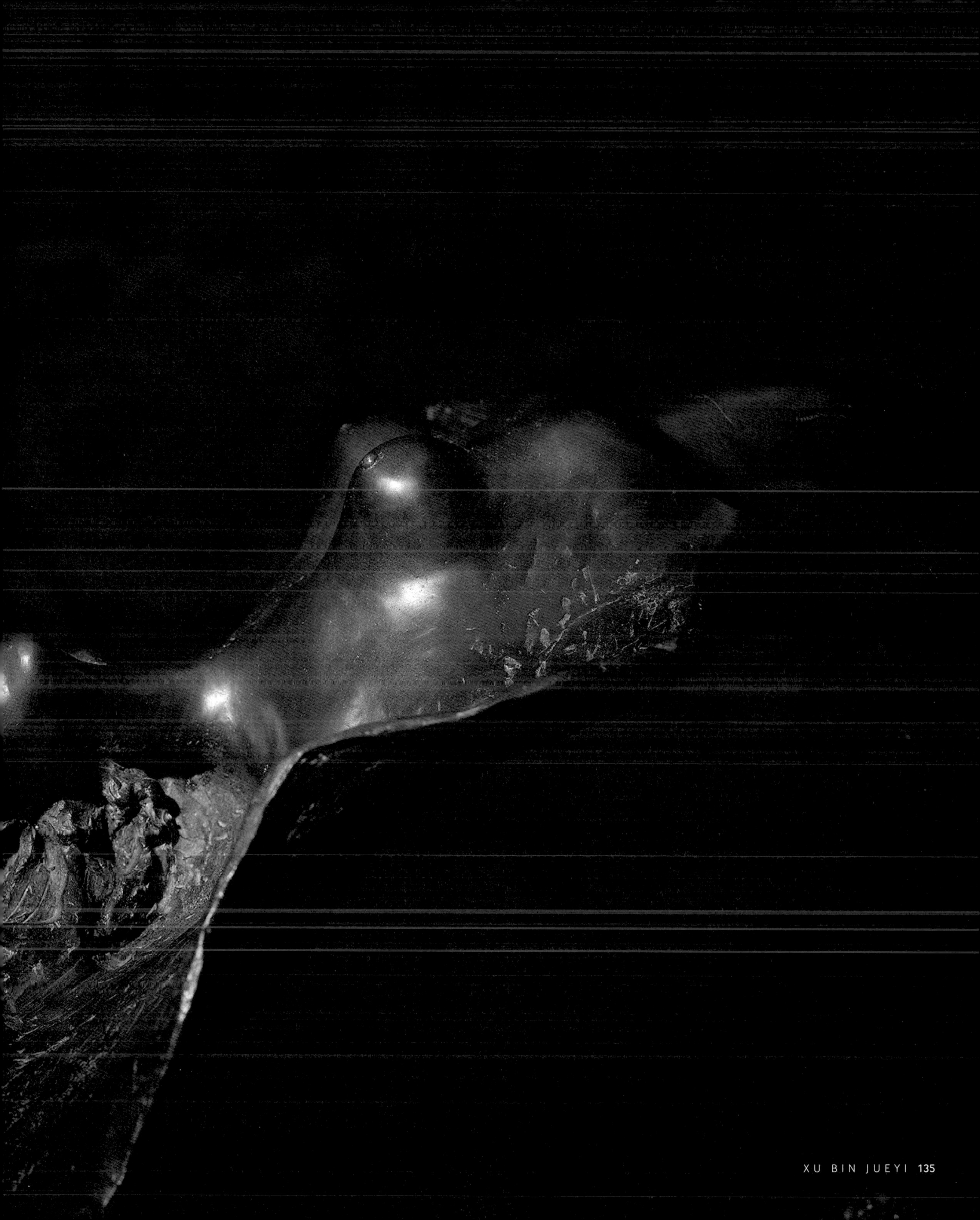

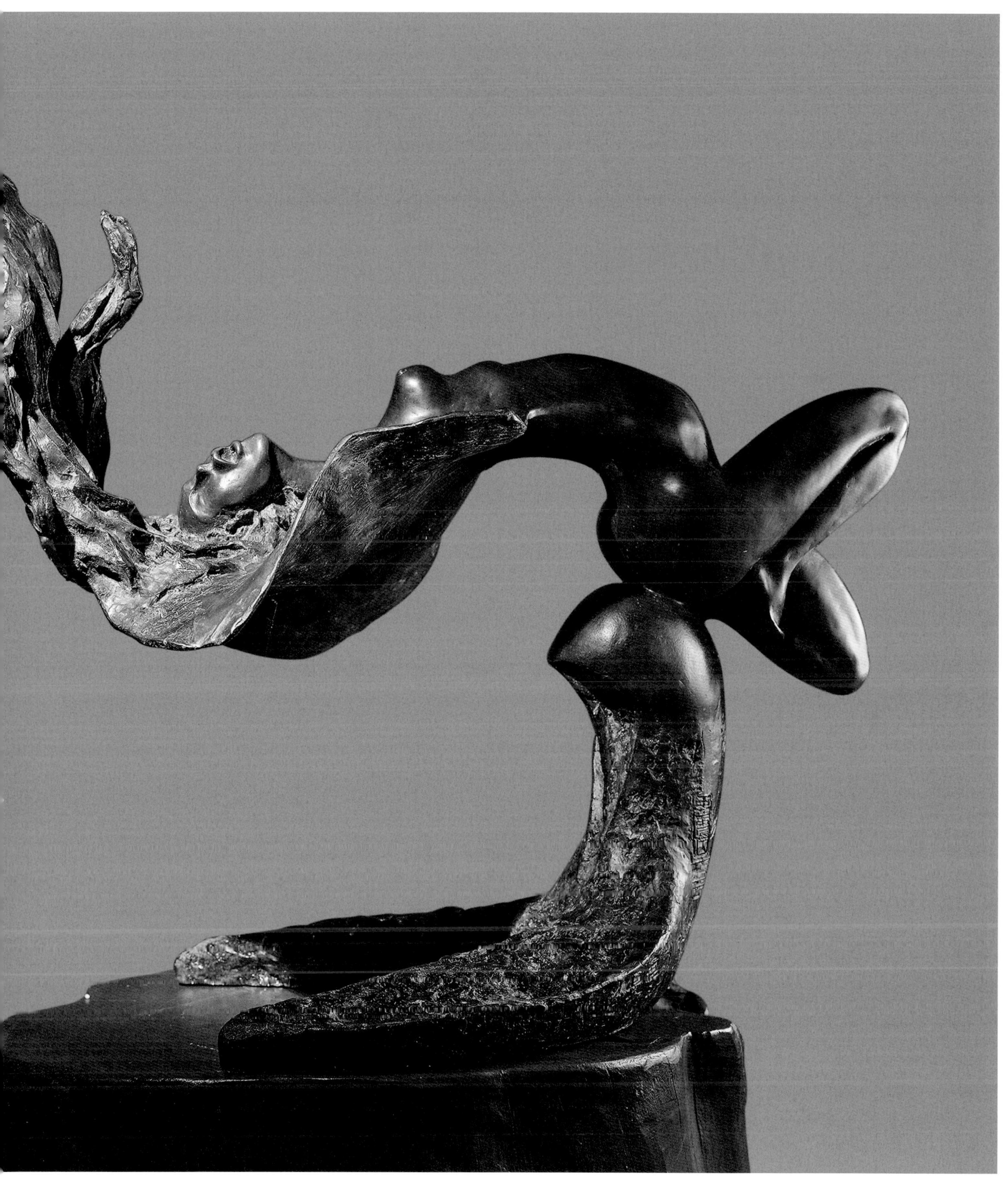

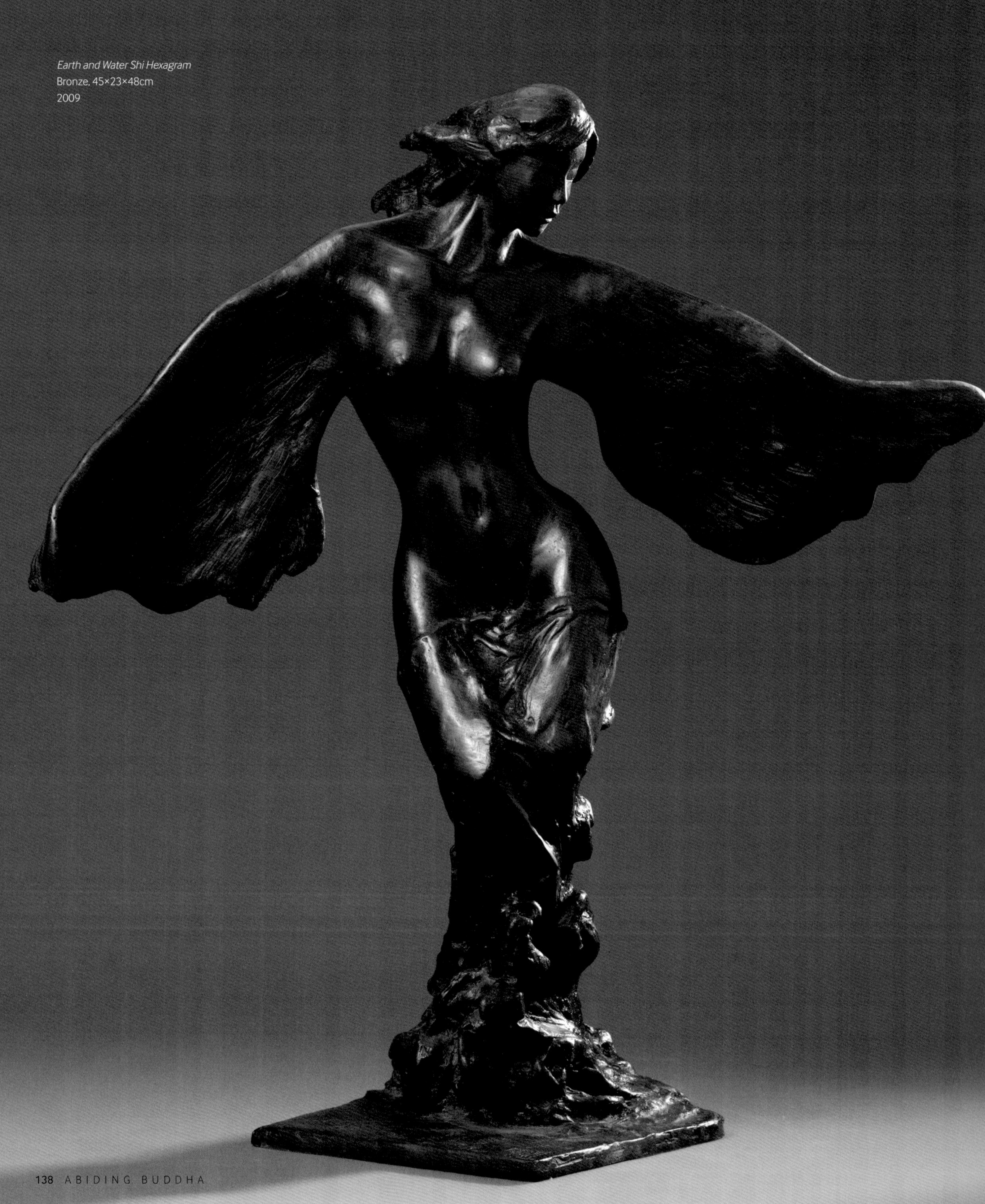

Earth and Water Shi Hexagram
Bronze, 45×23×48cm
2009

Before the Buddha, the heart warms and blossoms
- Commentary on Xu Bin Jueyi's contemporary Buddhist sculpture
- *Gao Ling*
1st-6th October, 2014

In our era, improvements in, and the enrichment of, our material life have unintentionally become like a high wall blocking out people's faith and morality. Relationships between people, and the connection between people and material things, are overshadowed and diminished by the relationships between things themselves. Nothing develops without the possession of material objects and the exchange of money, and nothing subsists except through the stimulation of desire and existence of consumption. This is an era lacking in faith and morality. It is also time when those with insight rouse themselves and courageously take on responsibility.

In the visual arts, some choose to replicate closely the pursuit of material things in an ironic way. Others choose to view our burgeoning desires from a distance in a critical way. Some opt for abstract languages and expressionist styles to escape or disengage from the heavy burden of this material world. Others simply treat things as things, seeing or setting up objects as objects, to express neutrality and indifference ... Some, though of course only a few, choose religious or pan-religious natural themes, attempting to calibrate the contradiction inherent in the serious conflict between the soul and materiality. Of course, such religious and pan-religious natural themes, if they simply copy traditional religious sculpture and compositions, or merely imitate the classical landscape painting style, achieve very little, as they offer nothing new.

There is one person, however, a sculptor, who is something of a maverick among the small number of artists of religious themes - Xu Bin Jueyi. He uses the suffix Jueyi ('Awareness of the One') to express his belief and trust in Buddhism. In metal, resin and wood, he models his understanding of and feeling for the Buddhist heavenly realm. If we enter Xu Bin Jueyi's artistic world, we seem to see the sculptor's mental journey as he moves increasingly deeper into reflection on and apprehension of the Buddha, the bodhisattvas and the believers.

We observe his personal interpretation of Buddhist art, and experience him accepting the Buddha in his heart, coming to regard human beings as buddhas, cultivating himself both internally and externally, and putting into practice a diligent re-shaping of the world.

The series *Pilgrims* and *Qinghai-Tibetan Plateau* represent a peripheral or preparation stage in his reverence for and sculpting of the Buddha. His numerous investigations and sketches of Tibetan landscape and folk customs gave him the opportunity to understand more fully the supreme place of religion in Tibetan life, and a strong impulse to sculpt the devotion of the believers. It is said, if you love a place, it is because you love the people. The piety of the Tibetan pilgrims – the way they place their palms together, and every third step prostrate themselves – deeply fascinated Xu Bin Jueyi. He saw purity and serenity in their (these women's) eyes, quite devoid of the pursuit of material desires of contemporary urban life! His wish was to use the ready medium of clay to create sculptures of these very ordinary, lowly believers. He wanted, while retaining a basically realistic approach, to add strong religious feeling and the language of harmony between humanity and the universe. Thus, he boldly used the symbol of the Falun wheel to replace the wrinkles on the pilgrim's faces, Tibetan landscape and clouds to represent the coloured stripes on the pilgrims' clothes, and Tibetan incense and incense ash to make a sacred and pure prayer path. Moreover, he created slender forms to highlight the pilgrims' physical and mental transcendence, rising from below up towards heaven. Although they (the women) are wearing jackets, giving a swaddled effect, in fact they are physically and mentally lithe and translucent – their spiritual world from youth like the tall prayer poles soaring high, leaving only long shadows to tell of their detachment from the physical world and devotion to the realm of heaven. With millions of incense offerings and endless ash, it is they (these women) who offer the best proof of cutting ties with the material world and dedication to the spirit. Xu Bin Jueyi skilfully handles the contrasts between the weight of bronze and the lightness of the sculpture, the substance of the spirit and the void of the ash, enabling the limited and necessary vehicle of the visual medium to convey the infinite and free, cleansed spiritual consciousness.

Why, for centuries, no matter how the world has changed, have Tibetans constantly been in awe of and devoted to Buddhism. What is it about Buddha, about Buddhist teaching and learning, that draws them in, cutting across space and time, offering a steady source of nourishment, an abundant supply to the hearts of generation after generation? The strong religious atmosphere of Tibet, and the devotion and purity of Tibetan religious practices, produced in Xu Bin Jueyi a greater thirst for knowledge about Buddhism. Although from youth he had travelled widely, and satisfied his curiosity about many novelties, while he possessed a singular love for philosophy and the *I Ching (Book of Changes),* and was an artist, before this time, it is true, he had not systematically studied Buddhism, nor researched Buddhist doctrines. He now started to think seriously about the issue of faith that led millions of people and generations to repent.

Faith is a kind of standard of consciousness in relation to the world. From the perspective of truth, it is correct consciousness in respect of the future, and morality is correct behaviour as governed by faith. In our time, the crisis of lack of faith and morality is often taken as synonymous with the deficiency known as the 'ultimate concern' in the academic field. Thus, in the context of the real-life transformation of contemporary Chinese society, the whole of the humanities pays special attention to the field of 'ultimate concern'. In the end, this field is in fact the same as faith. The essence of faith is people transcending the self, so faith is a sign of humanity's ultimate concern. If you speak of faith, then you cannot fail to speak of religion; and if you speak of religion, you cannot fail to speak of philosophy. There is a close internal relationship between these forms of consciousness that belong to the top level of spiritual awareness. Religion and philosophy are both forms of faith signifying humanity's ultimate concern. The difference is that, in explaining the overall view people have of the world and life, religion focuses on the soul, predestination, rituals, precepts, etc., while philosophy is an attempt at a more rational form of answering the fundamental questions about consciousness and existence. Interestingly, because religion and philosophy have different approaches to reality, as they have led spiritual belief over the millennia, when one subsides the other rises, both mutually dependent and mutually restrained, finally facing together this current precarious era of lack of faith.

Faith, religion, philosophy, and the ultimate concern, all these are ideas and expressions, and ideological issues and concepts, familiar to those who are educated and have experience of urban life. But for Tibetans who grew up on the Qinghai-Tibetan plateau, they are not such lofty matters, but more the physical basis of life itself. What Xu Bin Jueyi wants to do as an artist is to use visual forms to explore the infatuating and fascinating world of Buddhism, the world that has drawn in so many countless people and generations.

From the behaviour of this group of people he loves, to the object of their worship, on to the inner spirit and spiritual meaning of that object, Xu Bin Jueyi feels that religious faith is a spiritual bond for a people, organization or class, a cohesive and spiritual force for the members of a society or nation. He pondered on how to use art in contemporary life to carry forward the values of being detached from the material world, living a simple life, caring for others and being diligent in self-esteem, enabling art to play a unique role in the establishment of faith. So, he began to study the field of Buddhism, especially the history of the Buddha image. He did not conceal his admiration for the humanistic and Buddha sculpture of the Wei-Jin period: 'That kind of gentle, serene, unruffled presence and modest self-restraint obsessed me.' However, he had no intention, and indeed disdained, to copy traditional Buddha images. Instead, he undertook an internal dialogue with Wei-Jin culture, and made his own Buddhas inspired by the spirit of those of the Wei-Jin period. He said: 'I want to create "metaphysical" Buddhas, minimalist and empty, with a simple and unsophisticated appearance, but transcendent and bold in form. What I want to express is the Eastern aesthetic approach.' In other words, his work took the traditional Buddha images of the Wei-Jin period as its sculptural basis, but melded it with his own feelings about the times and form of language as a contemporary artist.

As a result, we have seen a series of elongated Buddhas, seemingly very different in form to traditional harmoniously round, sturdy Buddha images, and instead slender and delicate. This lengthening device marks a continuation of Xu Bin Jueyi's use of incense and ash in the installation series *Pilgrims* to highlight the Tibetans' cutting of ties with the material world and admiration for the realm of heaven. He wanted to use the length of material things and shadows in the space to emphasize the believers' persistence in their course of inner piety. Similarly, he intended the elongated Buddha images and their shadows to reflect people's journey through the barrier of materiality in pursuit and recognition of the unrestrained spiritual life of the Buddha. Not only is the form of the Buddha elongated, but Xu Bin Jueyi is also bold in the high degree of simplification and generalization in the facial features of the Buddha and bodhisattvas, and in the folds of their clothing. Nose, mouth, eyes and ears, etc., are for traditional Buddha making the necessary means for sculpting the Buddha's interior and harmonious confidence, serenity, delight and quiet, and in the hands of the artist they become ever more indistinct and smooth. Even the original drape of the garments becomes minimal and more clinging — all the detail in the representation gives way to the sculpting of the slender body, the form of which is so sparse that the only purpose is to lead to the void and ease at the heart of the Buddha. The qualities of confidence, serenity, delight and quiet are now absorbed and melded into the skin of these slender and smooth buddhas and bodhisattvas, transposed into the upward movement of the eyes and mind in contemplating these long bodies in space, and retained and recalled in the slightly raised noses, coils of hair and earlobes. Undoubtedly, this represents a breakthrough by the artist in traditional Buddhist sculptural language. It is a conscious transformation that aims to prolong the length of time that people mentally experience of the spiritual world of Buddha, replacing visual possession with psychological continuity, substituting the cumbersomeness of materiality for the length of the soul. For, in our era, the Buddha is often used in prayer and worship in a utilitarian manner, not for pursuing inner peace and simplicity, but for calibrating an indulgence for the material world — Buddha becomes an instantaneous Buddha and a secular Buddha. And without inner simplicity, even myriads of buddhas, however at ease and harmoniously round, cannot truly enable the giving up of materialism, nor genuinely return to naturalness of heart.

Mysteriously, Xu Bin Jueyi's conscious elongation technique goes so far as to combine the Eastern pursuit of the natural with a Western reverence for metaphysics. Western traditional religious sculptures, in attempting to represent the remoteness and sacredness of the kingdom of heaven, invariably suspend and elongate figures and clothing to emphasize a gazing upwards. Along with the high arches and stained glass in the churches, Western religious statues create for the mass of believers a consciousness space for soaring heavenwards. And Xu Bin Jueyi's buddhas, in casting aside the vulgarity and secularism of the times, pursue a contemporaneity with a loftier and more essential intention of freedom, unexpectedly coinciding with the Western reverence for transcendence and metaphysics — a genuine syncretism. That is, acknowledgement of the Buddha nature and reverence for God in truth transcend disparate cultural geographies and differences in faith, and achieve a true fusion. From this higher plane, his artistic works, embodying the common pursuit of people of different cultures and traditions over the millennia, are more in line with the [notion] that in the context of the different national and ethnic cultures of the the current information age, people transcend the barriers and enclosures of ideology and religious faith, and seek a vision of a common spiritual homeland. As we stand before these slender Buddha images, those draperies hanging to the floor enclose not only Buddhas in niches, but also angels and sisters of the church leading us up to heaven. Those long shadows, while calling us to look down, also summon our eyes up, following the Buddha's slender body, past abdomen, chest, head and coil of hair, to gaze at and meditate on the vault of heaven. Devotion and calm, yearning and introspection, ascent and return, transcendence and repose, the East and the West, all become undifferentiated — past and present, this life and what is to come, all exist in the moment. 'If you do not learn from the ancients, you can achieve nothing; if you are too similar to the ancients, you have no originality.' Xu Bin Jueyi has learnt from and emanates from the ancients, he seeks the new and achieves fusion, he sculpts Buddha with a Buddha heart, ultimately achieving a Great Buddha on earth, this is proof of respect for one's conscience and achievement of a different kind of Great Realm.

Minimizing the detail in the depiction of the facial expression of the Buddha provides Xu Bin Jueyi with a sculptural basis to explore boldly [the space] between the materiality of the figure and the spirituality of the soul. He has conducted a series of trials in the language of the Buddha form and gestures. Moreover, in the next three years, he intends to launch a huge and exciting 'Myriad Buddha Programme'. He would like to sculpt, and accumulate, a Buddha every day, and so take the lead in exemplary self-cultivation. One day, his sculpting of a myriad Buddhas will represent his best means of sharing spiritual practice with people and taking on the rebuilding of faith. We look forward to Xu Bin Jueyi achieving rich results in this new path of origin-seeking, practice and action, so that a myriad modern-style buddhas will soon become the spiritual images held deep in the hearts of people of our era.

Xu Bin Jueyi

Xu Bin Jueyi, ('Awareness-of-the-One') is an independent artist from Nantong in Jiangsu. He has had a passion for art from childhood, and spent many years travelling the world to well-known mountains and rivers, taking nature as his teacher, and responding to nature. He has created a large number of sculptures, paintings and photographs. Representative sculptural works include: the *I Ching* series, for example, *Heaven and Earth Tai Hexagram;* the Tibet series, for example *Qinghai-Tibetan Plateau* and *Pilgrims;* Buddhas, for example *Considering the Fracture* series, *Awareness* series and the '360-degree Redemption' *Beauty of Compassion* series. He blends Chinese and Western cultures to create his own unique artistic style.

Selected Exhibitions and Events:

2007:	Participated in an exhibition at the Art Museum of the Guangzhou Academy of Fine Arts
2010:	A joint exhibition with Mr Pan He
2011:	Created large group sculptures relating to the six Hakka migrations for the Hakka Cultural Park in Heyuan
2012:	'Treasures of the Snow Region Tibet Cultural Relics Exhibition' and 'Xu Bin Sculpture Exhibition' held at the Guangdong Provincial Museum, and twelve pieces retained by the museum. Also, the 'Xu Bin Sculpture Exhibition' held in Red Factory Art District, Guangzhou
Dec 2013:	'Sino-Italian Sculpture Dialogue: Sculpture Exhibition of Xu Bin and Italian Sculptor Moro' held at the Guangdong Provincial Museum
2013:	Invited to create a statue of Lady Xian, 6 metres high, for Lady Xian's hometown.
May 2014:	Took part in the Beijing airport art exhibition.
June 2014:	Participated in the Shanghai cross-border art exhibition.
2014:	Took part in the ArtePlace (Sanxuanshe) contemporary art exhibition.
2014:	Took part in an exhibition of contemporary art in Guangzhou.
10 Oct 2014:	Started the '360-degree Redemption' *Beauty of Compassion:* Myriad Buddha Programme.
Mar 2015:	Participated in an exhibition of works at Guangzhou Library.
May 2015:	Solo exhibition of '360-degree Redemption' *Beauty of Compassion* was held in the September Space.
2015:	Invited to create the memorial monument to the heroes of the Battle of Linyi in Tai'erzhuang.
2015:	Invited to create a huge sculpture of Lady Xian, 39 metres high and 69 metres wide.
Oct 2015:	Invited to participate in the 'Second China Contemporary Buddhist Art Exhibition' in Wuxi.
2016:	Invited to create eighty-eight statues for the Liurong Temple Flower Pagoda
2016:	Suzhou 'Gaia 2016 Life Art Exhibition'.
2016:	Guangzhou Four Seasons Hotel 'ZEN.Delight __ Xu Bin Jueyi Sculpture Exhibition'.
Dec 2016:	Artron (Shenzhen) Arts Centre, '360-degree Redemption: Xu Bin Jueyi Myriad Buddha Exhibition', and published collections of his works *Xu Bin Jueyi* and the *Beauty of Compassion.*
11 Jan 2017:	Guangzhou Baiyun Airport '360-degree Redemption: Xu Bin Jueyi Myriad Buddha Exhibition'.
11 May 2017:	Artron (Shenzhen) Art Centre Gallery 'Strange Treasures of the Snow Region: Selected Cultural Art Objects from the Potala Palace'.
2017:	Exhibition 'Beauty of Compassion' at the Taiyi Art Museum, Chengdu
2017:	The book *Xu Bin Jueyi* is exhibited at the Doha International Book Fair and acquired by the Doha Museum of Islamic Art
2017:	The book *Xu Bin Jueyi* is acquired by the Buddhist Association of China
2018:	Invited to create a large public sculpture *The Hermit Yan Feng* for the Yan Feng Academy
2018:	Invited to create a large public sculpture of the sixth Dalai Lama, Tsangyang Gyatso
2018:	Invited to hold an exhibition 'Xu Bin Jueyi' at the Liurong Temple